1901 ... **nt**

St... ...ollier
s... ...Rees

Series editors: Martin Collier • Rosemary Rees

Book 3

Cover image: *People at Play* by William Patrick Roberts (1895–1980). Roberts became an official war artist in 1917, through both world wars. He painted people in everyday situations.

www.heinemann.co.uk

✓ Free online support
✓ Useful weblinks
✓ 24 hour online ordering

01865 888080

Heinemann is an imprint of Pearson Education Limited, a company incorporated in England and Wales, having its registered office at Edinburgh Gate, Harlow, Essex, CM20 2JE. Registered company number: 872828

www.heinemann.co.uk

Heinemann is a registered trademark of Pearson Education Limited

Text © Pearson Education Limited 2009

First published 2009

13 12 11 10 09

10 9 8 7 6 5 4 3 2 1

British Library Cataloguing in Publication Data

A catalogue record for this book is available from the British Library

ISBN 978 0 435319 01 4

Freelance edited by Sandra Stafford
Designed and typeset by Jerry Udall
Original illustrations © Pearson Education Limited 2009
Illustrated by Tek-Art, Crawley Down, West Sussex

Cover design by Wooden Ark
Picture research by Elena Goodinson
Cover photo © The Bridgeman Art Library/Christie's Images
Printed in Spain by Graficas Estella

Acknowledgements

The authors and publisher would like to thank the following individuals and organisations for permission to reproduce material:

Photographs

AKG-Images pp. 30c, 73, 125h, 170a; Alamy Images / AKG-Images pp. 100–101; Alamy Images / Ariadne van Zandbergen p. 171b; Alamy Images / David Bagnall p. 77d; Alamy Images / Gregory Davies p. 94a; Alamy Images / Isifa Image Service SRD p. 66a; Alamy Images / Mary Evans Picture Library pp. 6a, 7c, 18b, 88a; Alamy Images / The Print Collector pp. 90–91; AP Photo pp. 62c, 176b, 184c; Australian National Archives pp. 144, 168a, 181d; Benjamin Zephaniah p. 165; British Cartoon Archive / David Low pp. 32a, 33c, 33d, 36a, 46a; British Library of Political and Economical Science pp. 147c, 182a; Camera Press pp. 7e, 63l; Contact Press Images / Li Zhensheng pp. 114a, 115e, 142c; Copyright Zapiro p. 174; Corbis pp. 54–55, 122a, 123a, 124a, 143e; Corbis / Bettmann pp. 77b, 113; Corbis / Hulton-Deutsch Collection p. 164f; Courtesy of the International Institute of Social History Amsterdam p. 112a; Courtesy Nordic Africa Institute p. 63i; Courtesy Yad Vashem Library pp. 98a, 99d; CROWN COPYRIGHT p. 123d; Dan Howarth p. 150a; Empics pp. 26, 56a, 58a, 69e, 86a, 161e; Francis Frith Collection p. 77c; Gandhi Foundation pp. 158a, 158b; Getty Images pp. 7f, 12a, 12g, 18a, 27a, 28a, 30a, 31g, 37d, 38b, 44b, 60a, 62d, 63f, 68a, 78b, 80a, 92a, 93g, 96a, 108a, 130a, 131e, 132c, 133f, 138, 156a, 161d, 165; Getty Images / AFP / Timothy A. Clary p. 179; Getty Images / Ben Stansall p. 166a; Getty Images / Forrest Anderson / Time & Life Pictures p. 115c; Getty Images / Hulton Archive pp. 8, 76; Getty Images / Popperfoto pp. 77a, 77c; Getty Images / Time & Life Pictures p. 62e; Getty Images / Topical Press Agency p. 130g; Illingworth Images p. 160a; Imperial War Museum pp. 19c, 82b, 84b, 147e, 154a, 155b, 155c, 184b; JFK Library pp. 120, 138; John Harris p. 137f; Library of Congress p. 85e; Lincolnshire Archives p. 85f; Magnum pp. 134, 172a; Manchester Evening News Syndication p. 167g; Mary Evans Picture Library pp. 14a, 146b; Mirrorpix / Philip Zec p. 97d; Museum of London pp. 7b, 10a, 11e, 146a, 181a; PA Photos p. 11f; Reproduced with permission of Kip Koss, President of JN 'Ding' Darling Foundation p. 41d; Reproduced with permission of Punch Ltd p. 33b; Reuters pp. 64, 66b, 175; Rex Features p. 63k; Rex Features / East News pp. 60b, 69h; Rex Features / Richard Gardner p. 53c; Rex Features / SIPA Press p. 157d; Robert Altman p. 133h; Time p. 136a; Topfoto pp. 7d, 59d, 63h, 79d, 99c, 128b, 131b, 138, 144, 162a, 184a; Topfoto / Ria Novosti p. 111g; United Nations p. 62a; USHMA pp. 153b, 153c; Warsaw Institute of History p. 99e; Weiner pp. 99b, 142a.

Written sources

p. 13f, Christabel Pankhurst, *Unshackled*, Hutchinson, 1959, reprinted by permission of The Random House Group Ltd; p. 19e, Lyn MacDonald, *The Roses of No Man's Land*, Penguin, 1993, reproduced by permission of Pollinger Limited and Lyn MacDonald; p. 24b, Anthony Babbington, *For the Sake of Example*, Pen and Sword Books, 1993; p. 40b, A. J. P. Taylor, *The Second World War*, Penguin, 1975; p. 45e, Paul Fussell, *Hiroshima: A Soldier's View*, New Republic, 1981, reprinted by permission of Sterling Lord Literistic, Inc.; p. 45f, Basil Liddell Hart, *History of the Second World War*, Cassell & Co. Ltd, 1970; p. 90d, Barbara Castle, *Fighting All the Way*, Pan Books, 1993; p. 115b, Gao Yuan, *Born Red*, Stanford University Press, 1987; p. 125g Andreas Ramos, *A Personal Account of The Fall of the Berlin Wall*, 11 and 12 November 1989, www.andreas.com/berlin.html; p. 147d, Jay Winter, *Remembering War*, Yale University Press, 2006; p. 167d, *Bend it like Beckham*, 2002, sourced from www.script-o-rama.com; p. 169b, *Hansard*, 9 February 1959, Crown copyright material is reproduced with the permission of the Controller of HMSO and the Queen's Printer for Scotland.

Every effort has been made to contact copyright holders of material reproduced in this book. Any omissions will be rectified in subsequent printings if notice is given to the publishers.

Websites

There are links to relevant websites in this book. In order to ensure that the links are up to date, that the links work, and that the sites are not inadvertently linked to sites that could be considered offensive, we have made the links available on the Heinemann website at www.heinemann.co.uk/hotlinks. When you access the site, the express code is 9014P.

Contents

Finding out about history

This book has been written to bring your Key Stage 3 History lessons alive and to make sure you get the most out of them! The book is divided into three sections:
Ruling, **Living and working** and **Moving and travelling.**

By looking at each of these big themes, you will build up a picture of what life was like for people living in the twentieth-century world. This was a time of great changes and great contrasts. You will find out about the two world wars, about the horrors of genocides and the struggle for civil rights, and your enquiries will focus on the impact these had on the lives of ordinary, and not so ordinary, people.

This book isn't just about Britain and the British people. While you will investigate events on a local and national scale, these will be in South Africa and the USA, in Australia, the USSR and China, as well as in the British Isles.

Doing history!

In each section of this book there are activities to help you get the most out of that topic. Most sections will have four different types of task, though some will have just the first three:

1 Everyone should be able to have a go at this task.

2 Next, have a go at this task.

3 Once you've completed the blue task, see if you can try this.

4 If you want to stretch yourself, you can have a go at this.

History detective

There will be chances for you to investigate topics in more detail and carry out your own investigations.

Back to the start

You will also be able to review and reflect on the bigger picture and on your own learning.

Practising historical skills

At the end of the book, you'll find a Skills bank. This is to remind you of some of the important historical skills you'll be learning. Use this section for useful hints and tips as you complete the tasks and the activities throughout the book.

Introduction

Who ruled the world in 1901? The short answer is: no one! The longer answer is a little more complicated. In 1901 the countries of the world were ruled in different ways by different people under different regimes. One hundred years later, a lot had changed.

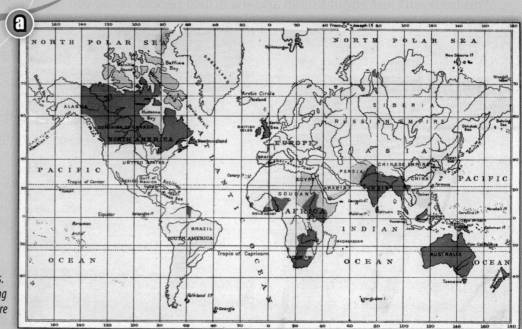

a A map of the world published in the 1880s. The countries belonging to the British Empire are coloured red and pink.

Timeline 1901–Present day

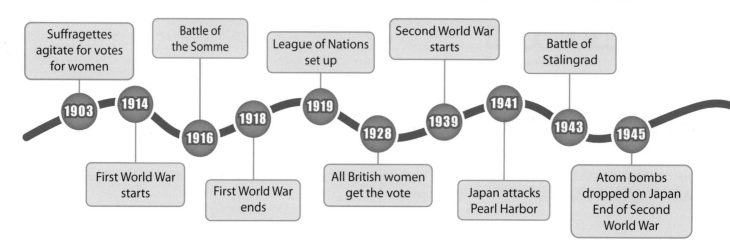

1903 Suffragettes agitate for votes for women

1914 First World War starts

1916 Battle of the Somme

1918 First World War ends

1919 League of Nations set up

1928 All British women get the vote

1939 Second World War starts

1941 Japan attacks Pearl Harbor

1943 Battle of Stalingrad

1945 Atom bombs dropped on Japan End of Second World War

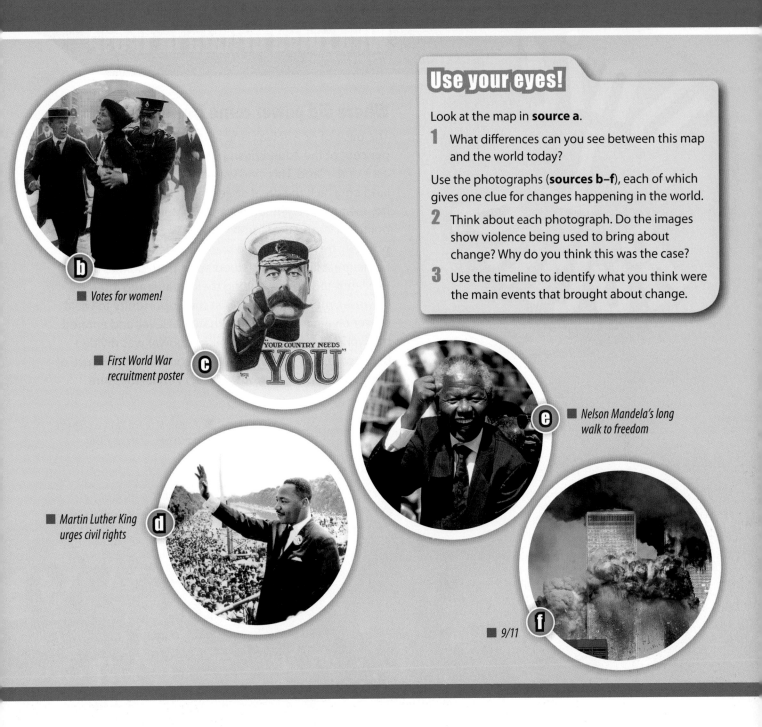

Use your eyes!

Look at the map in **source a**.

1 What differences can you see between this map and the world today?

Use the photographs (**sources b–f**), each of which gives one clue for changes happening in the world.

2 Think about each photograph. Do the images show violence being used to bring about change? Why do you think this was the case?

3 Use the timeline to identify what you think were the main events that brought about change.

■ *Votes for women!*

■ *First World War recruitment poster*

"YOUR COUNTRY NEEDS YOU"

■ *Nelson Mandela's long walk to freedom*

■ *Martin Luther King urges civil rights*

■ *9/11*

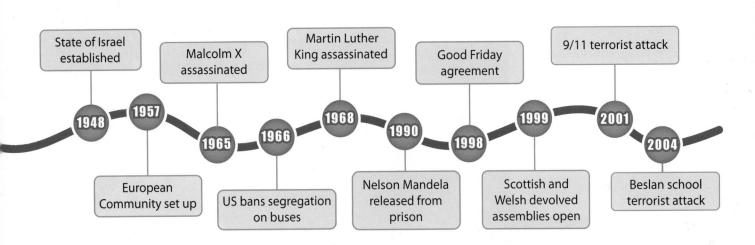

State of Israel established — 1948

European Community set up — 1957

Malcolm X assassinated — 1965

US bans segregation on buses — 1966

Martin Luther King assassinated — 1968

Nelson Mandela released from prison — 1990

Good Friday agreement — 1998

Scottish and Welsh devolved assemblies open — 1999

9/11 terrorist attack — 2001

Beslan school terrorist attack — 2004

Unit 1 Ruling

Where did power come from?

The basis of power was land and property. Roughly 10 per cent of the adult British population owned 95 per cent of the land. This land wasn't just farming land, but land on which the great streets and squares of London (for example, Regent Street and Russell Square) were built. Docks and ports, iron works and mines were mostly privately owned and the owners wielded power, too. Some great landowners stood apart from politics and concentrated on developing their estates and interests. However, most could not resist the opportunity to wield power on a national and international level, and entered the world of politics. Here, political power was divided between the Crown, the House of Lords and the House of Commons but not, as you will see, in equal measure.

■ *A photo of Queen Victoria's funeral procession, 2 February 1901.*

Think it over

4 Who, or what, had the most power in Britain in 1900?

5 Is the power structure fair? Remember that Parliament (the House of Lords and the House of Commons) will be making decisions that affect the lives of everyone in Britain.

6 If you wanted to change the balance of power, how could it be done?

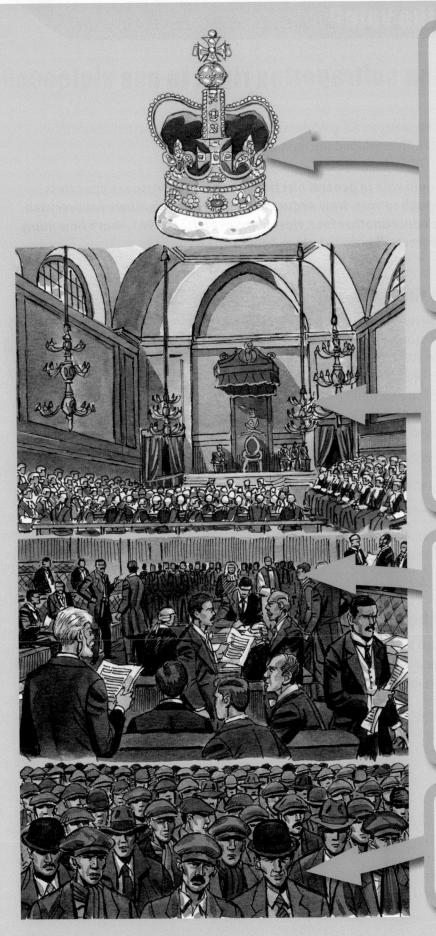

The Crown chose the prime minister (almost always the leader of the party that had a majority in the House of Commons), and this was the only real political power the Crown had. However, the monarch exercised a great deal of power as far as influence and patronage was concerned. Millions of people in Britain and the British Empire felt strong ties of loyalty to the monarch. Queen Victoria had died in January 1901 (after reigning for 63 years) and was succeeded by her son, Edward VII.

Dukes and earls, marquises and bishops sat in the **House of Lords**. Most were great landowners and many did not belong to any particular political party. Before any bill became law the House of Lords had to agree to it. In this way the Lords controlled the Commons.

The Conservative and Liberal parties dominated the **House of Commons**. The basis of any government's power was its ability to command a majority in the House of Commons. This majority was won at general elections. If its majority held up, a party could remain in power for seven years. The Labour Party had only come into being as a political party in 1900 and held just two seats in 1901.

In 1900, only men could vote in general elections. About six men in every ten had the right to vote, which was based on renting or owning property above a certain value.

In this lesson you will:

■ find out about the methods used by the suffragettes

■ investigate reactions to the suffragettes of those in authority.

○ Key words

MP or MPs
An abbreviation of Member or Members of Parliament.

Suffrage
The right to vote.

Suffragettes
Women who used militant, and sometimes illegal, ways of persuading people that women should have the vote.

Suffragists
Those who used peaceful, legal ways of persuading people that women should have the vote.

Were the suffragettes right to use violence?

Early in the twentieth century, women decided to be more assertive about their place in society. This included the right to vote.

? *Who could vote in general elections? Imagine everyone in your class is old enough to vote. Now deduct the number of girls. Then, for every ten boys, deduct another four. How many are left? In 1901, that's how many people were allowed to vote in general elections.*

Who were the suffragettes?

In 1903 Emmeline Pankhurst and her daughters set up a pressure group called the Women's Social and Political Union (WSPU). They had grown irritated by the lack of progress made by the National Union of Women's **Suffrage** Societies (NUWSS) towards getting the vote for women. NUWSS members, known as **suffragists**, used peaceful, legal methods.

● They held rallies and public meetings.

● They sent petitions to Parliament.

● They wrote letters to the newspapers and to their **MPs**.

However, WSPU members were determined to use more drastic methods. Their motto was 'Deeds, not words' and they became known as **suffragettes**.

a

■ *Emmeline Pankhurst being arrested outside Buckingham Palace, 21 May 1914. As part of a larger demonstration, she was trying to present a petition to the King, demanding votes for women.*

What did the suffragettes do?

The suffragettes were determined to attract as much publicity as possible. They designed their own banners and sashes in purple, green and white. They heckled politicians at public meetings, chained themselves to railings, poured chemicals into letter boxes, smashed windows, cut telegraph wires, slashed paintings and occasionally burned down buildings. They believed this was the only way to:

● make the government listen to them

● respond to what they saw as the violence of the police and therefore the government.

On 18 November 1910, about 300 suffragettes marched to Westminster (home of the Houses of Parliament) intending to speak with Prime Minister Herbert Asquith. They were met by a large force of police and trouble flared up.

Your turn ...

1 What surprises you about **source a**? Talk to the person next to you and see what ideas you both have.

2 What questions do you need to ask about **source a** so that you can fully understand what is happening and why? Work with the person next to you and make a list. Share the list with others in your class. (Your questions should be answered in the rest of this lesson!)

b

For hours I was beaten about the body, thrown backwards and forwards from one to another, until one felt dazed by the horror of it. Often seized by the coat collar and pushed into a side street while the policeman beat up and down my spine until cramp seized my legs, when he would release me with a vicious shove, and with insulting speeches, such as 'I will teach you a lesson; I will teach you not to come back any more. I will punish you, you ****, you ****. Once, I was thrown with my jaw against a lamp-post with such force that two of my front teeth were loosened.

■ *Extract from one of the 150 statements made by suffragettes complaining of their treatment on 18 November 1910, when they marched to Westminster.*

c

It was my intention to have these women removed from the scene of disorder as soon as possible, and then to prosecute only those who had committed personal assaults on the police or other serious offences. The directions I gave were not fully understood or carried out. I believe the Metropolitan police behaved on 18 November with the patience and humanity for which they are well known. I reject the unsupported allegations that come from that fountain of lies, the Women's Social and Political Union.

■ *Winston Churchill, who was Home Secretary at the time, gives the official version of events on 18 November 1910.*

Tit for tat?

When the courts fined suffragettes for crimes they had committed, the women almost always opted to go to prison instead. Many of them went on hunger strike once they were in prison. The authorities decided to force-feed the hunger strikers. The government hurried a bill through Parliament, which allowed hunger-striking suffragettes to be released, kept at home until they regained their strength, then imprisoned again.

Did you know?

In 1918, Parliament gave the vote to all men over the age of 21 and to all women aged 30 and over who were householders or married to a householder.

d

People were held down by force, flung on the floor, tied to chairs and iron bedspreads while the tube was forced up the nostrils. After each feeding the nasal pain gets worse. The wardress endeavoured to make one prisoner open her mouth by sawing the edge of a cup along her gums. The broken edge caused laceration and severe pain. Food into the lung of one unresisting prisoner immediately caused severe choking, vomiting and persistent coughing. She was hurriedly released the next day, suffering from pneumonia and pleurisy.

■ *Extract from* The Lancet, *a medical journal, which described the force-feeding in its August 1912 publication.*

Think it through

3 Read **sources b** and **c**. Should you believe the evidence of the Home Secretary, Winston Churchill, more than that of the suffragettes? Why?

4 Study **sources d** and **e**. What is the message of the WSPU poster?

5 Think about all the **sources (a–e)**. Do you think the reaction of the authorities to suffragette militancy was reasonable?

■ *A WSPU poster in response to the government's bill.*

e

THE CAT AND MOUSE ACT
PASSED BY THE LIBERAL GOVERNMENT

THE LIBERAL CAT
ELECTORS VOTE AGAINST HIM!
KEEP THE LIBERAL OUT!

f

■ *Lady White's house, burned down by suffragettes on 20 March 1913. The suffragettes made sure no people or pets were inside before firing it. Lady White was a well-known opponent of women's suffrage.*

Argue both sides

6 Imagine you are one of the suffragettes involved in burning down Lady White's house (**source f**). An investigative journalist has come to interview you. What would you say to justify your actions?

7 What would Lady White have said when she was interviewed by the same journalist?

What did the suffragettes do to get the vote?

In this lesson you will:

■ decide whether Emily Davison's death was suicide or an accident

■ consider the differing reactions to her death.

Key words

2/6 and 7/6
Pre-decimal currency; 2/6 is 12.5p in decimal currency and 7/6 is 37.5p.

Martyr
Someone who dies for a cause.

Propaganda
Information that deliberately misleads people about the true facts.

The Derby
Important horse race held once a year at Epsom, near London.

Emily Davison: suicide or accident?

? *Look at source a. What do you think is happening? Write down three things you can see. As a class, make a complete list.*

a

■ *From the front page of* Lloyd's Weekly News, *published on 8 June 1913.*

Did Emily Davison commit suicide?

Emily Davison was a militant suffragette. She gave up her career as a teacher to campaign for the rights of women. She died on 4 June 1913 when she was knocked over by a horse at the Epsom **Derby**. It is your job to decide whether Emily's death was suicide or an accident:

Over to you ...

1 If you watch live sports you will know that commentators make races as exciting as possible. If you had been an outside broadcaster at this event, what would you have said? Use **sources a** and **b** to help you write or record a commentary. Make it as lively and dramatic as you can.

Did you know?
In 1928, Parliament gave the vote to all women on equal terms with men.

b

Miss Davison, who was standing a few yards from me, suddenly ducked under the railings as the horses came up. This was very near Tattenham Corner, and there was a very large crowd of people on both sides of the course. The King's horse came up and Miss Davison went towards it. She put up her hand, but whether it was to take hold of the reins or to protect herself, I do not know. It was all over in a few seconds. The horse knocked the woman over with very great force, and then stumbled and fell, pitching the jockey violently on to the ground. Both he and Miss Davison were bleeding heavily, but the crowd that swarmed around her almost immediately was too much for me to see any more.

I feel sure that Miss Davison meant to stop the horse, and that she did not go onto the course thinking the race was over. The affair distressed the crowd very much.

■ *An account from eye witness John Irvine.*

What do you think?

2 Read **sources c** and **d**. In your judgement, did Emily Davison mean to die? Back up what you say with evidence from the two sources.

3 Now read **sources e** and **f**. How do you account for the differences between these two reactions to Emily Davison's actions?

What do you think? Was Emily Davison brave? Silly? Thoughtless? Calculating? Was she a **martyr**? Talk about this in your group.

c

On her jacket being removed, I found two suffragette flags, each consisting of green, white and purple stripes folded up and pinned to the back of her jacket on the inside.

On her person was found:

- 1 purse containing three shillings and eight pence three farthings
- 1 return half of a railway ticket from Epsom to Victoria
- 2 postal orders for **2/6** and **7/6**
- 8 postage stamps
- 1 key
- 1 helper's pass for the Suffragette Festival, Empress Rooms, High Street, Kensington, London, for 4 June 1913
- 1 memo book
- 1 race card
- some envelopes and writing paper
- 1 handkerchief.

■ *From a police report listing what was found in Emily Davison's jacket and pockets after her death.*

In conclusion

4 Look at **source g** and consider your own opinion of Emily Davison's death. Do you think the WSPU used Emily Davison's death for **propaganda** purposes?

d

Emily Davison and a fellow militant had planned a Derby protest without tragedy – a mere waving of the purple-white-and-green at Tattenham Corner, which, by its suddenness, it was hoped would stop the race. Her friend declares that she would not thus have died without writing a farewell message to her mother. Yet, she sewed the WSPU colours inside her coat as though to make sure that no mistake could be made as to her motive when her body was examined.

■ *Written by Sylvia Pankhurst in her book* The Suffrage Movement, *published in 1931. Sylvia was one of Emmeline Pankhurst's daughters.*

e

The case will, of course, become the subject of investigation by the police, and we may possibly learn from the offender herself what exactly she intended to do and how she fancied it would help the suffragist cause. A deed of this kind, we need hardly say, is not likely to increase the popularity of any cause with the ordinary public. We believe that yesterday's event did more to hurt the cause of women's suffrage than to help it.

■ *From a report in* The Times *newspaper on 5 June 1913, the day after the Derby.*

f

News came of Emily Davison's historic act. She had stopped the King's horse at the Derby and was lying mortally injured. We were as startled as everyone else. Not a word had she said of her purpose. Taking advice from no one, she had gone to the racecourse, waited her moment and rushed forward. Horse and jockey were unhurt, but Emily Davison paid with her life for making the whole world understand that women were in earnest for the vote. Probably in no other way, and at no other time and place, could she so effectively have brought the concentrated attention of millions to the cause of votes for women.

■ *Written by Christabel Pankhurst in her book* Unshackled, *published in 1959. Christabel was Emmeline Pankhurst's eldest daughter.*

g

■ *Emily Davison's funeral procession as it moved through London, 14 June 1913.*

Back to the start

You have read a lot about the actions of the WSPU. Do you think they were justified in being militant?

How did one assassination cause a war?

In this lesson you will:

- find out how assassination led to war in the Balkans
- explain the relationship between different causes.

Key words

Balkans
Area of south-east Europe that includes many present-day countries such as Albania, Serbia, Croatia and Bulgaria.

Slav
Ethnic group from eastern and central Europe with several related languages.

Why did a war break out in the Balkans?

The date is 28 June 1914. The heir to the throne of the Austro-Hungarian Empire, Archduke Franz Ferdinand, is travelling through the streets of Sarajevo in Bosnia-Herzegovina accompanied by his wife. As the car slows down, two shots ring out …

? *What is happening in source a? Describe the scene.*

Why did war break out?

The assassination of the Archduke and his wife was the trigger for a war in which around 9.7 million military personnel were killed. The war led to rulers being overthrown and the map of Europe being redrawn. The world was never the same again. But what were the reactions to the assassinations, and how and why did they lead to a war in the region of Europe known as the **Balkans**?

a

■ *The assassination of Archduke Franz Ferdinand and his wife by a Serbian youth, Gavrilo Princip, 28 June 1914.*

The Balkans had been controlled until the late part of the nineteenth century by the Turkish Ottoman Empire. As the Turkish grip weakened, many of the small countries in the region wanted to become nations in their own right. However, two of the most powerful empires in the world (Austria and Hungary) wanted to control the region.

The Austro-Hungarian Empire was made up of different nationalities including Serbians, Croats, Czechs and Germans. Austria-Hungary's rulers wanted to dominate the Balkans because they feared that any growth in the power of Balkan states such as Serbia might lead to demands for independence from ethnic minorities within the empire.

Russia wanted to protect fellow **Slavs** in Serbia and the rest of the Balkans region. It had lost out to Austria-Hungary in 1908 when they seized control of Bosnia-Herzegovina. Russia's rulers were determined that it would not be so humiliated again.

AUSTRO-HUNGARIAN EMPIRE

BOSNIA-HERZEGOVINA

ROMANIA

SERBIA

MONTENEGRO

BULGARIA

N

Adriatic Sea

ALBANIA

0   100 miles (161 km)

GREECE

■ *A map of the Balkans region in 1909.*

War or peace?

The assassination of Franz Ferdinand shocked politicians and military leaders in the Balkan countries and beyond. They put their ideas to their countries' rulers as to what should happen next.

1 Working in groups of three, read through the thoughts of key advisers from the countries involved (below). Make a note of the allies and enemies of:
- Austria-Hungary
- Germany
- Serbia.

2 In turn, each group member should choose a country and explain to the other two in the group the arguments for and against war for that country.

What do you think?

3 Working in the same groups of three, select one leader each:
- King Petar of Serbia
- Emperor Franz Joseph of Austria-Hungary
- Kaiser Wilhelm II of Germany.

In turn, read the opinions of your advisers. Then decide whether to go war or not. Tell others in your group:
- your decision (will you go to war or not?)
- the factors you took into account in making your decision.

Austria-Hungary: Count Hoyos

I have been to Germany to discuss the situation with the German leader, Kaiser Wilhelm. He has given us a 'blank cheque' to do whatever we want with Serbia. The Emperor agrees that now is our chance to deal with Serbia once and for all. If Russia threatens us, it will have to face the might of the Austrian and German Army.

Austria-Hungary: Count Tisza

I am worried that war will cause unrest in the Austro-Hungarian Empire. There are thousands of Slavs in the Empire and they will sympathise with Serbia. If we win the war, what will we do with Serbia? A war with Serbia might lead to instability in the region for years.

Serbia: Colonel Apis

We must seize this opportunity to fight a war against Austria-Hungary. They have issued us with an ultimatum that we must reject. Russia will support us militarily. This is our chance to create a greater and stronger Serbia.

Serbia: Prime Minister Pašić

Let's see what happens. Perhaps this crisis will sort itself out with an international conference. Maybe Britain can bring the leaders of the main powers together to agree a solution. Russia says it will support us, so perhaps Austria will think twice about using force against us. King Petar hopes we can avoid war.

Germany: Chancellor Bethmann Hollweg

Germany must support Austria in its argument with Serbia in any way we can. We must fight against Russia before its army becomes too strong, even if this means fighting against France as well. We should pretend to the outside world we want peace, but we should get ready for war. I think this is what the Kaiser wants.

Germany: Prince Heinrich

I am against war. As the Kaiser's brother, I am very worried that a war with Serbia will lead to a war with Russia and that this will result in war against Britain. The British navy is too strong for the German navy and will crush it if a war starts.

Give explanations

4 You have studied the decisions of each of the important rulers. Now answer the following question.

Why did war break out between Serbia and Austria-Hungary in 1914?

Try to find a way of explaining how the actions of one country had an impact on the decisions of others.

In this lesson you will:

- find out about the causes of the First World War

- use information from different sources to explain why war spread.

How did war a world war begin?

What is happening in this cartoon, published in 1914?

The countries of Europe were divided into two distinct groups or alliances. They were like gangs in the playground: when one member of the gang becomes involved in an argument, everyone else in the gang joins in on their side. The events of June 1914 triggered the alliance system into action.

The two sides were known as the Triple Entente and the Triple Alliance. This is how the two sides lined up.

Triple Alliance: Germany, Austria-Hungary, Italy. They were supported by the Ottoman Empire.

Triple Entente: France, Great Britain and Russia. They were supported by Serbia.

For some time tension had been rising between the two sides. Below are some of the events that raised the temperature.

Read and think

1 Read through the information in the table opposite (top of page) about the main countries involved. Then, in pairs, make an overall judgement about the strength of each country. Give each one a score from 1–5, where: **5** = very strong indeed and **1** = weak.

Note: although Italy was a member of the Triple Alliance, its rulers decided not go to war in 1914. When Italy did join the war in 1915 it was on the side of the Triple Entente.

2 Before you finalise your scores, discuss them with another pair. See if you can come to an agreement.

3 According to these agreed scores, which side looks stronger?

1898	**1905**	**1908**	**1911**	**By 1914**
Germany started to build warships to rival the British Royal Navy.	Kaiser Wilhelm visited Morocco, which was under French influence.	Austria seized Bosnia-Herzegovina – an action that upset Russia and Serbia.	Germany sent the gunboat *Panther* to Morocco to again challenge French claims on the country.	Most countries were heavily armed and ready for war.

Country	Soldiers available in 1914	Money spent on military 1913–14	Battleships	Population
Germany	2,200,000	£60 million	40	65 million +15 million in Empire
Austria-Hungary	810,000	£22 million	16	50 million
Italy	750,000	£10 million	14	35 million + 2 million in Empire
Ottoman Empire	360,000	£8 million	0	20 million
France	1,250,000	£37 million	28	40 million + 58 million in Empire
Great Britain	234,000	£50 million	64	45 million + 390 million in Empire
Russia	1,200,000	£67 million	16	164 million
Serbia	195,000	£1.25 million	0	5 million

How did war start ?

4 Read through the events on the right, then place them in date order on a timeline.

5 Use the events to describe, in your own words, the outbreak of war. You will need to refer to information from Lesson 1.2a to complete your account. You must mention every country named. In your description you should try to identify these turning points:

- the outbreak of war in the Balkans
- when a Balkans war became a European war
- when a European war became a world war.

In conclusion ...

6 You have described **how** war broke out in three different phases. You job now is to explain **why**. Complete, in no more than 70 words, each statement. Use the clues beneath the statements to help you.

Statement 1: War broke out between Austria-Hungary and Serbia because …

Clues: *assassination, ultimatum, blank cheque*

Statement 2: The war in the Balkans became a wider European war because …

Clues: *mobilisation, Russia, France, Germany, alliance system*

Statement 3: The war turned from being a European war to a world war because …

Clues: *Britain, invasion of Belgium, Empire*

1 August
France and Germany order mobilisation of their armies because of high tension between the two countries.

28 July
Austria declares war on Serbia and stops talking to Russia because it thinks it can destroy Serbia without starting a major war.

1 August
Germany declares war against Russia in response to Russian mobilisation. The war escalates.

4 August
Britain and its worldwide Empire declare war on Germany to protect Belgium and prevent Germany seizing the Channel ports, including Ostend.

2 August
Germany begins the invasion of Luxemburg

25 July
Serbia replies to Austria's ultimatum rejecting one of the points. Serbia and Austria mobilise.

24 July
Russia decides Serbia must not be attacked and devoured by Austria.

23 June
Austria sends Serbia a list of demands known as an ultimatum because it wants to provoke Serbia into war.

30 July
The Tsar gives the order to mobilise the whole of the Russian army in response to Austria's declaration of war on Serbia.

29 July
The German Chancellor, Bethmann Hollweg, tries to persuade Britain to stay neutral but fails.

3 August
Germany declares war against France and invades Belgium. It is now at war on two fronts against Russia and France.

Back to the start

You have read about the reasons for the outbreak of the First World War. In groups discuss the following statement:

Germany has often been blamed for starting the First World War. But to what extent should historians place all of the blame on Germany?

Next Lesson

We want to volunteer!

Britain declared war on Germany on 4 August 1914. But in order to fight a war, it needed soldiers. Many men were very willing to volunteer to fight for their country. And many women were happy to volunteer to work in supporting roles.

? *Look at source a. What is the mood of the crowd in Trafalgar Square?*

■ *A crowd in Trafalgar Square, London, gathered on 4 August 1914 to support Britain's declaration of war.*

Get into character

1 Imagine it is September 1914 and you are 18 years old.

  a) Choose a name for yourself from these lists.
    First name: Albert, Arthur, George, Thomas, Dorothy, Emily, Grace, May
    Last name: Cook, Edwards, Greaves, Jones, Kenyon, Marshall, Mitchell, Power

  b) Now choose your occupation:
    domestic servant, factory weaver, farm labourer, office worker, printer, student, typist, unemployed.
    Remember your name and occupation, as you will use them again later.

2 Look at **source a**. As your character, what might be your initial reactions to the outbreak of war?

3 Now look at **sources b** and **c**.

  a) How does each poster try to persuade people to volunteer to help with the war effort? Look for clues in the design of the posters, the colours used and the messages given.

  b) What are the similarities between these posters?

  c) Which poster would be most effective in persuading your character and why?

■ *A recruitment poster which first appeared on the cover of a weekly magazine, London Opinion, in 1914.*

c ■ *A recruitment poster for the Voluntary Aid Detachment (VAD), which gave medical help in times of war.*

d

We don't want to lose you but we think you ought to go,

For your king and your country both need you so.

We shall want you and miss you,

But with all out might and main

We shall cheer you, thank you, kiss you,

When you come back again.

■ *A popular song, entitled 'Your King and Country Want You', from 1914.*

Britain needs you!

To fight a war Britain needed an army. While it had a very large navy, its army in August 1914 was small at around 234,000 men in comparison to the German army of 1.7 million. On 6 August the Secretary of State for War, Lord Kitchener, was given permission by Parliament to recruit 500,000 soldiers for a new army. By 12 September 1914, 478,893 men had joined up. Most believed they would be home by Christmas.

Within a week of the outbreak of the war, the 100,000 strong British Expeditionary Force (BEF) had left England to fight the German army, which was advancing through Belgium. The fighting was fierce. Nine out of ten soldiers in the BEF were either wounded or killed by Christmas 1914.

The army needed nurses to help tend the wounded and dying. At the start of the war there were only 300 nurses in the army and 2,000 nurses in reserve. However, there were 2,500 branches known as Voluntary Aid Detachments (VAD), which were first set up in 1909 to give medical support to the armed forces. At the outbreak of war, thousands of women volunteered to join the VADs or similar organisations such as the Red Cross or St John's Ambulance.

Why did so many volunteer?

Sources d–g give some clues as to why so many men and women volunteered to serve.

Why I have volunteered

4 Using the identity you have chosen for yourself, write a letter to one of your parents explaining why you have chosen to volunteer for Kitchener's New Army or the VAD.

What was the impact?

5 Using **sources a–g,** describe in no more than 300 words the response of the public to the declaration of war. Here are some of the themes you might cover in your description: *Belgium, enthusiasm, volunteering, patriotism, opposition.*

e

Spurred on by the bad news of the BEF, now in full retreat in Belgium, a wave of enthusiasm swept the country. Many felt a strong pride in Britain and the Empire. Younger people were inspired by the thought of travel at a time when few people had travelled abroad. Many workers and the unemployed saw **joining up** as a means of escaping miserable jobs and conditions. This was a heaven-sent opportunity; away from mines, poor pay and slums and into a new life with fresh air, regular meals and good pay. Many joined units known as Pals battalions, with their friends.

■ *Adapted from Martin Middlebrook's book* The First Day on the Somme, *published in 1971.*

f

Faced with overwhelming odds, Belgium squared up to the invader and appealed to its allies for help. The public imagination in Britain was caught by the justness of the cause. Germany should not be allowed to get away with it. Public anger was fanned by stories that German soldiers were raping Belgian women and **bayoneting** Belgian children. It was no wonder that it was a popular war and everyone wanted to do their bit.

■ *Adapted from Lyn MacDonald's book* The Roses of No Man's Land, *published in 1993.*

g

I spent the evening walking round the streets, especially Trafalgar Square, noticing cheering crowds, and making myself sensitive to the emotions of passers-by. During this and the following days I discovered to my amazement that average men and women were delighted at the prospect of war. Meanwhile, I was living at the highest possible emotional tension. Although I did not foresee anything like the full disaster of the war, I foresaw a great deal more than most people did. War filled me with horror. But what filled me with even more horror was that 90 per cent of the population were delighted with the prospect of war.

■ *Adapted from the autobiography of Bertrand Russell, an anti-war protestor. He was imprisoned during the First World War for his* **pacifist** *activities.*

1.3b

In this lesson you will:

■ discover what life was like on the front line

■ evaluate how useful diaries are to historians.

● Key words

Gangrenous
When body tissue becomes infected and starts to rot. The answer to gangrene in the First World War was amputation, cutting the rotting part of the body off.

Shrapnel
Fragments of a bomb that scatter on explosion.

What was life like on the front line?

Diaries are very useful sources of information for historians. They give first-hand accounts and opinions of life and events at the time they were written.

? *Do you keep a diary? If so, what kind of things do you write in it? Read source a. Why is this extract useful to historians writing about life in the trenches in the First World War?*

Trench warfare

By the end of 1914, the armies on the Western Front faced each other along a front that stretched from the English Channel to Switzerland. To protect themselves, both armies dug trenches. For the next three and a half years, trench warfare was to produce millions of casualties but gain little territory for either side. The trench system made attacking very difficult, as the illustration shows.

a

14 June 1916: Returned to the company at 10am, and this afternoon two more men were buried in a dug-out. One, Private George Shaw (Chester), who joined the Battalion the same day as myself, was killed having both legs blown off. The other, Private Lol Beasley (Runcorn), had one leg blown off and was just alive when got out. I mounted guard this afternoon until 4pm the following day.

■ *From* The Diary of Thomas Fredrick Littler: January–June 1916.

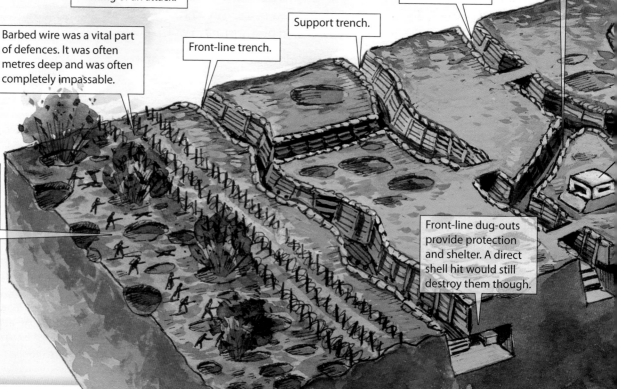

Aeroplanes and observation balloons are used to watch enemy troop movements and give warning of an attack.

Troops from the reserve trenches could be sent forward more safely through these communication trenches.

Reserve trench.

Support trench.

Front-line trench.

Barbed wire was a vital part of defences. It was often metres deep and was often completely impassable.

The area between the front-line trenches was known as No Man's Land. Constant shelling turned it into a mass of mud, making it even harder for troops to attack across.

Front-line dug-outs provide protection and shelter. A direct shell hit would still destroy them though.

1 Working in pairs, read the diary entries for this lesson. One of you should read **sources b** and **c**; the other should read **sources d** and **e**. Pick at least three things from each source about life on the front line. Share these points with your partner.

Daily life

Many people kept diaries of their experiences on the front line. Here are some extracts from some diaries.

4 December 1915: Marching to trenches 4.10, dusk, shells bursting, someone says, boys it is Saturday night. Men coming out of trenches up to their thighs in mud. Reached trenches 5.30 bullets and **shrapnel** bursting over our heads, slept in dug-out, lying with legs over one another and hundreds of rats as big as rabbits crawling all over us, biting holes in Haversacks for our rations.

■ *From the diary of Sergeant William Whitmore.*

30 October 1915: I hated it this afternoon. There was one boy who couldn't have been more than 20. His seven brothers were all killed and his mother had died – he said it was from grief. He wasn't ill enough to be sent back to Blighty [England]. He sat waiting to hear his fate from the Medical Officer. The decision came, he isn't fit but he isn't ill, it had to be off to the convalescent camp and 'Up the Line' once more.

■ *From the diary of VAD Kitty Kenyon.*

20 September 1914: You boarded a cattle truck, armed with a tray of dressings and a bucket; the men were lying on straw, had been in trains for several days. Most had only been dressed once, and many were **gangrenous**. If you found one urgently needing amputation or operation, or was likely to die, you called a medical officer to have him taken off the train for hospital. Most wounds came from shrapnel shells and are more horrible than anything I have ever seen or smelt.

■ *From the diary of Sister K. Luard.*

15 August 1917: Working day and night. Fortunately plenty of rum can be had as there are many jars lying about. Bombardment goes on all of the time; numerous cases of gassed men. At night the enemy sends over gas shells. Sometimes the gas does not affect the men for three or four days and then they just collapse. Corporal Service was helping a wounded man when a gas shell burst just in front of them. He shouted: 'Hold your breath and come on.'

■ *From the diary of Sergeant R. McKay.*

Artillery fires onto the front line from up to 10 kilometres (6 miles) away. Shellfire from these guns is used to try to destroy enemy fortifications and kill enemy troops.

Machine guns were placed in a concrete block house for protection. These would be placed in groups that provided covering fire for each other.

Both sides constructed deep dug-outs as much as 15 metres (49 feet) below ground. These were too well built to be damaged by shellfire and meant defended troops could emerge once shelling had stopped.

What questions shall I ask?

2 Imagine you have been asked to investigate life on the front line in the First World War. You have been given **sources a–e** as a starting point. Evaluate this information by compiling a list of six questions you need to ask of the sources. Here are three categories for your questions, the first one with an example. You will need to come up with two questions for each category.
Category 1: Content of the sources
What do the diaries not mention?
Category 2: Situation of the author
Category 3: Purpose of the author writing

3 Once you have drawn up your questions, compare them with someone else in your class.

How useful are the diaries?

4 Answer this question: *How useful are diary extracts for historians investigating life in the trenches in the First World War?*
To help with your answer, you will need to look at the strengths and weaknesses of using diaries.

1.3c

What happened on the first day of the Battle of the Somme?

The *Daily Chronicle* was one of the most popular newspapers in Britain during the First World War. **Source a** shows a headline and report written by journalist Philip Gibbs about the attack on 1 July 1916. Gibbs was not allowed to watch the battle but stayed some 8 kilometres (5 miles) behind the front line.

But had all gone well? The British and French attack on the German lines at the Somme was to see Kitchener's 'New Armies', which had been raised in 1914, put to the test. The attack along a 26-kilometre (16-mile) front was planned by Field Marshal Haig and General Rawlinson. They ordered the shelling of the German lines and barbed wire for seven days before the attack in the hope that the wire would be cut and the German defenders killed.

? *What impression does source a give of the attack?*

a

The Historic first of July

The attack launched today against the German lines on a 20-mile front began satisfactorily. It is not yet a victory, for victory comes at the end of a battle, and this is only a beginning. But our troops, fighting with very splendid valour, have swept across the enemy's front trenches along a great part of the line of attack, and have captured villages and strongholds which the Germans have long held against us. Many hundreds of enemy are prisoners in our hands. His dead lie thick in the track of our regiments. And so, after the first day of battle, we may say with thankfulness: All goes well.

At 7.30am on Saturday 1 July 1916, the men of the British divisions selected for the attack climbed out of their trenches and started to walk across No Man's Land towards the German lines. Ten minutes earlier, a huge mine had been set off under Hawthorn Ridge near Beaumont Hamel giving the German artillerymen and machine gunners more than enough warning of the attack. By the end of the day 19,240 British and Empire soldiers had been killed, 2,152 were missing and another 35,593 were wounded; a total of 56,985 men.

■ *An abandoned German position in Delville Wood, near the village of Longueval, during the Battle of the Somme. The photo was taken in September 1916.*

1 Sort **sources a–f** into the following categories:

- those that suggest the attack on 1 July 1916 was a success
- those that suggest it was a disaster
- those that are a mixture of the two.

1 July 1916: Reports up to 8am most satisfactory. Our troops have everywhere crossed the enemy's front trenches.

2 July 1916: I visit two casualty clearing stations. They were very pleased at my visit, the wounded were in wonderful spirits. Reported today that total casualties are estimated at over 40,000. This cannot be considered severe in view of numbers engaged and the length of front of attack. By nightfall the situation is much more favourable than when we started today.

■ *Extracts from Field Marshal Sir Douglas Haig's diary.*

British advance.

16 miles of German front.

Trenches stormed.

'The day goes well' for our heroic troops.

Special telegrams to the 'News of the World'

British Headquarters, 1 July – Attacks launched north of River Somme this morning at 7.30am in conjunction with French forces.

British troops have broken into German forward system of defences on a front of 16 miles. Fighting is continuing. On remainder of British front raiding parties again succeed in penetrating enemy's defences at many points, inflicting loss on enemy and taking some prisoners.

■ *Headlines and report in the* News of the World, *2 July 1916.*

d

I was shell-shocked and I couldn't stop crying. I was told to take B Company over the top. The shellfire was absolutely appalling. They were simply pouring shells down. We couldn't get across [to the German lines]. We didn't even get as far as the trench we had dug. We got orders to turn and make our way back to the village. A young officer jumped out of the trench to try to organise the men and he was killed; just disappeared in an explosion. So many men were killed, we were simply treading on the dead. It was murder.

■ *Captain Arthur Agius describing his experiences of 1 July 1916.*

e

I could see, away to my left and right, long lines of men. Then I heard the 'patter, patter' of machine guns in the distance. By the time I'd gone another 10 yards there seemed to be only a few men left around me; by the time I had gone 20 yards, I seemed to be on my own. Then I was hit myself.

■ *Captain R. Wood describing his experiences on 1 July 1916.*

f

The 20th Battalion Manchester Regiment left the trench and took the Sunken Road trench. We could see about 400 of our soldiers advancing. There were about 25 casualties on the left of the advance. German machine guns were firing on the other side of the hill. At 7.15 people could be seen moving about the German lines beyond Sunken Road. The 20th Battalion Manchesters have been held up there. A good number of prisoners have been brought in on our sector (it has been reported that there were several hundred).

■ *Captain Siegfried Sassoon describing his experiences from 1 July 1916.*

How do the sources differ?

2 Explain how **sources a–f** agree and how they differ. Write five sentences, then share them with a partner. Here is an example:

Source a *agrees with* **source f** *that German prisoners were captured on 1 July.* **Source a** *states that 'Many hundreds of enemy are prisoners in our hands.'* **Source f** *says, 'A good number of prisoners have been brought in on our sector.'*

Why do the sources differ?

3 Create a spider diagram to explain why **sources a–f** differ. Think about: situation, context, purpose and nature of the evidence.

1.3d

In this lesson you will:

- find out about soldiers executed by their own side
- investigate a historical issue.

Why were soldiers shot at dawn?

Some soldiers were executed by their own side. The reasons for this can be complex and each case is different, as this lesson explores.

? *Read source a. What is going on? Why do you think it happened?*

a The officer had loaded the rifles and had left them lying on the ground at our position. We got into position and were warned to fire straight, or we may have to suffer the same fate. The prisoner was taken out of a car and placed on the other side of the curtain.

As soon as the curtain dropped, the prisoner was tied in a chair five paces away from us, a black cap over his head, we got the order to fire. One blank and nine live rounds. It went off as one. I did not have the blank. The prisoner did not feel it. We went back to the Battalion Orderly Room and got a big tumbler of rum each, and we went back to our **billets**, ate, and went to bed. We had the rest of the day off. It was a job I never wanted.

■ *From the journal of Canadian soldier Deward Barnes.*

To pardon or not to pardon?

Deward Barnes was part of a firing squad that executed Private Harold Lodge on 13 March 1918. During the First World War, 346 soldiers from Britain and the Commonwealth were executed by their own side; 306 were from Britain. After the war the families of those who were shot campaigned for a pardon for their loved ones. In 2006 the British government agreed to a general pardon for the 306 British soldiers shot, which meant that, as a group, the executed soldiers were forgiven. However, the government refused to reconsider the cases of each individual soldier. This is a controversial issue that is still hotly debated, and which still stirs up strong emotions on both sides of the debate.

Your turn ...

Before you consider individual cases, you need to understand the background to the executions.

1 Read **sources b** and **c** and the factfile. Discuss with a partner what the sources tell you.

2 Quickly skim through the three case studies. Then write five questions you think could be asked about each of the executed soldiers.

b Few of the executed men received even basic justice. The cases were poorly presented and were often not properly investigated. In the British Army in 1914 a number of offences could be punished with death. These included mutiny, cowardice [being a coward], disobeying an order, desertion, sleeping or being drunk when on duty, hitting a superior officer, throwing away weapons in the presence of the enemy.

■ *Adapted from historian Anthony Babbington's book* For the Sake of Example, *published in 1993.*

c The number of rogues outnumbered those wrongly executed by about six to one. Many of those shot were repeat deserters who showed no sign of shell shock. An individual re-assessment of these cases would undoubtedly reconvict the majority. Life was much harsher then; **capital punishment** was still used in Britain. And while the military law was harsh every one of the soldiers signed up to those regulations.

■ *From an interview with historian Cathryn Corns, co-author of* Blindfold and Alone, *published in 2001.*

British Army Regulations 1914

Offences punishable by death included:

- mutiny
- sleeping on duty
- assisting the enemy
- cowardice
- hitting a superior officer
- desertion
- discarding your weapon in the face of the enemy.

Make a judgement

3 Re-read the three case studies. Now use your five questions from task 2 to discuss with a partner whether, in each case:

- the soldier should be given an individual pardon
- the decision to execute the soldier was the right one.

Remember, your partner may have written different questions. Make sure you discuss them all.

Case study 1:
Private Edward Tanner

Edward Tanner arrived in France at the start of the war. He fought in the bloody early battles of the war in which many of his colleagues died. Conditions by mid-October 1914 in France were very poor and Tanner spent a short period of time in hospital with dysentery. On 18 October, Tanner was with a small group of soldiers in the village of Halpgarbe on route to rejoining his regiment. This is his account of what happened next:

'I lost my party at the village on the night of 18 October and after they had left I went off on my own in the direction where I thought my regiment was, when I walked into a firing line of some troops, so I turned round and came back to the village and slept there till daylight. I was terribly overcome by nervousness from heavy firing and do not know what I was doing at the time. I had just left hospital suffering from dysentery and my nerves were shattered by the Battle of the Aisne.'

The next day Tanner was stopped and questioned by a British Army officer. He was dressed as a civilian and he had hidden his rifle. He was arrested and tried by court martial. Tanner was not defended in court. His trial lasted 15 minutes, and his health and past record were not taken into account. Tanner was found guilty and was executed as an example to others.

Case study 2:
Private John Thomas Rogers

John Rogers joined the army in August 1915 but almost immediately went missing for eleven days. He was eventually arrested and imprisoned for a short period of time. This was a pattern that continued for the next year. In April 1916 he was sentenced to 56 days detention for going missing. In November 1916 Rogers was posted to France, but in February 1917 he disappeared after being told his battalion was going up to the front line. At his court martial, Rogers was not defended by a lawyer and he pleaded guilty to the charge of desertion. His only defence was that:

'I am very sorry it occurred. I had some drink on the night before and in consequence I was rather confused on the following day.'

Rogers's court martial lasted little more than 20 minutes. He was found guilty and shot.

Case study 3:
Private Harry Farr

Harry Farr served in the trenches and had fallen victim to shell shock. The symptom of this illness was uncontrollable shaking. He was in hospital for five months in 1915 and two weeks in 1916 with the condition. In September 1916 he was ordered to go up to the front line with a ration party, but he stayed behind the lines. It was well known that he was suffering from nerves. At his court martial, Farr gave the following evidence:

'On 16 September 1916, when going up to the trenches with my Company, I fell out sick. The Sergeant Major told me to go to the **advanced dressing station**. However, they would not see me there as I was not wounded. The Sergeant Major told me to go up with the ration party at night. I started with this party and had to fall out sick. I returned to the 1st Line Transport, hoping to report sick to some medical officer there. On the Sergeant Major's return I reported to him and said I was sick and could not stand it. The Sergeant Major then told Lance Coporal Form to fall out two men and take me up to the trenches. They commenced to shove me. I told them not to as I was sick enough as it was. The Sergeant Major then grabbed my rifle and said, "I'll blow your brains out if you don't go." After this I do not know what happened until I found myself back in the 1st Line Transport under a guard.'

Farr had served for nearly two years in France. It was clear that he suffered from a nervous disorder. Despite the evidence of good character from witnesses, the court martial found that Farr was guilty of cowardice and he was shot.

In conclusion ...

4 Discuss the following questions. Then write full answers to the questions, explaining your decisions.

- *Should British soldiers have been executed by their own side in World War One? (Be careful not to apply the values of today.)*
- *Was the government right to give a general pardon in 2006?*
- *Should the government have investigated individual cases?*

History detective

This is your chance to be a history detective! Find out more about those executed by visiting www.heinemann.co.uk/hotlinks. Put in the express code 9014P. Then find this lesson for a website that provides a good starting point.

Back to the start

Resume the character you chose in Lesson 1.3a. Remember how you felt about the war in 1914. How do you feel after the first day of the Battle of the Somme? How would you feel if you heard about the 'examples' set by these executions?

1.3e

Taking it further!

Remembering the war

Describe what you can see in **source a**.

The memorial in this photograph was built near the village of Thiepval, which saw some of the fiercest fighting during the Battle of the Somme. The memorial carries the names of the 73,000 British and Commonwealth soldiers whose bodies were not found and who have no grave. Each name listed on the wall was once a real person who left family, friends and loved ones behind.

Your task is to investigate the life of a person who lived during the First World War. This person might have been directly involved in the war effort as a soldier, nurse or factory worker, but do not worry if this was not the case. You might not get too far in your investigation but that does not matter; it is undertaking the investigation that counts. You can, if you like, investigate more than one person, or even a group of people.

To begin with, you need to ask yourself 'Who shall I investigate?' and 'How shall I investigate?'

a

■ *Thiepval War Memorial.*

Who shall I investigate?

You might attempt to investigate one or more of the following:

● a member of your family or of your carer's/guardian's family

● a member of a friend's family

● a name from a war memorial close to where you live.

How shall I investigate?

There are a number of leads you might follow. Here are some suggestions (and you might have some of your own).

● **Ask at home:** you might ask a parent, carer/guardian or another member of your family.

● **Library:** your local library might be able to help with information about people from your community.

● **Internet:** there are a number of very good websites you might visit. One of the best websites is the Commonwealth War Graves Commission. Another is a site that gives all kinds of useful information and stories about people's lives during the First World War. You can find details of both of these on www.heinemann.co.uk/hotlinks (express code 9014P).

Try to collect as much information as possible about your chosen person (or people). If you are given valuable photographs or medals to look at, you should try to photocopy or photograph them rather than keep them.

Questions and answers

1 What questions should you ask about the person (or people) under investigation? Draw up a list of at least five questions you want answered. Here are a couple of examples.

● What was your chosen person's job before the war?

● What did your chosen person do during the war?

2 When you have finished your investigation you should present your results. You will also need to explain:

● the process of your investigation – how you went about it and how successful you were (if you were not very successful try to explain why)

● the results – outline the questions you asked as part of your investigation, why you chose them and the answers you found.

You should also present your findings in full.

Next Lesson

What was the impact of the end of the First World War?

Key words

Demobbed
Someone who has left the armed services and has returned to civilian life.

Slum housing
Housing that is badly built, in bad condition and is often overcrowded.

What are your demands?

1 Get back into the character you created in Lesson 1.3a. Imagine it is 1921 and you are attending a public meeting for ex-servicemen with a small group of people who also served in the war.

  a) Before the meeting, write a list of demands which, if accepted by the government, will make Britain a 'land fit for heroes'.

  b) Compare your list with one written by another group.

A land fit for heroes?

The First World War ended on 11 November 1918. On 23 November, Prime Minister David Lloyd George made a speech to an election rally in Wolverhampton. In his speech he stated clearly: 'What is our task? To make Britain a fit country for heroes to live in.'

? *Look at source a. What problems did Britain face after the war? What other problems do you think there might have been? How successful had Lloyd George been in creating a country fit for heroes?*

■ *A group of unemployed ex-servicemen carry a banner demanding work in September 1919.*

What changed?

The sacrifice of life and limb was huge; Britain and its Empire lost just under 1 million men, with a further 2 million wounded. Around 9 million men had been mobilised to fight and 38,000 women had become VADs (see Lesson 1.3a). For many people, life before the war was tough, with poor healthcare, bad housing, unemployment and low wages.

What did the government do?

Politicians realised that, after four years of sacrifice, some reform to improve the lives of British people was necessary.

● In Lesson 1.1a, you learned how women were given the vote in 1918.

● Many workers benefitted from a reduction in working hours to eight hours a day. But many others were made unemployed as the British economy struggled to readjust; in 1921 more than 20 per cent of Britain's workforce were out of a job. The government responded in 1923 by extending national insurance to 60 per cent of the workforce. This meant you would receive some money if you were out of work. But 40 per cent of the workforce were not covered and the government did not provide jobs.

● The government tried to improve housing conditions. A series of Housing Acts meant that by 1921, 214,000 new homes had been built, and by 1933, another half a million new homes had been built and paid for by the government. But these new homes did not help the poorest people who could not afford the increased rent of this new housing. The government did nothing to tackle the problem of **slum housing**.

Private C. A. Turner, 1921

Many is the time I've gone to bed after a day of 'tramp, tramp' looking for work, on a cup of cocoa and a penny worth of chips between us; I would lay puzzling, why, why, after all we had gone through in the service of our country, we have to suffer such poverty, willing to work at anything but no work to be had.

2 In small groups, and still in your character, discuss the following questions.

- Has the government introduced the changes you wanted?
- What issues face ex-servicemen?
- How far has Lloyd George created a 'land fit for heroes'?

Lance Corporal P. J. Evans, 1923

Of course I have been angry and bitter about the betrayal of promises made to the men of the First World War. Wages have stayed low, which means many can't afford the rent of some of the new homes that have been built. Many of my miner friends suffered unemployment and poverty. They even had to watch their own children line up at soup kitchens.

Write a speech

3 Look back at task 1. You have been chosen to address the rally. In your speech you should explain:

- your war record
- the changes you expected after the war
- the extent of change which has taken place
- what you think of Lloyd George. (Remember, this is a public meeting and you must not be offensive.)

You may be asked to read your speech out.

Private F. W. A. Turner, 1928

More than anything I hated to see crippled men standing in the gutter selling matches. We had been promised a land fit for heroes; it took a hero to live in it. I'd never fight for my country again.

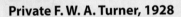

Captain Robert Graves, 1929

Ex-servicemen were continually coming to the door selling boot-laces and asking for cast-off shirts and socks. One day, an out-of-work ex-serviceman came calling with his three children and a baby. His wife had died in childbirth. We offered to adopt his eldest daughter.

Private Frank Richards, 1933

Living not far from me is an old artilleryman. He served for three years in France and was wounded and gassed. He suffers with his health and receives his pension of five shillings a week [25p, which might be worth £40 a week now]. No man has been treated with greater contempt than he was.

Corporal George Coppard, 1969

*No steps had been taken to look after the **demobbed** men and I joined the queues for jobs as messengers or window cleaners. It was a common sight in London to see ex-officers with barrel organs, trying to earn a living as beggars. The government looked after the high-ranking officers; Field Marshal Haig and Admiral Beatty were each given £100,000, an earldom and an estate for doing a job they were already paid to do.*

In this lesson you will:

- find out the reaction to the end of the war in Germany

- reach a judgement about the significance of defeat.

Key words

Communist
Person who believes in government by a single party that controls the country in order to bring about equality for the people.

What was the reaction in Germany to the end of the war?

Imagine an old suitcase belonging to someone called Wolfgang Schmidt has recently been discovered in a loft in the German city of Munich. It contains several scraps of paper and photographs. The photo shown in **source a** is of returning German soldiers marching through Munich in 1919. It is the first item removed from the suitcase.

? *What do you find so surprising about this photograph?*

What does it tell us?

1 Investigate the remaining contents of the suitcase (**sources a–g**). What does each item tell us about the impact of the end of the First World War? The significance of these items can sometimes be assessed:

- either on their own
- or along with other items.

b Our field-grey heroes return to the *Heimat* [homeland] undefeated, having protected the native soil from the horrors of war for four years. Everywhere a festive reception should be prepared for the returning troops. This will show the gratitude of the *Heimat* towards the undefeated heroes who stood their ground up to the last minute.

- *Poster issued by the German War Ministry, November 1918.*

- *A membership card from the German Workers' Party, which later became the Nazi Party.*

Write your memoirs

2 Imagine you are Wolfgang. Use all the items in your suitcase (**sources a–g, plus the letter from Hans**) to write a section of your memoirs about your reactions to the end of the war.

d

When we were told that we must now end the long war, that now that it was lost and we were throwing ourselves upon the mercy of the victors, I threw myself on my bunk, and dug my burning head into my blanket and pillow. And so it had all been in vain. In vain all the sacrifices; in vain the hunger and thirst of months which were often endless; in vain the hours in which, with fear in our hearts, we nevertheless did our duty; and in vain the death of two millions who died. The politicians who have surrendered are miserable and shameful criminals!

■ *A page from Adolf Hitler's book* Mein Kampf, *written in 1924.*

e

There will be a just and lasting peace. There shall be no annexations of land, no contributions, no punishing damages. The hopes of nations must be respected; people should only be ruled by their own consent. Self-determination is a very important principle which all statesmen shall note.

■ *Adapted from a German newspaper version of a speech by American President, Woodrow Wilson, 8 January 1918. The speech covered 14 points that would help to achieve world peace.*

f

Article 27: Germany to lose German-speaking Posen and West Prussia to Poland.

Article 198: The armed forces of Germany must not include any military air force.

Article 231: Germany must take responsibility for the war.

Article 232: Germany must pay reparations for the damage done.

Article 233: The amount that Germany should pay will be established by a Reparation Commission.

■ *Adapted from the Treaty of Versailles, 1919. This treaty set out terms for the end of the First World War.*

g

■ *German tank being dismantled as a result of the terms of the Treaty of Versailles.*

Berlin

21 November 1919

Dear Wolfgang,

I hope that you are well. It is strange to think that the war has been over for more than one year. Much has happened in that year, including Kaiser Wilhelm II's departure. There is another war that we are bravely fighting; the war on the streets against the **communists** *must continue. I hear that you bravely helped to crush the communist uprising in Munich in May, just as we had to in Berlin in January. We ended up killing the leaders of the revolution – Karl Liebknecht and Rosa Luxembourg – and we threw their bodies into the canal.*

Did you hear about Field Marshal Hindenburg's comments made a few days ago? He says that the German army was not defeated in the war by the English and French. He had made it clear that we were stabbed in the back by politicians and revolutionaries. What a great man the Field Marshal is.

Keep in touch.

Hans

What's the significance?

As you have seen from the items in Wolfgang's suitcase, the end of the war had a huge impact on Germany.

3   With a partner, use the items in Wolfgang's suitcase to identify four aspects that made the defeat so significant.

4   Discuss the significance of each one in as much detail as you can, then write them down.

What was the impact of the end of the First World War?

In this lesson you will:

- **examine the founding and actions of the League of Nations**

- **assess the meanings in contemporary cartoons.**

How was the League of Nations perceived?

The Great War was over and many were calling it the 'War to end all wars'. People now looked to the future to see what they could do to try to make sure this statement became true.

(?) *Look at source a. What can you see in this cartoon? Make a list of the images and what you think they represent.*

What was the League of Nations?

In 1919 the League of Nations was set up by the Treaty of Versailles with two main aims: to ensure that the world would not go to war again; and to make the world a better place.

In the 1920s the League of Nations successfully sorted out a number of disputes between smaller nations. It also created committees that took on a range of tasks from improving people's health to improving working conditions across the world. However, it had a number of weaknesses, including the fact that three major areas (the USA, Germany and the **Soviet** Union) did not become members in 1919. The American people did not want to get involved in world affairs. So even though the the US President, Woodrow Wilson, helped to establish the League of Nations, the **US Congress** decided that the USA would not join. Germany was not allowed to join because of what had happened in First World War. The Soviet Union was not allowed to join because there had been a revolution there in 1917 and the country was now run by communists, led by Lenin.

The League relied on collective security; the idea was that if one member of the League was attacked, then other members would come to its aid. The League did not have its own army, so it relied on powerful members such as Britain and France to enforce its decisions. Despite its limited successes in the 1920s, most nations put their own interests first, ahead of the interests of the League.

THE FLOWER.

■ *Cartoon by David Low published in* The Star *newspaper, 11 November 1919.*

Using cartoons

Cartoons can tell historians about attitudes at the time towards the League of Nations. The artist who drew the cartoons in **sources a, c** and **d** is David Low. He was a supporter of the League of Nations, which he felt was one of the best ways to keep the peace. David Low's cartoons were very popular and reflected the views of many people in Britain. The same can be said of the work of Leonard Raven-Hill (see **source b**), who worked for the very popular magazine *Punch*.

Look and think

1 Working in pairs look closely at **sources b–d**. What does each one tell us about the League of Nations? Try to come up with at least four points for each source.

Cartoon by Leonard Raven-Hill from Punch, 10 December 1919.

"Young Feller, the report has been greatly exaggerated."

Cartoon by David Low published in the Evening Standard, 5 September 1922. The seated figure represents War.

Cartoon by David Low published in the Evening Standard, 19 January 1933.

Problems facing the League

In 1929 the stock market on Wall Street, New York, crashed and the world fell into an economic depression. As a result, the League of Nations found it even harder to persuade the more powerful countries to spend money to support it.

In 1931, Japan invaded and conquered Manchuria, which was part of neighbouring China, despite the fact that both countries were members of the League of Nations. Japan had suffered during the depression and now wanted control of Manchuria's rich supply of raw materials, which included coal and wood. The Japanese government was heavily influenced by the Japanese army, which wanted to conquer as much of South-East Asia as it could. The League's response was to set up a commission led by Lord Lytton to investigate the invasion. In 1933, the commission criticised the actions of Japan, which promptly left the League.

Worse was to follow. In 1935, Italy, led by the dictator Benito Mussolini, invaded the African country of Abyssinia (now Ethiopia). As with the invasion of Manchuria, the League failed to stop Italy's aggression.

By the mid-1930s, the League had been shown to be weak and powerless, and aggressive countries now felt they could act as bullies without anyone doing anything about it.

Low opinions

2 Using the information you have from **sources a–d**, explain in writing how David Low's depiction of the League of Nations changes over time.

3 In pairs, discuss the following question. Then give a written answer.

   Why does Low's depiction of the League of Nations change?

Useful or not?

4 Decide whether **sources a–d** are useful to modern historians trying to find out about the League of Nations. For each cartoon, state which of the following two statements is more accurate. Give full reasons for your decisions.

   Statement 1: *Low's cartoons are exaggerated and are not useful to historians.*

   Statement 2: *Low's cartoons are really useful to historians.*

What was the impact of the end of the First World War?

In this lesson you will:

- find out why Britain adopted a policy of appeasement

- investigate a historical problem.

Key words

Appeasement
Give in to demands to keep someone happy.

Conscription
Making someone join the armed forces.

Isolationist
Remaining separate from the political affairs of other countries.

Nazis
Extreme right-wing Fascist party in power in Germany 1933–45.

Was appeasement the right policy?

Imagine a fight in a school playground. A well-known bully is picking on one of the smaller children. You are quite strong and brave, but do not have many friends you can rely on to help you tackle the bully. Your teachers don't take much notice of what goes on in the playground.

? *What would you do in the above situation? Discuss with a friend the best course of action.*

Look and think

1 Using the map and your own knowledge: why were so many Germans upset with the terms of the Treaty of Versailles?

2 Why did the British and French governments not use military intervention when Germany broke the terms of the Treaty of Versailles in the mid-1930s?

What happened in Germany?

Most people in Germany expected that the post-First World War settlement would be based on Woodrow Wilson's Fourteen Points towards peace (see Lesson 1.4b), which they thought to be fair. When the Treaty of Versailles was presented to the world in May 1919 it was clear that the reality was going to be different, as map 1 shows.

In 1933, the leader of the **Nazi** Party, Adolf Hitler, became Chancellor of Germany. Three of his aims were to destroy the Treaty of Versailles, to re-arm, and to seize living space in the east for Germans.

What about Britain?

Britain was hit hard by the Depression in the early 1930s. Unemployment was high and living conditions in many areas were very poor. There was little enthusiasm for any action that might lead to war. The Great War had led to the death of just under 1 million people from Britain and its Empire and thousands of people now campaigned for peace and disarmament. This did not mean that Britain's rulers were doing nothing. The priority for the British government was the protection of its Empire. By 1936 it had decided that Britain needed to re-arm. However, rearmament was expensive and could not happen overnight. Britain needed time, perhaps three years, to build up the strength of its armed forces.

PRINCIPAL GERMAN LOSSES
100% of its pre-war colonies
80% of its pre-war fleet
48% of all iron production
16% of all coal production
13% of its 1914 territory
12% of its population

Memelland
Memel
Danzig
Northern Schleswig
Southern Schleswig
Kiel
Stolp
Königsberg
Hamburg
Stettin
Schneidemühl
Bromberg
Allenstein
GERMANY
Berlin
Posen
Marienwerder
Essen
Glogau
Kielce
Polish Corridor (West Prussia & Posen)
Eupen-Malmedy
Cologne
Leipzig
Weimar
Dresden
Breslau
Upper Silesia
Demilitarised Rhineland
Weisbaden
Mainz
Frankfurt
Darmstadt
Beuthen
Gleiwitz
Pless
Saarland
Metz
Mannheim
Karlsruhe
Strasbourg
Stuttgart
Alsace-Lorraine
Freiburg
Munich
Mülhausen

N

0   200 miles (322 km)

Territory lost by Germany after its defeat.

Territory lost by Germany following voting by the local population.

Territory retained by Germany, but within which no fortifications could be built or soldiers stationed.

■ *The Versailles Territorial Settlement.*

Who might support Britain?

If Britain was about to take on Germany, it would need the support of other countries. However, it was clear that such support was not guaranteed.

● France was in a very similar position to Britain.

● The USA, led by President Franklin D. Roosevelt, was **isolationist**. In 1937 the US Congress passed a Neutrality Act promising that the USA would remain neutral in time of war.

● The British prime minister, Neville Chamberlain, did not like or trust the Soviet Union.

● The Empire did not promise much help either. In September 1938, both Australia and South Africa declared that they would not help Britain in a war.

Germany on the march

Against this background, Germany decided to take the following action. In 1935 the German government reintroduced **conscription**, which had been banned by the Treaty of Versailles. In March 1936 the German army marched into the Rhineland, which had been demilitarised by the Treaty of Versailles. In March 1938 Austria became part of Germany; this union had been forbidden by the Treaty of Versailles.

The British and French governments did not try to stop these events and the League of Nations had already proved it was too weak to intervene (see Lesson 1.4c).

What was the Czech Crisis?

There were 3 million German speakers in Czechoslovakia, known as Sudeten Germans. In September 1938 tension in the area increased when the Sudeten leader, Konrad Henlein, ordered the use of violence against Czechs and Jews. This violence was part of his campaign to force the Czech government to transfer Sudetenland to Germany. Hitler believed Germany was ready to fight Czechoslovakia and hoped to use this growing political crisis as an excuse for war. He did not believe Britain or France would intervene, even though they were both allies of Czechoslovakia.

What happened next?

Chamberlain agreed to talk to Hitler and travelled twice to Germany. At Munich, in September 1938, Chamberlain and the French prime minister, Edouard Daladier, agreed on **appeasement** – that the Sudetenland should be transferred to Germany. On 1 October 1938 German troops marched into the Sudetenland. But Hitler did not stop there. In March 1939 he ordered the invasion and seizure of the rest of Czechoslovakia. It was clear to many politicians that his next target was Poland. In the light of Hitler's actions, Chamberlain promised Poland that, if Germany attacked, Britain would go to war to support the Polish. In September 1939 Germany invaded Poland, and Britain and France finally declared war.

What should Chamberlain do?

The Czech crisis placed Neville Chamberlain in a difficult position.

3 What are the strengths and weakness of the following suggestions to him?

● *Threaten Germany with war and prepare to fight.*

● *Agree to support the transfer of the Sudetenland to Germany.*

● *Try to persuade Hitler to change his mind.*

What do you think?

4 Which of the following interpretations do you agree with?

● The policy of appeasement was a mistake.

● Appeasement was a reasonable policy that made sense given the circumstances.

You might write your views first, then later be given the opportunity to debate them in class.

Back to the start

Make a list of the factors that prevented governments from creating a new peaceful world, 'fit for heroes'.

In this lesson you will:

- find out about Dunkirk in 1940

- discover that one event can be interpreted in different ways.

Dunkirk: victory or defeat?

On 10 May 1940 the German army launched a huge attack to the west. Six weeks later it had swept through Belgium, Holland and northern France. Sensing defeat, the British army, along with some of its French allies, withdrew to Dunkirk on the coast of northern France. Just as the German army was about to catch up with them, Hitler ordered his tanks to halt, giving them a two-day rest before the planned attack south towards Paris. As a result of this stroke of good fortune, from 26 May to 4 June 340,000 British and French soldiers were rescued from Dunkirk's beaches by an armada of small and large ships and were transported to England. France surrendered on 25 June; Britain was now alone.

a

"VERY WELL , ALONE"

■ *Cartoon by David Low published in the* Evening Telegraph, *18 June 1940.*

? *Look at source a. What five words would you use to describe the message of this cartoon?*

What are the views?

1 Was Dunkirk a victory for the British or was it a defeat? Look at **sources b–g**. Each one gives an interpretation, or view. Write one sentence about each interpretation that sums up what the author or photographer thinks about Dunkirk.

b

For us Germans the word 'Dunkirchen' will stand for all time for victory in the greatest battle of annihilation in history. But for the British and French who were there, it will remind them for the rest of their lives of a defeat that was heavier than any army had ever suffered before.

■ *From the German magazine* Der Adler, *5 June 1940.*

c

The story of that epic withdrawal will live in history as a glorious example of discipline [among our troops]. Every kind of small craft – destroyers, paddle steamers, yachts, motor boats, rowing boats – have sped here to the burning ruins of Dunkirk to bring off the gallant British and French troops betrayed by the desertion of the Belgian king. Here in these scenes off the beaches of Dunkirk you have one of the dramatic pictures of the war. Men wade to a vessel beached at low tide, its crew waiting to haul them aboard. Occasional German planes fleck the sky, but where was the German Navy? Of German sea power there was little trace.

■ *From the script of the* British Movietone News, *June 1940.*

e

So long as the English tongue survives, the word 'Dunkirk' will be spoken with reverence. In that harbour, such a hell on earth as never before blazed before, at the end of a lost battle, the rags and blemishes that had hidden the soul of democracy fell away. There, beaten but unconquered, in shining splendour, she faced the enemy, this shining thing in the souls of free men, which Hitler cannot command. It is in the great tradition of democracy. It is a future. It is victory.

■ *From the* New York Times, *1 June 1940.*

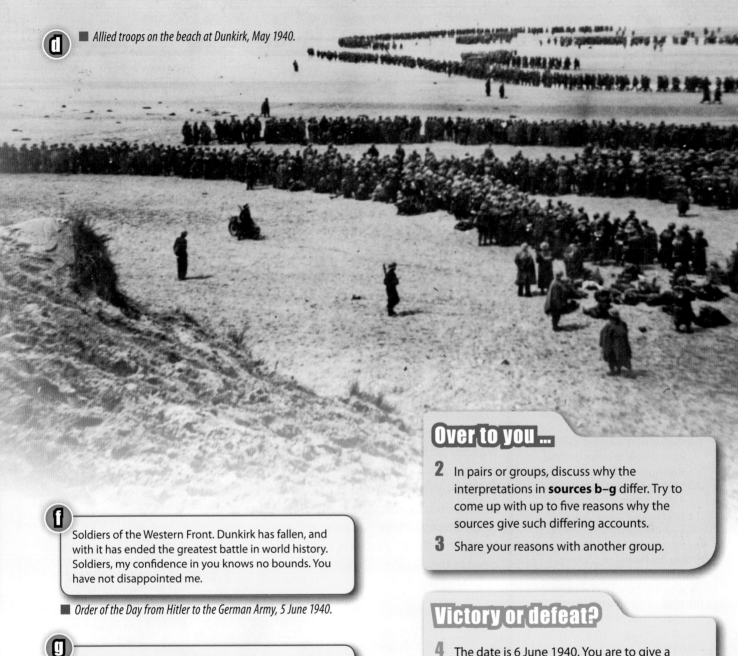

d ■ *Allied troops on the beach at Dunkirk, May 1940.*

f

Soldiers of the Western Front. Dunkirk has fallen, and with it has ended the greatest battle in world history. Soldiers, my confidence in you knows no bounds. You have not disappointed me.

■ *Order of the Day from Hitler to the German Army, 5 June 1940.*

g

The Royal Air Force engaged the main strength of the German Air Force, and inflicted on them losses of at least four to one; and the Navy, using nearly 1,000 ships of all kinds, carried over 335,000 men, French and British to their native land. We must be very careful not to call this a victory. Wars are not won by evacuations. But there was a victory of a kind that was gained by the Air Force … but the escape of our army and so many men, whose loved ones have passed through an agonising week, must not blind us to the fact that what has happened in France and Belgium is a colossal [huge] military disaster.

■ *Extract from a speech about Dunkirk given by the British prime minister, Winston Churchill, to the House of Commons, 4 June 1940.*

Over to you …

2 In pairs or groups, discuss why the interpretations in **sources b–g** differ. Try to come up with up to five reasons why the sources give such differing accounts.

3 Share your reasons with another group.

Victory or defeat?

4 The date is 6 June 1940. You are to give a speech about Dunkirk. First, choose to be one of the following characters:

● a British politician talking to munitions workers

● a German army commander addressing troops

● an American radio commentator.

In your speech you will explain what happened at Dunkirk. Remember, you will need to keep your audience in mind when writing your speech.

In this lesson you will:

- find out why the USA joined the Second World War

- tell the story of Pearl Harbor.

(?) *What do you think Churchill means in this part of his speech? What is he referring to when he mentions the 'New World'?*

Pearl Harbor: what is the story?

In Lesson 1.5a you found out that in June 1940, Britain stood alone. You also read an extract from a famous speech made by British prime minister, Winston Churchill, on 4 June 1940 (**source g**). **Source a** gives the end of that speech. Of particular interest is the mention of the 'New World'.

Pearl Harbor

In 1940, Franklin D. Roosevelt was re-elected as President of the USA. As you learned in Lesson 1.4d, the USA was strongly isolationist. But Roosevelt and many other Americans were sympathetic towards the British and, in 1940, the USA lent Britain 50 warships. In 1941 a system known as Lend-Lease was agreed, and large amounts of food and weapons were sent from America to Britain. Despite this help, the USA did not join the war.

On the other side of the world, the government of Japan had ambitions to extend the Japanese Empire. It was keen to conquer parts of the French and British Empires in South-East Asia. However, the Japanese were aware that any such attack might bring war with the USA. Key to the Japanese success was control of the Pacific Ocean. Japan's rival for this control was the USA, which had a large fleet based at Pearl Harbor in Hawaii. By 1941, the Japanese government was convinced that if it was to conquer South-East Asia, it would need to destroy the US fleet at Pearl Harbor.

Tell the story

The run up to the attack at Pearl Harbor was confusing. While American intelligence knew that the Japanese were up to something, they did not know what.

1 Imagine it is your task to sort out what actually happened at Pearl Harbor. Begin by putting the telegrams opposite into chronological order.

Did you know?

There was no Internet in the 1940s. Urgent information was usually sent by telegram. Many messages were coded, which meant they could not be read by the enemy.

(a)

We shall go on to the end, we shall fight in France, we shall fight on the seas and oceans, we shall defend our Island, whatever the cost may be. We shall fight on the beaches, we shall fight on the landing grounds, we shall fight in the fields and in the streets, we shall fight in the hills; we shall never surrender, and even if, which I do not for a moment believe, this Island or a large part of it were subjugated [conquered] and starving, then our Empire beyond the seas, armed and guarded by the British Fleet, would carry on the struggle, until, in God's good time, the New World, with all its power and might, steps forth to the rescue and the liberation of the old.

■ *From a speech by Winston Churchill to the House of Commons, 4 June 1940.*

(b) ■ *The USS* Shaw *exploding during the Japanese attack on Pearl Harbor.*

Who knew what?

2 Many people claim that President Roosevelt knew in advance about the attack on Pearl Harbor and have criticised him for it. After reading the telegrams, which of the following statements do you agree with and why?

- *Roosevelt knew in advance about the attack on Pearl Harbor.*
- *Roosevelt's policy was to wait and see what the Japanese were up to.*
- *Roosevelt did not know where the Japanese were going to attack.*
- *The Japanese had decided on attacking Pearl Harbor by the end of December.*

3 Some historians believe that Prime Minister Churchill knew that the Japanese were going to attack Pearl Harbor, but did not tell Roosevelt. What would have been his motives for staying quiet?

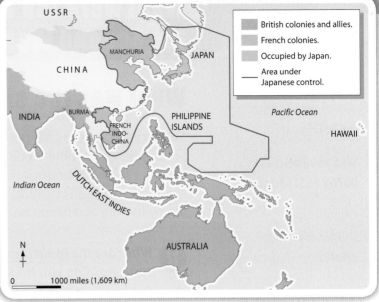

■ *South-East Asia in the 1940s, including Japan, British and French colonies, and Hawaii.*

---

4 December 1941

From President Roosevelt

To British Ambassador Lord Halifax

The Japanese are likely to attack Thailand. Britain must go to Thailand's aid. If the Japanese attack British territory, the USA will support Britain.

---

29 November 1941

From Foreign Office in Tokyo

To Japanese Ambassador in Berlin

Secretly advise the German government that war between Japan and the Anglo-Saxon nations (Britain and USA) is likely to come soon.

---

1 December 1941

From American official Sumner Welles

To Japanese Ambassador Nomura

Please would you inform the US government why there are significant movements of Japanese troops in South-East Asia?

---

30 November 1941

From British Prime Minister Winston Churchill

To President Roosevelt

I disagree with your decision not to issue a joint warning with us to the Japanese about their large naval force, which is moving south from Japan. I understand you are concerned about the opinion of those in our country who do not want to be involved, but the Japanese threat is real.

---

19 November 1941

From Japanese government

To Japanese embassy in Washington

Listen to the Toyko weather forecast. If you hear the words in the weather forecast 'east wind, rain', it means that relations between Japan and the USA are close to breaking down. At this point you must destroy all code books.

---

7 December 1941

From naval command in Honolulu

To all posts in Hawaii

Hawaii is under attack. Japanese air force is attacking the American fleet. This is no drill; repeat, this is no drill.

---

2 December 1941

From the Japanese High Command

To Pearl Harbor task force

7 December has been fixed as the day hostilities will commence. Attack as planned. 'East wind, rain.'

---

6 December 1941

From President Roosevelt

To Japanese Emperor Hirohito

A real emergency seems to be emerging. We want to keep the traditional friendship between Japan and the USA but, for this to happen, Japan must not threaten South-East Asia.

In conclusion ...

4 From your understanding of the events surrounding the attack on Pearl Harbor, answer the following question:

Did the Americans know in advance that the Japanese were going to attack Pearl Harbor?

---

5 December 1941

From General Miles of US intelligence

To the US government

The probable line of action for the Japanese task force is Thailand.

What were the key moments of the Second World War?

In this lesson you will:

- find out about the battle at Stalingrad

- explain the significance of an event.

Key words

Army Group South

A number of German army groups in the Second World War, further subdivided into smaller groups.

Caucasus

Mountain range that runs between the Caspian Sea and the Black Sea. It used to be part of the Soviet Union.

Fascist

A racist who supports the rule of a dictator.

Hypothesis

Statement to be further investigated and proved or disproved.

Turning point

Event after which things are never the same again.

What was the significance of Stalingrad?

Source a is taken from a report produced by the Security Service of Hitler's bodyguard, the SS, in February 1943. It provides us with a **hypothesis** about the battle of Stalingrad, which we can then test by looking at different historical information.

? *What are the main points made in source a? Can you think of any other turning points in history?*

People are saying that the enemy's strength must have been underestimated, otherwise the risk of continuing to occupy Stalingrad even after it was surrounded would not have been taken. There is a general belief that Stalingrad signifies a **turning point**. Some people believe it to be the beginning of the end.

■ *From a report by the Security Service of the SS, 4 February 1943.*

What happened?

Before you begin to test the hypothesis that Stalingrad was such a significant turning point, it is important to have some background information.

In the early hours of 22 June 1941 a huge artillery barrage signalled one of the largest military invasions ever to take place. More than 3 million German soldiers supported by half a million troops from allied countries including Romania and Hungary invaded the Soviet Union. The soldiers were supported by 3,600 tanks and 2,700 aircraft. Hitler's aim in invading the Soviet Union was to crush communism, create living space for Germans and win the war by defeating Britain's last potential European ally.

In August 1939 the Soviet Union had signed a military agreement with Germany, the Nazi–Soviet Pact. Therefore, the Germans' invasion surprised the Soviet army, which fell back in disarray. Millions of Soviet soldiers were captured, most of whom later died in German captivity. But the Soviet Union was a vast country and the Soviets were not quickly defeated. By October 1941, German armies were within sight of the Soviet capital, Moscow. Heavy rains followed by freezing weather and stiffening Soviet resistance halted the German advance.

The following May the Germans renewed their attack. The main thrust of their advance was south towards the Caucasus and their vitally important oilfields. Hitler subdivided **Army Group South**, sending Army Group A to finish off the Soviet forces in the **Caucasus**, while Army Group B, the Sixth Army, was ordered to take the strategically important city of Stalingrad. The battle that followed resulted in defeat for the Germans and their allies with 100,000 of their soldiers killed and 235,000 taken prisoner.

b

The sacrifice of the Sixth Army was not in vain. German forces were able to regroup, then strike back. Stalingrad was not the decisive battle of the Second World War that some believe. The Germans still stood on the line from which they had started their offensive of 1942. They had recovered their fighting spirit and showed at the Battle of Kharkov [in March 1943] that they were still masters of the [battle]field. It was they, not the Russians, who took the offensive when the fighting season of 1943 opened.

■ *Written by historian A. J. P. Taylor, in* The Second World War, *1975.*

Look carefully

1 **Sources b** and **c** are both written by British historians. How similar are their views about the importance of Stalingrad? Why might their views differ?

Put information together

2 In pairs, divide **sources b–f** into three groups:

- those that fully support the hypothesis in **source a**
- those that partly support the hypothesis
- those that disagree with the hypothesis.

e The battle for Stalingrad has come to an end. The sacrifice of the army was not in vain. It tied down strong enemy forces for a number of weeks. By doing so, the army gave the German Command time to set up defences on which depended the fate of the whole Eastern Front. Officers and men fought shoulder to shoulder to their last bullet. They died that Germany might live. Their example will have consequences long into the future.

■ *From a German radio broadcast, 3 February 1943.*

f From the end of 1942 the Great Patriotic War [Second World War] entered a new phase. The Red Army passed to the attack, and began the massive expulsion of the German-**Fascist** invaders from our soil. The battle for Stalingrad was the greatest military and political event of the Second World War. This victory turned out to be the beginning of a vital change in the course of the war to the advantage of the USSR and the anti-Fascist allies. From the banks of the River Volga, the Red Army began its advance which ended in the surrender of Germany.

■ *From* Istoryia SSSR, *the official Soviet History textbook for schools used in the 1960s.*

c From early 1943, the early belief across Europe that there was no alternative to German domination was beginning to disappear. At the heart of the preparedness of Europeans to resist was the understanding that Hitler might lose the war. The turning point was provided by a single battle that more than any other showed that the German armed forces could be defeated: Stalingrad.

■ *Written by historian Richard J. Evans, in* The Third Reich at War, *2008.*

d

■ *'Caught in his bear trap' by American cartoonist Jay Darling, 28 November 1942. The bear in the picture represents the Soviet Union.*

■ *The Eastern Front in March 1943.*

Look at both sides

3 Think about the provenance for each **source (b–f)** before you decide whether to trust it or not. Once you have discussed this with your partner, answer the following question:

According to the sources, how significant was the Battle of Stalingrad?

In your answer you will need to look at both sides of the argument. Then write up your response as a presentation.

In this lesson you will:

■ learn about D-Day through the eyes of one person

■ evaluate the usefulness of the evidence.

Questions for Martha

On 6 June 1944, the largest ever amphibious invasion fleet set sail from England, bound for the coast of France. Troops from countries including Britain, Canada, the USA and France set sail with the aim of liberating continental Europe from occupation. The day was to become known as D-Day. On board one of the hospital ships heading for France was the American journalist and writer Martha Gellhorn. She told the story of her D-Day experiences in *The Face of War*, which was published in 1959. Read **source a**, which is an extract from her book.

What have we learned?

1 What have we learned about D-Day from **source a**? Working in pairs try to list at least ten points, which you should write in your own words. Share these points with another pair.

What is left out?

Source a gives plenty of information. However, there are some aspects of D-Day which the author has not described.

2 Still working in pairs, list six questions you would like to ask about D-Day that have not been covered by Martha's story.

How useful is Martha's story?

3 Divide a page in your exercise book lengthways into two columns headed: 'Useful' and 'Not useful'. Write points in each column about whether Martha's evidence is useful or not to historians researching D-Day. Remember, when writing your points to think of:

● the content of the source

● the context/situation of the author

● the purpose/nature of evidence.

Here are examples of the kinds of points you might make.

Useful	Not useful
Martha gives a clear picture of the size of the invasion fleet.	Martha does not describe the fighting.

Martha's story

There were 422 bunks covered with new blankets, and a bright, clean, well-equipped operating room, never before used. Everything was ready and any moment the big empty hospital ship would be leaving for France. There were six nurses aboard. Three weeks ago they were in the USA completing their training for this overseas assignment.

We had pulled out of the harbour in the night, but we crossed by daylight and the morning seemed longer than other mornings. The only piece of news we had, so far, was that the two hospital ships ahead of us struck mines on their way over. Then we saw the coast of France and suddenly we were in the middle of the invasion. People will be writing about this sight for a hundred years and whoever saw it will never forget it. First it seemed incredible; there could not be so many ships in the world. There were destroyers and battleships and transports, a floating city of huge vessels anchored before the green cliffs of Normandy. Small craft beetled around in a curiously jolly way. Troops were unloading from big ships to heavy cement barges or to light craft, and on the shore, moving up four brown roads that scarred the hillside, our tanks clanked slowly and steadily forward.

Then we stopped noticing the invasion because the first wounded had arrived. Everything happened at once. We had six water ambulances, light motor launches, which swung down from the ship's side and could be raised the same way when full of wounded. Wounded were pouring in now, hauled up in the lidless coffin or swung aboard in the motor ambulances.

Below deck was a vast ward with double tiers of bunks. From two o'clock one afternoon until the ship docked in England again the next evening at seven, none of the medical personnel stopped work.

It will be hard to tell you of the wounded, there were so many of them. There was no time to talk; there was too much else to do. They had to be fed, as most of them had not eaten for two days; shoes and clothing had to be cut off; they wanted water; the nurses and orderlies, working like demons, had to be found and called quickly to a bunk where a man suddenly and desperately needed attention; plasma bottles must be watched; cigarettes had to be lighted and held for those who could not use their hands; it seemed to take hours to pour hot coffee, via the spout of a teapot, into a mouth that just showed through bandages.

On A deck in a bunk by the wall lay a very young lieutenant. He had a bad chest wound and his face was white and he lay too still. Suddenly he raised himself on his elbow and looked straight ahead of him, as if he did not know where he was. His eyes were full of horror and he did not speak. Later he spoke. He had been wounded the first day, had lain out in a field and then crawled back to our lines, sniped at by the Germans. He realised now that a German, badly wounded also in the chest, shoulder and legs, lay in the bunk behind him. The gentle-faced boy said very softly, because it was hard to speak, 'I'd kill him if I could move.'

The wounded looked much better in the morning. The ship moved steadily across the Channel and we could feel England coming nearer. Then the coast came into sight and the green of England looked quite different from the way it had looked only two days ago; it looked cooler and clearer and wonderfully safe. The beaches along this coast were only lovely yellow sand. The air of England flowed down through the wards and the wounded seemed to feel it.

American ambulances were waiting on the pier. Everyone felt happy and you could see it in all their faces. Now they would restock their supplies, clean the ship, cover the beds with fresh blankets, sleep whatever hours they could, and then they would go back to France. But this first trip was done; this much was to the good; they had made it.

■ *From Martha Gellhorn's book* The Face of War, *published in 1959.*

In this lesson you will:

- learn about the use of the atom bomb on Hiroshima in August 1945

- debate the arguments for and against the use of the bomb.

Hiroshima: use of the bomb, right or wrong?

In 1939 the US government set up the Manhattan Project to develop a nuclear weapon: the atom bomb. Such a weapon would be more destructive than any previously known. The project cost US$2 billion and was undertaken in secret at a number of locations including Richland, Washington. On 16 July 1945, the first atom bomb was tested in secret in the desert in New Mexico.

Throughout 1945 the Japanese army had continued to put up strong resistance. The battles for the islands of Iwo Jima and Okinawa, which were within striking distance of Japan, had cost the Americans 75,000 casualties. From May to August, American bombers pounded Japanese towns and cities, including an attack on the Japanese capital Tokyo, which created a firestorm that killed 120,000 people. On 6 August an atom bomb was dropped on the Japanese city of Hiroshima killing 70,000 people outright with perhaps a further 70,000 dying by the end of the year as a result of their injuries. On 9 August the US airforce dropped a second atomic bomb, this time on the Japanese city of Nagasaki. Approximately 40,000 people were killed immediately by the explosion, a further 40,000 dying by the end of the year.

What is your view?

1 What questions do you think need to be asked by historians about the dropping of the atomic bomb? Start your list when you have read **source a**. Then add to it as you read through the remaining sources in this lesson.

? *Read source a. What does it tell us about the impact of the bomb?*

a

THE VILLAGER

PEACE!

OUR BOMB CLINCHED IT!
JAPS SURRENDER

How large a part did 'Our Bomb' have in ending the war quickly? This was a question on many village lips today. The final answer is up to history, but there is no question here but that the bomb was an important factor in the quick termination of the war. Many national commentators and writers gave much credit to 'Our Bomb' for convincing the Japs that further resistance was useless. Some day the answer will be given by those who know but if you ask a Villager they will tell you, 'Our Bomb' clinched it.

■ From the front page of a newspaper published in Washington, USA, called The Villager, 14 August 1945.

b

■ Photo of the devastation caused at Hiroshima as a result of the atomic bomb dropped by US armed forces on 6 August 1945.

c Once it had been tested, President Truman faced the decision as to whether to use it. He did not like the idea, but he was persuaded that it would shorten the war against Japan and save American lives. It is my opinion that the use of this barbarous weapon at Hiroshima and Nagasaki was of no help in our war against Japan. The Japanese were already defeated and ready to surrender because of the effective sea blockade and the successful bombing with conventional [normal] weapons. My own feeling was that in being the first to use the atom bomb we were acting like the barbarians of the Dark Ages. I was taught that wars cannot be won by destroying women and children.

■ *Extract from Admiral William D. Leahy's book* I Was There, *published in 1950. Leahy was one of President Harry S. Truman's top military advisers.*

e When the bombs dropped and news began to circulate that [the invasion] would not, after all, take place, that we would not be obliged to run up the beaches near Tokyo assault-firing while being mortared and shelled, for all the fake manliness of our facades we cried with relief and joy. We were going to live. We were going to grow up to adulthood after all.

■ *From an account by Paul Fussell, a 21-year-old soldier who had been assigned to the invasion force in 1945.*

d The enemy now possesses a new and terrible weapon with the power to destroy many innocent lives and do incalculable damage. Should we continue to fight, not only would it result in an ultimate collapse and obliteration [complete destruction] of the Japanese nation, but also it would lead to the total extinction of human civilisation. Such being the case, how are we to save the millions of our subjects? This is the reason why we have ordered the surrender.

■ *From a radio broadcast by Japanese Emperor Hirohito announcing the Japanese surrender, 14 August 1945.*

f The Americans were already aware of Japan's desire to end the war. But President Truman and his main advisers were keen on using the atomic bomb to speed up Japan's collapse. Why else was the bomb used? America and Britain's ally, the Soviet Union, was due to declare war on Japan on 8 August [1945]. The Soviet leader [Josef] Stalin had demanded to share in the occupation of Japan. The US government were keen to prevent this. The atomic bomb was used to help solve the problem; it was dropped two days before the Soviets were due to enter the war against Japan. The second reason for the bomb's use at Hiroshima was that it had cost a lot of money and simply had to be a success.

■ *Adapted from Basil Liddell Hart's book* History of the Second World War, *published in 1970.*

What are the arguments?

2 Were the Americans right to drop the atom bomb on Hiroshima in 1945? Divide a page in your exercise book lengthways into two columns headed: 'Arguments for' and 'Arguments against'. Read through all the sources, making notes in each column.

g The Japanese began the war from the air at Pearl Harbor [in 1941]. They have been repaid many times over. It was to spare the Japanese people from utter destruction that the ultimatum of 26 July [demanding that Japan surrender] was issued. Their leaders promptly rejected the ultimatum. I shall give further consideration as to how atomic power can help maintain world peace.

■ *Statement made by President Truman, 6 August 1945.*

What do you think?

3 Write an argument in response to the question: *Were the Americans right to drop the atom bomb on Hiroshima in 1945?*
Take one of these stances:

● strongly in favour of the dropping of the bomb
● strongly against the dropping of the bomb
● a balanced view that sees reasons for and against.

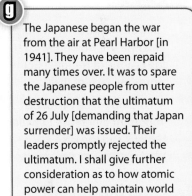

Back to the start

In **Lessons 1.5a–e** you have studied five key moments of the Second World War.
In your opinion, which is:

● the most significant
● the least significant?

Next Lesson

How did governments respond after the Second World War?

In this lesson you will:

- consider how strong and effective the United Nations has been since 1945

- compare and contrast a range of case studies to reach an overall judgement.

Has the United Nations helped to create a better world?

The United Nations (UN) was created on 24 October 1945 to replace the old League of Nations (see lesson 1.4c) with the aims of achieving world peace and helping to spread human rights.

? *What one thing would you do to make the world a better place? Create a class list of all your ideas. How many ideas are similar?*

■ *A cartoon by David Low on the intervention of the UN in the Korean War, first printed on 30 October 1950.*

Use your eyes

1 Look at **source a**. What words would you use to describe the women who represent the UN and the League of Nations? Come up with three words for each of them.

2 According to the cartoonist, what was the most important difference between the League of Nations and the UN?

New and improved?

The League of Nations had ended in great failure: no one even bothered to tell the League that the Second World War had started! However, there were some important differences between the League and the UN.

- The UN could take action with a majority (rather than unanimous) vote on the Security Council (although the USA, UK, France, China and Russia had a **veto**).

- The UN had an army made up of soldiers donated by member countries. UN soldiers are called 'Peacekeepers' and are only sent out if a nation asks for their help. The UN soldiers have to obey the Security Council's **mandate** at all times.

Many people hoped these differences would mean that the UN would succeed in stopping wars where the League had failed.

Make the grade!

3 You are about to write a report on the UN (a bit like one you might get from school) to decide whether or not it has helped to make the world a better place.

   a) Read the case studies on the UN report card opposite.

   b) For each case study, award the UN a grade from A–E for achievement (where A = excellent result and E = poor result) PLUS a number from 1–5 for effort (where 1 = excellent effort and 5 = poor effort).

   c) Explain your grade using the details given.

4 Think about the grades you have awarded. Are there any similarities in the type of case studies where you gave the UN a high grade? What about where you gave the UN a low grade?

UN REPORT CARD

	grade

1950–53: Korea

The problem: Korea was split in half after the Second World War, with the Soviets in the North and US troops in the South. In 1950, the communist North Koreans invaded South Korea. The South Korean leader, Syngman Rhee, asked the UN for help.

What happened: UN forces, led and largely supplied by the USA, landed in South Korea to help drive back the North Korean invaders. The UN forces helped to defend South Korea and set up a ceasefire in 1953.

☐

1956–67: Egypt and the Suez Canal

The problem: In October 1956, Britain, France and Israel invaded Egypt to regain the Suez Canal from the Egyptian leader Colonel Nasser, who had taken the Canal earlier that year. Nasser asked the UN for help.

What happened: The UN quickly sent a peacekeeping force to make sure the invading troops left. They were successful and peace was kept for ten years. In 1967 the Egyptians forced the UN troops to leave. The 'Six-Day' War broke out soon after between Egypt and Israel.

☐

1960–64: Central Africa, the Congo

The problem: The Congo had been ruled by the Belgians. When the Belgians left in 1960 many parts of the country tried to set up their own government. The new prime minister, Patrice Lumumba, asked for UN soldiers to help keep the country stable.

What happened: At first, the UN helped to run the country, but refused to get involved in a civil war. In 1961 the Security Council agreed to allow UN soldiers to fight to keep the Congo as one country. By 1964, the Congo was stable but 100,000 people had been killed in the civil war. A brutal general called Joseph Mobutu seized power when the UN forces left.

☐

1949–present: India–Pakistan border

The problem: Kashmir is a region on the border between India and Pakistan. In 1947, the King of Kashmir had to decide whether to join India or Pakistan (see Lesson 3.3a). Although, like the people of Pakistan, 90 per cent of Kashmiris were Muslim, the king was a Hindu and decided to join India. In 1948, Pakistani soldiers invaded Kashmir. India asked the UN to help solve the conflict.

What happened: The UN managed to get both sides to agree to a ceasefire on 1 January 1949. The UN also wanted the Kashmiris to hold a public vote to decide which country they should belong to. It was never held. The UN sent observers to make sure the ceasefire line was held. However, the UN could not stop more fighting over Kashmir in 1965–66 and 1971–72. India refused to recognise the observers after 1972.

☐

1956–68: Eastern Europe

The problem: In 1956, the Hungarians tried to break free from the control of the Soviet Union. The Soviet Union sent in tanks to crush the opposition. The Hungarian leader, Imre Nagy, asked the UN for help. In 1968, the people of Czechoslovakia protested for more freedom from the Soviet Union. Again, the Soviets sent in tanks to crush opposition. The Czech leader, Alexander Dubcek, asked the UN for help.

What happened: In 1956, the UN called for the Soviet Union to withdraw from Hungary, but nothing happened. The issue was dropped in 1962. In 1968, the invasion of Czechoslovakia was discussed for three days at the UN but nothing was done as the Soviets used their veto to block action.

☐

1945–today: the world

The problem: Poverty and disease continue to affect millions of people all over the world.

What happened: The UN High Commissioner for Refugees (UNHCR) has helped more than 50 million refugees to restart their lives. The UN Children's Fund (UNICEF) has spent billions of pounds to improve the health, safety and education of the world's poorest children. All the work is paid for by donations. The World Health Organization (WHO) helps to fight diseases and improve health. In 1980 it helped to rid the world of the smallpox virus.

☐

● Key words

Mandate
Orders that set out what a person or group has the power to do.

Veto
Negative vote that blocks a decision for action.

Report time

5 Use the grades you awarded and other information on the UN to write a full end-of-term report. In your report:

- explain where the UN has done well
- explain areas that need improvement
- make recommendations about how the UN ought to try to improve.

In this lesson you will:

- explore the reasons for and against British membership of the European Community

- make judgements about who was to blame for the delay in British membership.

Why did it take sixteen years for Britain to join the European Community?

In 1957, the **European Community** (EC) was formed by the Treaty of Rome. This was an agreement between 'the Six' (Belgium, France, Germany, Holland, Italy and Luxemburg) to: set up a European 'Council of Ministers' that could make some laws for all EC members; set up a '**common market**'; and support farmers in the EC from a common budget.

In the same year, Harold Macmillan became the British Prime Minister. He had fought in the First World War and had seen much of Europe destroyed in the Second World War. As a result of his experiences, he saw the EC as a good way to bring Europe together and stop future wars.

? *Do you think Britain has more in common with Europe or with other parts of the world, like the USA or the Commonwealth?*

The British public

We don't know much about Europe. We'll join the EC if it is in our best interest, but we hear such mixed messages from the government and the media.

Commonwealth countries

Our livelihoods depend on trade with Britain. If Britain joins the common market, the EC will tax our exports so the British won't buy them. And don't forget our common history, our British roots.

The lawyers

We have one of the oldest Parliaments and legal systems in the world. If Britain joins the EC, our Parliament will have to accept the laws made by the European Council of Ministers. The European Court of Justice could overrule our own courts. We will lose our hard won sovereignty.

British farmers

The French want to use EC money to help their farmers make cheap food. If we join the EC, the common market will mean loads of cheap food coming from Europe. We'll go bust and Britain will have to rely on foreigners for all her food!

The Cabinet

The French are jealous of our Commonwealth and want us to abandon it to join the EC. We must not join the EC until 'the Six' have changed the rules to suit our Commonwealth trade. If we say that Britain wants to join the EC too early, the French will think we are desperate and won't agree to change the rules.

A turnaround

In 1957, 'the Six' wanted Britain to join the EC to make it even stronger, but Macmillan refused. Macmillan had many reasons to join the EC, but also a lot of pressure not to join! In 1963, Britain tried to join the EC, but was turned down! How can we explain this turnaround?

Sort it out!

1 Prime Minister Macmillan has travelled to Paris to meet the French President, General de Gaulle, who wants to know whether the British want to join the EC or not. Imagine you are Macmillan's top adviser. What will you tell him to say?

2 Look at the illustration. Decide which reasons are more important than others. Arrange the reasons in a 'zone of decision'.

Your final answer?

3 a) In your zone of decision, do the more important reasons seem to suggest that Macmillan should tell de Gaulle that Britain wants to join the EC, or does not want to join?

   b) Write a short report for Macmillan that gives your answer and explains the most important reasons for this answer.

4 Why do you think Macmillan decided not to join the EC?

America is not the friend we once thought. Look at the way it stopped our efforts in the Suez Crisis.

Russia is growing stronger and stronger. If it can put satellites into space, surely it can send missiles to our door!

Now that we have lost India and Ghana, how much life is really left in the British Empire?

Will the Commonwealth guarantee Britain's status as a world power in the years to come?

The European Community will be a huge new trading area of 160 million people. Can British industry afford to be left out of this Common Market?

If we stay out of the EC, will France or Germany dominate this new Europe in future?

A tale of two leaders?

General de Gaulle was scared that the British, with their links to the English-speaking world, would control the EC if they joined. On 14 January 1963, he used his veto to stop the British joining the EC. Macmillan did not expect this at all, and became so ill with stress that he retired.

Many historians blame de Gaulle for Britain not joining the EC in 1963. Others blame Macmillan for not leading Britain more positively into the EC soon after 1957. They compare the failures of 1957–63 with Britain's successful entry in 1973 when the President of France, Georges Pompidou, liked Britain, and the prime minister of Britain was Edward Heath, a passionate supporter of the EC.

Key words

Common Market
Large trading area made up of many smaller ones (such as countries). Members agreed to get rid of taxes on trade between themselves, and to have the same taxes on imports from outside the EC.

Commonwealth
Organisation of former members of the British Empire.

European Community
Organisation that binds the governments, laws, economies and people of Europe together. It is now known as the European Union (EU).

An ongoing argument!

Historians still argue about how far Macmillan was to blame for Britain's failure to join the EC for 16 years.

5 Judging by what you have read, do you think it is fair to blame Macmillan for Britain's failure to join the EC in 1963? Make sure you back up your reasons with evidence.

How did governments respond after the Second World War?

○ Key words

Devolution
Transfer of some powers from central government to regional governments.

Read all about it!

1 With a partner, decide whether to investigate Scottish or Welsh devolution. Once you have decided, use the factfiles opposite and your own knowledge to do the following:

a) One of you must find reasons for independence, the other against independence for your country.

b) List your reasons, then share notes.

Devolution: what's in it for us?

The United Kingdom has not always been united; some people think it should not remain united any longer! Until 1999, England, Scotland and Wales were ruled from London by the British Parliament. Northern Ireland is part of the UK, and is dealt with separately in Lesson 1.8d.

? *Think of an event where you might have your face painted with a flag. What flag would you choose to have? Try to explain why!*

One nation or three?

Since 1999, some powers have been given to a Scottish Parliament in Edinburgh and to a Welsh Assembly in Cardiff. This process is called **devolution**. Big decisions – such as those on most taxes, foreign policy and the armed forces – are still made in London. Other decisions – such as those on education, healthcare and local transport – are now made in Cardiff for Wales, and Edinburgh for Scotland.

Devolution has, however, caused a lot of arguments, with people divided into having three main views:

● Devolution is not necessary and things should go back to how they were before 1999.

● Devolution is a fairer system and a good way of keeping the UK together.

● The UK is no longer needed, and it would be better for Scotland and Wales to become completely independent.

Decisions!

2 Now you have all the facts, prepare for the debate. You are about to debate the same question three times:

● once in your pair

● once in a group of four (with another pair who chose your country)

● and finally in an eight!

The question is: *Should this country try to become completely independent from the UK?*

Make sure each pair gets a chance to argue for their point of view. Remember, the whole group has to agree on either a 'Yes' or 'No' answer.

Wales factfile

1284 Wales was conquered by Edward I and ruled by England under the Statute of Rhuddlan.

1400 Owain Glyndŵr led the last major revolt against the English. It was unsuccessful.

1536 Henry VIII's Act of Union meant that Wales had no national church and no separate laws.

1925 Foundation of Plaid Cymru, the Party of Wales, which wanted independence for Wales.

1955 Cardiff was recognised as a Welsh capital for the first time.

1957 The Tryweryn Valley was flooded to create a reservoir for the people of Liverpool. Every Welsh MP voted against it, and it caused great anger.

1967 The Welsh Language Act gave Welsh and English equal status in government business in Wales.

1979 A total of 12 per cent of Welsh voters wanted a National Assembly in Wales.

1982 A new Welsh language TV station was set up after many members of Plaid Cymru went on hunger strike in support of the new channel.

1950–1990 Wales was awarded many government jobs including the Licensing Office in Swansea and the Passport Office in Newport. The Welsh Development Agency led to many factories being set up in Wales.

1999 The Welsh Assembly was created and given devolved powers.

2007 Population: 3 million (UK 61 million).
Total earnings: £55 billion (UK £2,200 billion).

Scotland factfile

1100–1603 Many English kings tried, but failed, to conquer Scotland.

1603 Scotland and England became ruled by one king: James VI of Scotland (or James I of England!).

1707 In the Act of Union, England and Scotland became united as Great Britain. The Scottish nobles agreed to get rid of their Parliament and to be ruled from London. The Scots still kept their own legal system and church.

1934 The Scottish National Party (SNP) was formed. It called for complete independence from the UK.

1949 A Scottish Covenant was signed by 2 million Scots asking for a Scottish Parliament.

1950–70 Not much call for devolution as Parliament in London ordered several factories to be set up in Scotland.

1970 A huge oil field was found 177 kilometres (110 miles) off the coast of Aberdeen. The oil, worth around £200 billion, belonged to the UK! It is now beginning to run out.

1976–87 This period saw a 31 per cent drop in Scottish industry, a 64 per cent drop in textile factories in Scotland, and the collapse of mining and ship-building. Many Scots blamed Margaret Thatcher's Conservative government for favouring London.

1980–1999 The British government spent 20 per cent more on every person in Scotland than in England.

1997 63.5 per cent of Scots voted for devolution (not independence).

1999 The Scottish Parliament was created and given devolved powers.

2007 Westminster awarded Scotland £11.3 billion as part of a scheme to distribute public spending more evenly.

2007 Population: 5.5 million (UK 61 million)
Total earnings: £86 billion (UK £2,200 billion).

The SNP argues that Scotland could exist as part of the European Union, because smaller and less wealthy countries like Latvia and Lithuania do. Scotland could also join the UN, NATO and other international groups.

The big debate!

3 You know the facts and you have heard the arguments. Now it is time for the whole class to decide!

Scotland and Wales can only become totally independent if a majority of MPs in Westminster agree to let this happen. Imagine your classroom is now the House of Commons. A debate is about to take place that will decide the future of the UK: *This House believes that Scotland and Wales should be given full independence from the UK.*

● Two people will propose (support) the motion.

● Two people will oppose (speak against) the motion.

● The rest of the class are MPs. You can decide whether you are a Scottish, Welsh (or English) MP.

After the speeches for and against the motion, you can ask questions. You can either stand or raise a hand to ask a question.

Your teacher is the Speaker; as Speaker, they have the power to say who is allowed to speak at any time.

After all the questions, and perhaps a few last words from the supporters and opposition, the Speaker will call for a vote. The future of the UK is in your hands!

Back to the start

Look back over all the lessons in this enquiry. Do you think it would be better to be part of a 'United States of Europe'? Or do you think we should go back to being smaller, but independent, countries?

Next Lesson

1.7a

Who had an impact in the struggle for civil rights in the USA?

In this lesson you will:

- identify reasons why an individual protest became a national phenomenon

- reflect on the importance of events surrounding the actions of an individual.

○ Key words

Boycott
To protest by refusing to do something (e.g. go to work or school).

Civil rights
Rights that are considered to be unquestionable; deserved by all people under all circumstances, especially without regard to race, creed, colour or gender.

NAACP
National Association for the Advancement of Colored People – an organisation that strives for civil rights for all.

Proposition
Statement that affirms or denies something and is either true or false.

Segregation
Separation of groups of people based on race.

How did Rosa Parks transform America?

We may well think, from time to time, that individuals cannot make a real difference in the world. But that's not true of Rosa Parks. Her actions as an individual gained enormous attention and have found their way into many history books over the years.

? *What rights do you have? Which are the most important of those rights? Make a list of the rights you feel everyone should have, then compare them to the list a partner has drawn up. Between you identify the five most important ones. How similar are they to other people's lists in your class?*

a

*Four score and seven [87] years ago our fathers brought forth on this continent a new nation, conceived in Liberty, and dedicated to the **proposition** that all men are created equal.*

■ *Spoken by President Abraham Lincoln in his Gettysburg Address, November 1863.*

Civil rights

In the 1860s America was involved in a civil war between the states in the south that wanted to keep slavery and those in the north that opposed them. Abraham Lincoln, the president of the USA, used his Gettysburg Address to show that his country had been founded on the idea that all Americans had clear civil rights.

Not everyone agreed with him, however, and during the next 100 years many of the states passed laws that were collectively known as 'Jim Crow' laws. These divided the country on a racial basis and led to protests from large numbers of American citizens.

Did you know?

In some southern states black Americans travelling on public transport had to sit separately from whites in a special 'Jim Crow Car', even if they had bought first class tickets.

Look and think

1 Study **sources b** and **c**, which show some of the effects the 'Jim Crow' laws had.

  a) What do you think the purpose of the signs in **source c** were?

  b) In what ways do the sources help you to understand what life would have been like for black Americans under the 'Jim Crow' laws?

"WHO' DAT SAID DE NIGGER AM FREE?"

THEATRE · WHITES ONLY · LIBRARY · COURT HOUSE · ALL NEGROES ARE GUILTY. JUSTICE FOR WHITES ONLY · NEGROES TAKE A BACK SEAT

■ Cartoon from the early twentieth century showing the effects of the 'Jim Crow' laws.

Louisiana

ALL CIRCUSES, SHOWS AND TENT EXHIBITIONS, TO WHICH THE ATTENDANCE OF MORE THAN ONE RACE IS INVITED, SHALL PROVIDE NOT LESS THAN TWO TICKET OFFICES AND NOT LESS THAN TWO ENTRANCES.

Alabama

EVERY EMPLOYER OF WHITE OR NEGRO MALES SHALL PROVIDE FOR SUCH WHITE OR NEGRO MALES REASONABLY ACCESSIBLE AND SEPARATE TOILET FACILITIES.

Florida

THE SCHOOLS FOR WHITE CHILDREN AND THE SCHOOLS FOR NEGRO CHILDREN SHALL BE CONDUCTED SEPARATELY.

Arizona

THE MARRIAGE OF A PERSON OF CAUCASIAN BLOOD WITH A NEGRO SHALL BE NULL AND VOID.

North Carolina

BOOKS SHALL NOT BE INTERCHANGEABLE BETWEEN THE WHITE AND COLORED SCHOOLS, BUT SHALL CONTINUE TO BE USED BY THE RACE FIRST USING THEM.

Alabama

THE CONDUCTOR OF EACH PASSENGER TRAIN IS AUTHORISED AND REQUIRED TO ASSIGN EACH PASSENGER TO THE CAR OR THE DIVISION OF THE CAR, WHEN IT IS DIVIDED BY A PARTITION, DESIGNATED FOR THE RACE TO WHICH SUCH PASSENGER BELONGS.

■ Some of the 'Jim Crow' laws passed by separate US states between the 1870s and 1960s.

REST ROOMS
Aug. 2, 1924
WHITE ONLY

DRINKING FOUNTAIN
WHITE — COLORED
MONTGOMERY, ALA.
14 JULY 11

■ Public signs, indicating the separation of white and black people.

Think it through

2 Look at **source d**.

a) Why do think this source might have been produced?

b) Where do you think it might have been published?

c) What point is the artist trying to make?

Changing times

Many black Americans hated the 'Jim Crow' laws. They felt that being told where they should sit, and what facilities they were allowed to use, made them second-class citizens. But after the Second World War, when blacks as well as whites had given their lives for their country, things began to chnge. Black Americans began to join civil rights groups like the **NAACP** that challenged the laws that kept them separate from whites. They had some successes but attitudes towards blacks were still hostile – especially in the former slave-owning states in the south of the USA. It was in this atmosphere that one event made people begin to think more about how the USA should change.

Rosa Parks

On 1 December 1955 the actions of a black woman helped to spark a **boycott** of public transport in the town of Montgomery, Alabama, that lasted 381 days and virtually bankrupted the local bus companies. As a result the fight for civil rights in the USA became national headline news and Rosa Parks became known across the country.

e

Q: What made you decide not to get up from your seat?

'I did not sit at the very front of the bus; I took a seat with a man who was next to the window – the first seat that was allowed for "coloured" people to sit in. At this point a few white people boarded the bus, and one white man was left standing. When the driver noticed him standing, he spoke and told me to let the man have the seat. The driver saw me still sitting there. He said would I stand up, and I said, "No, I will not." Then he said, "I'll have you arrested." And I told him he could do that. So he didn't move the bus any further.

'Two policemen got on the bus in a couple of minutes. The policeman walked down and asked me why I didn't stand up, and I said I didn't think I should stand up. "Why do you push us around?" I asked him. And he said, "I don't know. But the law is the law and you are under arrest." As soon as he said that I stood up, and the three of us left.

■ *Interview with Rosa Parks, February 1997.*

Over to you ...

3 Read **source e**. Imagine you are interviewing Rosa Parks. What questions would you ask that help you to understand why she chose not to give up her seat on the bus.

Did you know?

During the Montgomery bus boycott black churches raised money to pay for new shoes for black workers who were walking to work rather than taking the bus.

Timeline 1875–1956

States restrict black voters by introducing 'poll taxes'

States begin to pass 'Jim Crow' laws to separate blacks from whites in public spaces

National Association for the Advancement of Colored People (NAACP) founded

1875

1880s

1890

1890s

1896

1909

1910

Civil rights act gave many blacks the vote

Mississippi sets a literacy test – reducing the black vote

Supreme Court states that education for black and white should be separate but equal

All southern states have passed laws to legalise **segregation** of white and black

Rosa Parks, who refused to give up her seat to a white passenger.

Tell the story

4 Imagine you are a reporter from the local newspaper following up the story of Rosa Parks. Your editor has asked you to write a balanced article for your paper, which will hopefully sell to a wider audience.

You need to include the views of a black representative of the Montgomery Civil Rights movement and white representatives of the local community about what happened and whether they feel it is important.

Finish this piece with your own conclusions about the importance of Rosa Parks' actions and how they affected the USA.

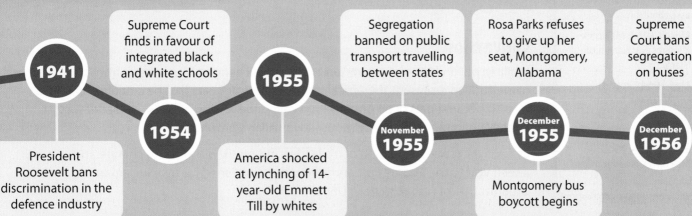

1941 President Roosevelt bans discrimination in the defence industry

1954 Supreme Court finds in favour of integrated black and white schools

1955 America shocked at lynching of 14-year-old Emmett Till by whites

November 1955 Segregation banned on public transport travelling between states

December 1955 Rosa Parks refuses to give up her seat, Montgomery, Alabama — Montgomery bus boycott begins

December 1956 Supreme Court bans segregation on buses

1.7b

Who had an impact in the struggle for civil rights in the USA?

In this lesson you will:

- understand why a civil rights leader was assassinated

- use sources to provide evidence for the motive behind Malcolm X's murder.

Why was Malcolm X assassinated?

On the 21 February 1965 a 39-year-old black civil rights activist was shot dead while giving a speech in the Harlem district of New York. His name was Malcolm X. More than 1,500 people attended his funeral, 500 of them standing outside the church. So why was such a popular man shot?

? *With a partner think of someone who is very famous at the moment. What makes them so well known? Draw a spider diagram to identify the main points.*

Factfile

Malcolm X

Real name: Malcolm Little

Born: 19 May 1925 in Omaha, Nebraska.

1931: Malcolm's father is found dead on the town's trolley tracks rumoured to be killed by white supremacists.

1946: Malcolm is sentenced to eight to ten years in prison for armed robbery.

1953: Becomes a convert to the Nation of Islam and changes name from Malcolm Little to Malcolm X.

1963: Nation of Islam orders Malcolm X to be silent, allegedly because of remarks concerning President Kennedy's assassination.

March 1964: Malcolm X leaves the Nation of Islam.

May 1964: Starts the Organization of Afro-American Unity (OAAU), a secular political group.

21 February 1965: Malcolm X is assassinated.

a

■ *Malcolm X, an outspoken civil rights activist in the 1950s.*

Conversion

While in prison Malcolm converted to Islam. He changed his surname from his 'slave name' to 'X' to represent the African name of his forebears that he could never know. He also became part of an organisation called the Nation of Islam. Its leader was Elijah Muhammad who many thought was Allah's prophet.

By 1964, Malcolm X's opinion of his leader and his views began to change and, after a visit to the Middle East and Africa, he established his own organisation, the Organization of Afro-American Unity.

Read and think

1 Read **sources b** and **c**.

a) What did the Nation of Islam and Malcolm X believe in?

b) What sort of views would people who listened to Malcolm X have had about him?

c) Who might have been angered by what Malcolm X was saying?

Over to you ...

2 Read **sources h** and **i**, which show that Malcolm X's views had changed. What opinion do you think people who had followed his career would have had about him by the beginning of 1965, and how strongly do you think their views would be held?

3 Imagine you are an assistant to Malcolm X. Write a brief memo to him advising him on the way you believe people are seeing him, and the course of action he might wish to take.

Solve the mystery

4 Malcolm X was an important and outspoken figure in the fight for civil rights in America. Imagine you are the senior detective investigating his murder. Use evidence from this lesson to determine:

a) the chief suspects

b) the motive for his murder.

b It doesn't mean that I advocate violence, but at the same time, I am not against using violence in self-defence. I don't call it violence when it's self-defence; I call it intelligence.

■ *Malcolm X, in a speech to the US domestic Peace Corps, 1964.*

c While a member of the Nation of Islam, Malcolm attacked the civil rights movement and rejected both integration and racial equality, calling instead for black separatism, black pride, and black self-reliance.

■ *Malcolm X's view of the black struggle, outlined on the Malcolm X Online website.*

d Malcolm X, a leader of the Black Muslims, yesterday characterised the assassination of President Kennedy as an instance of 'the chickens coming home to roost'.

■ *Extract from the New York Times, 2 December 1963.*

e We believed in the divinity of Elijah Muhammad, that God had taught him and all of that. I always believed that he believed it himself. And I was shocked when I found out that he himself didn't believe it.

■ *Spoken by Malcolm X after he became aware that Elijah Muhammad had fathered children by different women.*

f We never refer to the Honorable Elijah Muhammad as a prophet.

■ *Malcolm X, in a speech in 1963.*

g I feel like a man who has been asleep … Now I think with my own mind, sir!

■ *Spoken by Malcolm X in 1965.*

h It is a time for martyrs now, and if I am to be one, it will be for the cause of brotherhood. That's the only thing that can save this country.

■ *Spoken by Malcolm X on 19 February 1965, two days before he was murdered.*

i This was a brother you could believe. There was the sense that he was not in it for something. That was the extraordinary thing about him. He was in it because of his commitment to our liberation.

■ *James Turner, founding director of Africana Studies at Cornell University, giving the eulogy at Malcolm X's funeral, 27 February 1965.*

1.7c

Who had an impact in the struggle for civil rights in the USA?

In this lesson you will:

- find out the impact Martin Luther King had on the civil rights movement

- be able to use evidence to develop and present a historical conclusion.

Why was Martin Luther King seen as a threat?

Civil rights activist Dr Martin Luther King was the pastor of a Baptist church in Montgomery, Alabama. He made his name as the leader of the successful bus boycott in 1955, made famous by the actions of Rosa Parks that ended segregation on public transport (see Lesson 1.7a). He gained a reputation both for his powerful public speaking and for his use of non-violent protest against the 'Jim Crow' laws that kept white and black Americans apart. Using the policy of non-violent protest against 'unfair' laws, Dr King targeted Birmingham, Alabama, a city known for its racist attitudes.

? *Look at source a. What newspaper headlines do you think would have been written to describe the scene? In pairs discuss what else you need to help you understand the scene.*

Key words

Nobel Prize
An international award for outstanding achievement.

a

Look and think

1 a) Look again at what's happening in **source a**. This photograph was taken during April 1963 in a city called Birmingham, Alabama, in the USA.

b) Now read **sources b** and **c**. In what ways do they help your understanding of the incidents in Birmingham, and Dr King's role in them?

b
I have no fear about the outcome of our struggle in Birmingham, even if our motives are at present misunderstood. We will reach the goal of freedom in Birmingham and all over the nation, because the goal of America is freedom.

■ *From a letter written by Martin Luther King while he was in Birmingham Jail, 16 April 1963.*

c
This was the worst scenario he had envisioned: The [National] Guard would arrest thousands of black people, put them in camps, then greet a flood of protesters, hundreds of thousands, from around the country.

■ *Extract from Diane McWhorter's book* Carry Me Home: Birmingham, Alabama, *published in 2001.*

Victory for civil rights movement

After days of protest, the jails in Birmingham were full to overflowing. With the world's media noting every development, the decision was taken by the town's leaders to end the policy of segregation. It was a great victory for the civil rights movement.

King then went on to organise other marches and non-violent protests to gain black Americans the vote and workers' rights. The most famous of these was a march of 250,000 people on Washington in 1963, where he delivered his most famous speech.

■ Martin Luther King addressing the civil rights protesters who marched on Washington, 28 August 1963.

e

I have a dream that one day this nation will rise up and live out the true meaning of its creed: 'We hold these truths to be self-evident: that all men are created equal.'

I have a dream that one day on the red hills of Georgia, sons of former slaves and sons of former slave-owners will be able to sit down together at the table of brotherhood.

I have a dream that one day, even the state of Mississippi, a state sweltering with the heat of injustice, sweltering with the heat of oppression, will be transformed into an oasis of freedom and justice.

I have a dream that one day, down in Alabama … little black boys and black girls will be able to join hands with little white boys and white girls as sisters and brothers.

… And when we allow freedom to ring, when we let it ring from every village and hamlet, from every state and city, we will be able to speed up that day when all of God's children – black men and white men, Jews and Gentiles, Catholics and Protestants – will be able to join hands and to sing in the words of the old Negro spiritual, 'Free at last, free at last; thank God Almighty, we are free at last.'

■ Adapted from Martin Luther King's 'I have a dream' speech, 28 August 1963.

King's support and opposition

By 1964 the USA had passed civil rights laws that banned discrimination in public buildings, allowed mixed race schools and allowed qualifed blacks to vote in elections.

Even so, not everyone agreed with King and his methods. Black civil rights leader Malcolm X (see Lesson 1.7b) called the Washington march, the 'farce on Washington'. King's opposition to the Vietnam War and his support of laws to reduce poverty made him many enemies, and on 4 April 1968 he was assassinated.

Make a judgement

2 Read **source e**. Why would some have considered that Dr King's 'dream' would be a threat to the way people lived in the USA? Discuss your answer in pairs.

In conclusion …

3 The **Nobel Prize** committee of 1964 said that Martin Luther King was 'not only the symbolic leader of American blacks but also a world figure'. Using the evidence from this lesson, in what ways does King deserve this honour for the work he did?

Back to the start

Look back over this enquiry. Of the three people you have studied (Rosa Parks, Malcolm X and Martin Luther King), who do you think had the biggest impact in the struggle for civil rights in America and why?

Next Lesson

? *What ways are there to protest about things you don't like? How would you protest about things at school level, local level, national level and international level? Is there anything you would not do to protest, despite how unfair the issue is, and why?*

Why is Tamerlan Satsayev afraid to go to school?

How would you feel if another country was imposing its ideas on yours, and what would you do to gain independence for your country? Some people would start by organising petitions or becoming involved in protest movements in order to publicise their case. Others might go much further, as this lesson shows.

Background to Chechnya

Chechnya is a small republic that declared independence from Russia in 1991. After a brief conflict with the Chechens, the Russian government agreed to allow local politicians to run the country. However, these Chechen politicians found they could not control local armed groups and it became a place where law was ignored and hostage-taking became normal. Fearing the republic would collapse into chaos, Russia largely retook control, thus encouraging some Chechens to launch attacks against Russian targets, because they did not want any Russian involvement in their affairs.

■ *Russian troops storm Beslan School No 1, North Ossetia, September 2004.*

How Tamerlan's life was changed

The 1 September 2004 was the first day of school for many students in North Ossetia, a republic close to Chechnya. In the small town of Beslan, Tamerlan Satsayev was one of those excited children, but what happened next was to change his life.

■ *Russian soldiers rescue children from Beslan School No 1, 3 September 2004.*

c On Tamerlan Satsayev's first day of school one year ago, he wore a new suit and a white shirt and carried a bouquet of flowers. Two days later, he escaped death, almost naked, in the arms of an unknown rescuer, his mother severely wounded in the debris behind him.

■ *From a report by Peter Finn in the* Washington Post, *28 August 2005.*

Look and think

1 Study **sources a** and **b**, which were taken between 1 and 3 September 2004. Looking only at the photographs, what do you believe happened in Tamerlan's school?

2 Now read **source c**. In what ways does this help you to understand what happened?

3 In groups of four use the information below to build up a picture of what happened at Tamerlan's school from 1–3 September 2004.

4 Imagine you are a television reporter. You have been asked to go to Beslan to produce a balanced three-minute broadcast on the incident at the school for your audience at home. Use the information below to plan what you are going to say to the camera.

5 Imagine in a later bulletin you have been asked by the producer to include short eyewitness accounts from the soldiers, parents and one of the captured rebels. You only have time for two questions to ask each witness.

a) What questions would you ask?

b) What do you think their answers would be?

6 What sort of reaction do you think people around the world would have had after seeing this story and why?

Tamerlan attended the welcoming ceremony for new arrivals at the school.

Tamerlan wore a new suit and white shirt on his first day at school.

Russian special forces stormed the building.

There were 1,000 hostages.

The gym was wired with bombs.

Russia wanted to stop Chechnya becoming a separate country.

Local men now protect the school.

Hundreds of bodies were found in the rubble of the gym.

31 rebels were killed.

Beslan School No 1 was taken over by Chechen rebels.

26 hostages were released on the second day.

Tamerlan Satsayev went to Beslan School No 1.

Hostages were refused water.

On the third day Tamerlan was carried almost naked from the school.

The roof of the gym collapsed following an explosion.

186 children and 145 adults were killed.

Russian special forces surrounded the building.

The forces outside the building heard an explosion.

The rebels attacked the welcoming ceremony and took hostages.

What do you think?

The Chechen rebels took hostages at the school to bring the world's attention to the issue of Chechen independence. Afterwards the rebel leader Shamil Basayev said: 'What happened in Beslan is a terrible tragedy.'

7 Besayev was not apologising for the attack on the school. How would he have justified the attack, and in what circumstances do you feel he might be right?

In this lesson you will:

■ find out about the role of an individual in a struggle for justice

■ decide on the status of an individual.

● Key words

Amnesty
An official pardon.

Apartheid
Means 'apartness' in Afrikaans (the language of the Afrikaners).

Afrikaner
Means 'African' in Dutch; the Dutch settled in southern Africa in the seventeenth century.

ANC
African National Congress; a black political organisation.

Sanctions
Measures taken to improve conduct or behaviour.

Treason
Betraying your own country.

Nelson Mandela: activist or terrorist?

In 1943 Nelson Mandela, then aged 25, joined the African National Congress (**ANC**), an organisation that aimed to achieve equal rights for black people in South Africa. Over the next 50 years he was described as both a terrorist and a freedom fighter.

? *Think quickly about when you have seen Nelson Mandela on the news. Which do you think he was: terrorist or freedom fighter?*

Look and think

1 Look at **sources a–e**. How and why do you think Mandela changed his form of protest?

2 By 1961 do you think that you could have called Mandela a terrorist? Explain your answer to a partner.

a 1948 **Afrikaner**-*dominated South African government introduces the* **apartheid** *policy of racial segregation across the country.*

b
South Africa belongs to all who live in it, black and white.

The people shall govern!

All national groups shall have equal rights!

All shall be equal before the law!

There shall be houses, security and comfort!

These freedoms we will fight for side by side, throughout our lives, until we have won our liberty.

1955 *The ANC produces the Freedom Charter, which calls for equal rights. It is launched at the 'Congress of the People'.*

c **1956–61** *After the 'Congress of the People', Mandela and 155 others are charged with treason. After five years they are found 'not guilty'.*

d **1960** *The ANC holds a demonstration against apartheid in Sharpeville. The police react by killing 69 protestors. The ANC is banned and Mandela goes into hiding.*

e **1961** *Mandela becomes leader of the ANC guerrilla movement. He leads acts of sabotage against public buildings – he goes on the run.*

Truth and reconciliation

Soon after he became president, Mandela issued a statement that said: 'Only the truth can put the past to rest.' In 1996, in order to end the bitterness over the years of oppression, the new government set up the 'Truth and Reconciliation Commission'. This allowed people who had been victims of apartheid to make their stories public and grant **amnesty** to those who who had committed abuses – as long as the crimes were politically driven, did not involve extreme violence and full details were given.

The final report blamed both sides for the violence, but it also allowed South Africa to begin a new multiracial future.

Put information together

3 Imagine it's five years after Nelson Mandela was elected president. You have been asked to provide a visitor to South Africa with a short document that outlines the key moments in the struggle to end apartheid. Select four sources from **a–l** that you consider are vital to explaining the story. In 100 words say why you feel they are so important.

Make a judgement

4 Read **source m**. Mandela doesn't deny using bombs to draw attention to his cause. Does this make him a terrorist or a freedom fighter?

5 How important do you think the terrorist acts of Mandela and the ANC guerrilla movement were in bringing about the end of apartheid?

m The explosions took the government by surprise. We planned and executed another set of explosions two weeks later on New Year's Eve. The combined sounds of bells tolling and sirens wailing … symbolised a new era in our freedom struggle.

■ From Nelson Mandela's book Long Walk to Freedom, published in 1995.

f **1964** *Mandela is caught and convicted of sabotage and* **treason**. *He is jailed for life on Robben Island; he spends 18 years there.*

g *We first broke the law in a way which avoided violence; when this form was made illegal, and the government resorted to force, we decided to answer violence with violence.*

1964 *Spoken by Nelson Mandela at his trial on 20 April.*

h **1976–77** *In continuing protests against the government more than 600 students are killed by police in Soweto. The death of leading anti-apartheid activist Steve Biko in police custody is condemned around the world.*

i **1986 Sanctions** *against the South African government are tightened, making it difficult for the country to play sport or trade with the rest of the world and costing millions in revenue.*

j **London Herald** SPECIAL EDITION
MONDAY 12th FEBRUARY 1990

NELSON MANDELA FREED

50,000 Celebrate in Cape Town
South Africa Enters New Age of Hope

1990: *New president F. W. de Klerk lifts the ban on the ANC and Nelson Mandela is released from prison after 27 years. The ANC and the white government begin talks on forming a new multiracial government.*

k **1993:** *In recognition of the achievement of the two men in ending apartheid, Mandela and de Klerk are awarded the Nobel Peace Prize.*

l **1994:** *Free elections allow black South Africans to vote for the first time. Nelson Mandela becomes president and appoints de Klerk as deputy president.*

In this lesson you will:

- **learn why people commit acts of terrorism**
- **be able to explain why acts of terrorism can be seen from different perspectives.**

Why should we learn about terrorism?

For hundreds of years there have been acts of terrorism against governments, people and places. These acts can be seen from different points of view, as this lesson will help you to understand.

? *What do you understand by the word 'terrorism'? List all the terrorist attacks you can remember. Which do you believe was the earliest? Compare your earliest date with a partner. As a class, which was the earliest attack listed?*

What more would we like to know?

What do we probably know?

What do we know for definite?

Look and think

1. Look at this photograph of a person who was involved in a terrorist act in 2003. Looking just at the image, list answers to these questions.

   a) What do we know for definite?

   b) What do we probably know?

   c) What more would we like to know?

2. With a partner, write a definition of 'terrorism'. Use a spider diagram to write descriptions of terrorism, which will help you with your definition.

■ *'The Holy Land' after 1948.*

Mediterranean Sea

Haifa

Nazareth
GALILEE

Tel Aviv

West Bank

Jerusalem
Bethlehem

Gaza

Hebron

Gaza Strip

N

0   30 miles (48 km)

King David Hotel bombing, 22 July 1946

After the Second World War and the events of the **Holocaust**, the demand by Jews for a homeland in the British-controlled area of Palestine increased. In 1946 members of the **Irgun** were angered when the British arrested more than 2,000 Jewish activists throughout Palestine and captured detailed information about organisations seeking a Jewish homeland. In response they targeted the King David Hotel in Jerusalem where the information was taken, and on 22 July 1946 a huge explosion destroyed the hotel.

Did you know?

The bombs that caused the destruction of the King David Hotel were hidden in milk cans and placed in the basement of the building.

a

Members will have learned with horror of the brutal and murderous crime committed yesterday in Jerusalem. Of all the outrages which have occurred in Palestine, and they have been many and horrible in the last few months, this is the worst. By this insane act of terrorism 93 innocent people have been killed or are missing in the ruins. The latest figures of casualties are 41 dead, 52 missing and 53 injured.

■ *Speech by the British Prime Minister Clement Attlee in the House of Commons on 23 July 1946.*

b

Irgun leader Menachem Begin stressed his desire to avoid civilian casualties and said calls were placed, warning that explosives in the King David Hotel would soon be detonated.

The call into the hotel was apparently received and ignored. Begin quotes one British official who supposedly refused to evacuate the building, saying: 'We don't take orders from the Jews.' As a result, when the bombs exploded, the casualty toll was high: a total of 91 killed and 45 injured. Among the casualties were 15 Jews. Few people in the hotel proper were injured by the blast.

■ *Extract from a modern Jewish history website.*

Over to you ...

3 With a partner, read **sources a** and **b**.

   a) In what ways do they agree about what happened?

   b) Why and in what ways do the sources differ about what happened?

Independence for Israel

The state of Israel gained its independence in 1948, when land that had previously been part of Palestine was given to the Jews to create their own homeland. In the years that followed there was a great deal of conflict between the Israelis and the Palestinian Arabs over who rightfully owned the land. Israel has always felt under attack and has fought wars against its Arab neighbours. However, in recent years the way that Palestinians have shown their anger has changed.

The Haifa explosion

On 4 October 2003 an enormous explosion blew apart a popular restaurant in the Israeli coastal town of Haifa.

c

On 4 October 2003, Hanadi Tayseer Jaradat, a 29-year-old attorney from Jenin, detonated a bomb in a restaurant in Haifa, Israel, killing herself, 19 Israelis and injuring 50 others. Hanadi Tayseer Jaradat wrapped her waist with explosives and fought her way past a security guard at the restaurant. Hanadi Tayseer Jaradat was a single woman whose younger brother Fadi, a 25-year-old, and older cousin, 34-year-old Salah, had been killed by Israeli forces in the raid on Jenin in June of 2003.

■ *Taken from a pro-Palestinian website.*

d

Twenty-one people were killed, including three children and a baby girl, and 60 wounded in a suicide bombing carried out by a female terrorist in the Maxim Restaurant in Haifa. The Islamic Jihad claimed responsibility for the attack.

The bomber, Hanadi Jaradat, a 29-year-old lawyer from Jenin, managed to get past Maxim's security guard before blowing herself up in the middle of the restaurant. It was packed mostly with regular Saturday customers.

■ *Taken from the Israeli Ministry of Foreign Affairs website.*

Make a comparison

4 Look at **sources c** and **d**.

   a) In what ways do the two sources agree about what happened?

   b) Why and in what ways do the sources differ about what happened?

Note: We met Hanadi Jaradat earlier in this lesson. She is the woman in the photograph on page 64.

What has been learned?

5 As part of a radio programme, the producer has brought together two witnesses: one from the 1946 terrorist incident, and one from the 2003 incident. As the interviewer you have been asked to focus on the similarities and differences between the two incidents. You must ask the two interviewees what they feel are the lessons to be learned from the events.

   a) Would the interviewees describe either the Irgun's or Hanadi Jaradat's actions as terrorism or as part of a fight for freedom?

   b) Do you agree with them? Why?

In this lesson you will:

- learn about terrorist activity in Ireland 1966–97

- conclude the key factors in bringing an end to terrorist conflict.

Ireland 1966–1997: why did 'the Troubles' last so long?

We all have arguments, but some arguments go on for much longer than others. In fact, some can go on for decades, even centuries, and feel as if they are getting worse rather than getting better.

? *Why do people argue? Compare your reasons with the rest of the class. Which reasons are likely to make an argument the hardest to resolve? Why?*

Ireland and 'the Troubles'

We tend to take for granted that the homes and streets we live in will be peaceful and safe, but in part of the UK between 1966 and 1997 that was not the case. In Northern Ireland disagreements between the Protestant and Catholic communities spilled out into incidents of violence and terrorism. This period is known in Ireland as 'the Troubles'.

a

■ *A wall mural marking the start of a Loyalist area in Belfast.*

b

■ *A wall mural supporting the Republican cause.*

Key words

IRA
Irish Republican Army; Catholic terrorist group that wanted a united Ireland.

Loyalist
Supporter of the idea that Northern Ireland should remain part of the UK.

Nationalist
Supporter of the idea that there should be greater independence for Ireland from the UK.

Republican
Supporter of the idea that there should be a united Ireland.

RUC
Royal Ulster Constabulary; name of the police force in Northern Ireland until 2001.

UVF
Ulster Volunteer Force; a Loyalist terrorist group.

Compare sources

1 Look at **sources a** and **b**, painted during 'the Troubles'; they can still be seen today in Northern Ireland.

   a) What similarities do you think the two murals have?

   b) What are the differences?

2 Choose either **source a** or **b**. Then write a sentence to explain what impression the mural gives you about life at the time.

3 Now complete the same exercise with the second mural.

Why did it start?

In 1966 the **UVF** killed two Catholics and a Protestant. It was an attempt to blame the **IRA** and encourage **Loyalist** Protestants to increase opposition to the Northern Irish government's reforms to give Catholics equal rights. The effect was to encourage Catholic communities to develop their own organisation and to demonstrate on the streets for civil rights.

Some of the demonstrations became so violent that organisations formed to 'defend' the rights and people of loyalist and **Republican** communities alike. The violence on the streets led the British government to send troops to the province to re-establish law and order.

Group the information

4 Look at the information boxes below. Using a spider diagram like the one below, group the information into categories to help you find reasons why 'the Troubles' in Northern Ireland continued for so long. Some have been started for you. Add additional arms as you need them.

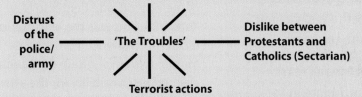

Distrust of the police/ army — 'The Troubles' — **Dislike between Protestants and Catholics (Sectarian)**

Terrorist actions

5 Look again at your spider diagram. What links can you find between pieces of information? Join them up with lines and write along each line what the connection is.

Civil Rights Demonstration 1968
A demonstration for Catholic civil rights in Londonderry was met with violence by the police.

Birmingham pub bombings, 21 November 1974
Explosions in two pubs in Birmingham town centre killed 21 people and injured 182. The **IRA** were blamed.

Peace Movement 1976
This movement used mass demonstrations to show the desire for peace of ordinary people on both sides of the divide.

Hunger Strikes, March 1981
Bobby Sands led a protest with other inmates in the Maze Prison, against being treated as 'ordinary prisoners' because he did not believe they were criminals. He said: 'We admit no crime unless, that is, the love of one's people and country is a crime.'

Orange Marches
Parades by the Protestant Orange order through Catholic areas of Belfast resulted in heightened tension between the two communities.

The RUC and B Specials 1970
The police and reserve police force were seen by the Catholic population as being pro-Protestant.

Internment 1971–1975
The policy of imprisonment without charge or trial of people accused of being members of illegal paramilitary (terrorist) groups. During the policy 1,874 Irish **Nationalists** and 107 Ulster Unionists were held.

Brighton bombing 12 October 1984
The IRA detonated a bomb at the Grand Hotel in Brighton where the (Conservative) government were at a conference. Although five people were killed, no government ministers died in the blast.

The Peace Line
Wall-like barriers were built to separate Protestant and Catholic areas of the cities of Belfast and Londonderry.

Bloody Sunday, 30 January 1972
During a civil rights march in Londonderry, 26 protesters were shot by the British army, 14 of whom died of their wounds.

Good Friday Agreement

After two decades of violence, the two sides of the conflict, plus the British and Republic of Ireland's governments, came together during Easter 1998 to sign 'The Good Friday Agreement'. This set up a government in Northern Ireland, based on power sharing in which both Catholics and Protestants were represented. In addition it brought about a ceasefire in which the IRA and UVF made their weapons unusable. 'The Troubles' were at an end.

Answer the question

6 Imagine you are a journalist. You have been asked to write an article for a magazine that answers this question: *How and why was it difficult for the people of Northern Ireland to end the conflict and reach a final agreement?*

You only have a short column for your piece, so you must write no more than 200 words. Your answer must cover the perspectives of two sets of interviews you have conducted:

- one with representatives from the Catholic community
- one with representatives from the Protestant community

In this lesson you will:

■ consider the effectiveness of the methods of dealing with terrorism

■ assess and reach conclusions as to possible solutions to terrorism.

Is there any solution to terrorism?

On 11 September 2001 (**9/11**) the world was shocked to see two planes deliberately crash into the twin towers of the World Trade Center in New York, USA. This was the worst terrorist incident in American history. The Muslim extremist group **Al-Qaeda** later claimed responsibility for the attack that killed more than 3,000 people.

? *Look at source a. If you had been on the street below at the time these planes crashed, what would be your immediate reaction to this scene?*

■ *Terrorist attack on the World Trade Center towers in New York, 11 September 2001.*

Key words

9/11
How the attacks on the World Trade Center are commonly known. In the USA, the dates are written with the month first, then the day; September 11 is the day the attacks took place.

Al-Qaeda
Islamic extremist group that has used terror to try to achieve its aims.

How should we respond to terrorism?

Throughout the twentieth and early twenty-first centuries there have been many examples of terrorist attacks in which people have been killed and property has been destroyed. Terrorists and terrorism are not easy to deal with because they can strike anywhere, at any time, with or without warning to their targets. Making a place safe means that those in charge of security have to:

● think about every possible threat

● devise methods of dealing with all types of threat.

The question of how to respond to terrorists and terrorist attacks has troubled many governments around the world for many years. They have often reacted in different ways.

Look and think

1 Look at **source a**. A first reaction to this image might be disbelief. But how do you think people's emotions changed in the days following this terrorist attack?

b
The enemy of America is not our many Muslim friends; it is not our many Arab friends. Our enemy is a radical network of terrorists, and every government that supports them. Our war on terror begins with Al-Qaeda, but it does not end there. It will not end until every terrorist group of global reach has been found, stopped and defeated.

■ *Extract from a speech by US President George W. Bush, 20 September 2001.*

c
Jerusalem
Israeli security instructed embassies and Jewish institutions around the world to go on alert Thursday for fear of revenge attacks for a car bomb that killed a top-wanted terrorist, Imad Mughniyeh, [who] was the suspected mastermind of several attacks that killed hundreds of Americans in Lebanon and of cruel kidnappings of Westerners.

■ *Extract from the Fox News website, 14 February 2008.*

d
Protesters try to storm Bali jail
Angry Indonesians have tried to break into a jail which houses convicted Bali bombers, on the third anniversary of the 2002 attacks on the island. Hundreds of protesters stormed the prison, demanding the immediate execution of three militants sentenced to death for their role in the attacks.

■ *Extract from BBC News, 12 October 2005.*

e

■ *Aftermath of Bali Bombing, 12 October 2002.*

f

Militant leader Abu Musab al-Zarqawi has been killed, Iraqi Prime Minister Nouri Maliki has announced. 'We have eliminated Zarqawi, ' Mr Maliki said at a news conference in Baghdad, sparking sustained applause. Zarqawi was considered the figurehead of the Sunni insurgency. He was the leader of Al-Qaeda in Iraq, blamed for killing thousands of Shias and US forces.

■ *Spoken by Iraqi Prime Minister Nouri Maliki, at a news conference in Baghdad, 8 June 2006.*

g

The Good Friday Agreement of 10 April 1998 launched a 'power sharing' accord between Catholics and Protestants that persists in Northern Ireland to this day. Yet what made the Northern Ireland peace process successful was a series of cold, hard calculations about the future made by politicians, who decided that their children would be doomed to misery if they did not compromise. 'The Troubles' had cost about 3,500 people their lives, maimed or scarred 40,000 others, pinned down 18,000 British troops and ruined the economy.

■ *Written by Michael Moran, Executive Editor of the Council on Foreign Relations, 30 March 2008.*

h

■ *Schoolchild being rescued from Beslan School No 1 after Russian police storm the buildings, 3 September 2004.*

In conclusion ...

5 Terrorism has been a problem throughout history. Look at the questions below and write down your first thoughts.

   a) In what circumstances do you think people feel they need to resort to terror as an action?

   b) Who does terrorism affect more, and why?

   ● Individuals

   ● Groups of people

   ● Governments

   c) In order to halt terrorism, what are the problems that both sides face in reaching a solution?

6 Share your ideas with a partner, then with another pair. How different is their answer from yours?

7 In your pair, look at this statement: *The only way of dealing with terrorists is to use the full force of the law.*

   As part of a debate, produce a short presentation on how far you agree with this statement.

Your turn ...

2 Look at **sources b–h**, which show some reactions to terrorists and terrorism. In pairs, copy the table below and complete columns 1 and 2. Then, using a scale of 1–5, rate how effective you think the solution was in bringing about an end to further terrorist attacks.

Description of the terrorist act	Reaction/method of dealing with the incident	How effective a solution to terrorism, 1–5 (1 = good; 5 =bad)
Planes crash into buildings in New York		

3 **Sources b–h** all show ways in which terrorism and terrorists can be addressed. Which way of dealing with the problem did you rate as the best solution? Explain your thinking to your partner.

4 People tend to disagree about the way terrorism should be dealt with. Look at all the examples you have been given. What solution would you have tried to use for each of the examples, and why?

Back to the start

The editor of a national newspaper wants to have a debate on the topic of terrorism. She has suggested the title: *'There are no terrorists, only freedom fighters.'*

Think carefully, then write TWO articles of no more than 200 words each. One article should agree with the title and the other should disagree. Both need to use evidence from this enquiry to back up the arguments you put forward.

Who had the most effect?

In this unit you have explored the changes that have taken place in the way in which individuals and governments affected how people were ruled. Throughout the period 1901–present who do you think had the greater influence – individuals or governments?

Think back over the work you have completed in this unit. For each of the sections think about whether it was the work of a single person, groups of people or governments that brought about change.

Look and think

1 Use a graph like the one below to help answer the question: 'Who had the most effect?' Take care to look at all of the events you have covered within a section before reaching a conclusion. Record your ideas by placing a cross on your graph to indicate who was the most influential, and to what extent, in bringing about changes to the way people were ruled.

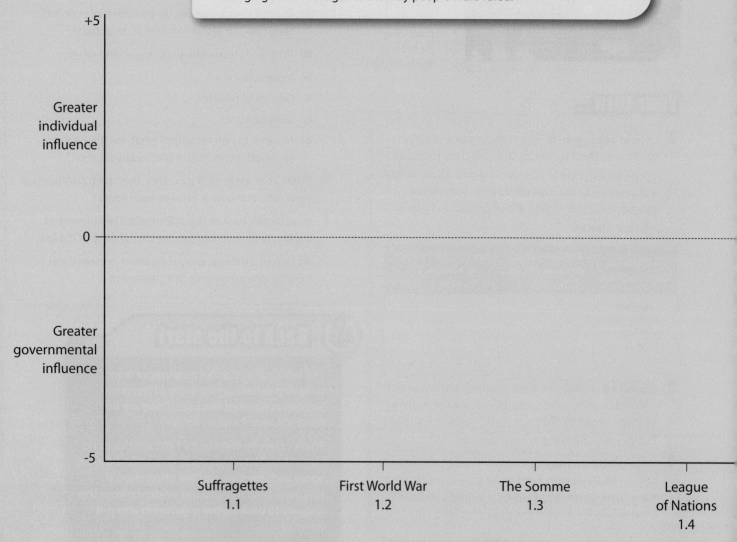

Your turn

2 Join up the crosses that you have put on to your graph.

3 Compare your graph with that of a partner. Look for any differences there might be. How would you account for the differences between the two graphs?

4 Based on what you have discovered from the graph, which of these statements would you agree with and why?

- During the period 1901–present it was, on the whole, the influence of actions taken by individuals that was responsible for most of the change in the way people were ruled.

- During the period 1901–present it was, on the whole, a combination of actions taken by both individuals and governments that was responsible for most of the change in the way people were ruled.

- During the period 1901–present it was, on the whole, the influence of actions taken by governments that was responsible for most of the change in the way people were ruled.

For whichever statement you select, support your choice with at least two examples from the sections you have covered.

In conclusion ...

5 Look back at the graph that you have completed. What circumstances do you think there are that encourage the actions of an individual or group of individuals, rather than those of a government, to influence bringing about a change in the way that people are ruled?

| Second World War 1.5 | Post-Second World War 1.6 | Civil rights 1.7 | Terrorism 1.8 |

Assessment 1

Why have there been different interpretations of Lenin?

One person whose life and work changed the way that millions of people were ruled in the twentieth century was Vladimir Illyich Ulyanov, or Lenin as he called himself.

This assessment focuses on different interpretations of Lenin. As a historian, you need to:

- explain why interpretations differ
- explain which interpretations are the most reliable or convincing

1 In what ways do **sources a** and **b** agree with each other?

Lenin was the creator of the tragedy of our era, the rise of dictatorships. He introduced to the twentieth century the practice of taking an ideology and forcing it on an entire society quickly and without mercy. He created a regime that erased historical memory and erased opposition. In his short career in power, from 1917 until his death in 1924, Lenin created a model for later dictators like Hitler and Chairman Mao.

■ *By David Remnick for* Time Magazine, *published in 1998.*

Lenin justified dictatorship and terror. Lenin applauded strong leadership. Lenin convinced his party that his ideas were pure and always correct. He had a lasting impact upon communism in Russia and all over the world.

■ *By Robert Service in his book* Lenin, *published in 2000.*

Vladimir Lenin, a big, real man of this world, has passed away. His death is a painful blow to all who knew him, a very painful blow! But there is no force that could dim the torch he has raised for the people of the world. Never has there been a man who deserves more to be remembered forever by the whole world. His wisdom and his will are living. They are alive and working more successfully than anyone on Earth has ever worked before.

■ *By Maxim Gorky from his book* V.I. Lenin, *written and edited between 1924 and 1931.*

Lenin is a pathetic, bald little man, whose only use is to write endlessly. Lenin is also unpleasant. If he visited the countryside to investigate an outbreak of cholera, he would probably ban the disease and order the villagers who caught it to be punished! I hope that Lenin's power withers and fades away.

■ *By Yevgeni Zamyatin for a newspaper called* Delo Naroda, *published in 1918.*

An American journalist's viewpoint

David Remnick is an American journalist; as Russian correspondent for the *Washington Post*, he lived in Moscow from 1988–92. **Source a** is his view of Lenin.

A modern British historian's viewpoint

Robert Service is Professor of Russian History at Oxford University. He has written many books about Lenin and about communism. **Source b** is his view of Lenin. He uses lots of new information that has been released by the Russian government.

The viewpoint of one of Lenin's contemporaries

Maxim Gorky (1868–1936) was a Russian writer. He was a friend of Lenin's. He lived in Italy for many years, but, having been promised a mansion and the Order of Lenin medal by the Russian dictator Stalin, he returned to communist Russia in 1931. **Source c** gives his view of Lenin.

The view of another of Lenin's contemporaries

Before Lenin managed to enforce tight censorship in Russia, many people criticised his ideas and actions. **Source d** shows what Yevgeni Zamyatin, a member of the Socialist Revolutionary Party, thought of him. He opposed Lenin's Bolshevik Party until he was banned in 1918.

2 a) In what ways do **sources c** and **d** disagree about Lenin?

b) Why do **sources a** and **b** differ in their interpretation of Lenin?

c) Why do **sources c** and **d** differ in their interpretation of Lenin?

d) Which interpretation of Lenin do you think is the most reliable?

Factfile

Vladimir Illyich Lenin

In 1870, when Lenin was born, Russia was ruled by tsars (emperors) from the Romanov family.

In 1887, Lenin's brother was hanged for trying to kill the Tsar. From this moment on, Lenin became a revolutionary, determined to end the personal rule of tsars. Lenin believed the best way to overthrow the tsars was by following the ideas of Karl Marx (see Lesson 2.5b).

In October 1917, Lenin inspired and led a revolution that replaced rule by the elites with rule by representatives of the workers and peasants.

By the time he died in 1924, Russia had become the world's first communist country. In time, China, North Korea, Cuba and much of Eastern Europe would be ruled by communist governments. Clearly, Lenin was a very important person. But what was he really like?

How will you set about a task like this?

Here are some handy hints.

1 This question asks you to make comparisons between the sources.

● As you read **source a**, pick out as many points that the author makes about Lenin as you can. You can underline these points, or even draw arrows to show where each point is in the source.

● Repeat the process with **source b**.

● Now compare the points that you have picked out from both sources. In your answer, state the point that the sources agree on, then back it up with a short quote from both sources.

2 a) This question is very similar to question 1. Start by picking out as many points as you can that the author makes about Lenin in **source c**. Do the same with **source d**. This time you are asked to identify the ways in which the sources *disagree* about Lenin. Again, use short quotes to back up your answer!

2 b) and c) These questions ask you to consider **the provenance** of the source – that is:

● its nature (What type of a source is it?)

● its origin (Who wrote it? When and where did they write it?)

● its purpose (For what reason or audience did the author write this?).

In your answers, use these ideas to make contrasts between the provenance of the sources.

2 d) To answer this question you need to explain why one source is more trustworthy than another. To do this:

● compare the tone of the content (Is it dramatic, over the top, or even and neutral?)

● compare the provenance of the source (Is the author of the source a reliable judge of Lenin and his legacy?).

How will your work be marked? Have you:

Level 5

Suggested reasons for different interpretations of Lenin?

Evaluated sources to establish evidence?

Selected and used information and used the correct historical words to support and structure your work?

Level 6

Begun to explain how and why different interpretations of Lenin have been made?

Evaluated sources to establish evidence important to your enquiry?

Selected, organised and used information, including the correct historical words, to produce structured work?

Level 7

Explained how and why different interpretations of Lenin have been made?

Begun to explain why views on the significance of Lenin have differed according to different viewpoints?

Established evidence for an enquiry by considering the origin, type and purpose of the sources?

Selected, organised and used the right information and the correct historical words to produce well-structured work?

Made judgements about the process of constructing history.

Who had the most success in changing the way people were ruled in the twentieth century?

You have seen that many people tried to change the way that people were ruled in the twentieth century. They used different methods and had different aims in mind, but who do you think had the most success?

Step 1: Choose your criteria

- Look back through the lessons in Unit 1.

- Think of criteria you could use to compare the success of individuals who tried to change the way people were ruled. Try to think of at least three different criteria. Here are some examples.
  - *Did their actions change the way that lots of people were ruled?*
  - *Did they have a long-lasting impact on the way people were ruled?*

- For each criterion, explain how it will help you to decide which person had the most success.

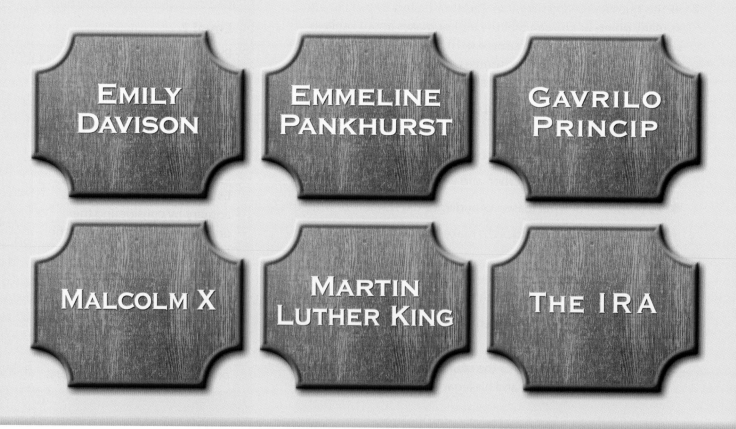

EMILY DAVISON

EMMELINE PANKHURST

GAVRILO PRINCIP

MALCOLM X

MARTIN LUTHER KING

THE IRA

Step 2: Make your choice

Now you have your criteria, decide who had the most success in changing the way people were ruled. Below are some people who tried to change things.

You might not have studied all of them, but put the ones you have studied into the order of how successful you think they were, with 1 for the most successful, 2 for the next successful, and so on. When you have your final order, use your criteria to explain what makes each person more successful than the one below them.

Step 3: Make your case

Every year a book called *Who's Who* is published. It contains information on the most important people in the world today. Imagine that there is only one space left in the next edition. Write a letter to the editor that explains why the person or group you chose as the most successful should be included in the book.

● Remember to use your criteria to structure each paragraph in the letter.

● Use comparisons with other people who have tried to change things, to get your points across!

NEVILLE CHAMBERLAIN

HAROLD MACMILLAN

NELSON MANDELA

HANADI JARADAT

How will your work be marked? Have you:

Level 5

Described some of the changes people tried to make in the twentieth century?

Suggested reasons for different interpretations of who was the most successful person?

Selected and used information and used the correct historical words to support and structure your work?

Level 6

Investigated historical problems and begun to ask your own questions as part of the enquiry?

Evaluated sources to establish evidence important to your enquiry?

Selected, organised and used information, including the correct historical words, to produce structured work?

Level 7

Explained how change and continuity differed over time and between places and peoples?

Explained how and why different interpretations of the past have been made?

Established evidence for an enquiry by considering the origin, type and purpose of the sources?

Selected, organised and used the right information and the correct historical words to produce well-structured work?

Unit 2
Living and working

Introduction

Imagine that someone from 1901 would be able to travel to the present day. The world that they would be visiting would be much changed, but what would surprise them most about the way we work and live?

? **Look at sources a–d, which are photographs of shopping centres taken during the period 1901–present day.**

? **In what ways have shops and the way that people shop changed over the period?**

? **If these were the changes in the way people shopped, what other changes do you think there would have been for ordinary people over this time?**

? **How typical do you think these images are of life at the time, and to what extent do you think there have been similar changes in other countries?**

■ *Market Street, Manchester, 1930s.*

Timeline 1901–Present day

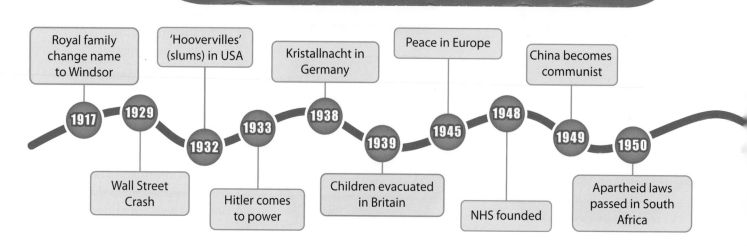

Royal family change name to Windsor — **1917**

'Hoovervilles' (slums) in USA — **1929**

1932 — Wall Street Crash

1933 — Hitler comes to power

Kristallnacht in Germany — **1938**

1939 — Children evacuated in Britain

Peace in Europe — **1945**

1948 — NHS founded

China becomes communist — **1949**

1950 — Apartheid laws passed in South Africa

a ■ A shopping street in Leeds, 1901.

b ■ A grocery shop in the 1940s.

c ■ Birmingham Bullring, 1960s.

d ■ The Bullring centre, Birmingham, 2008.

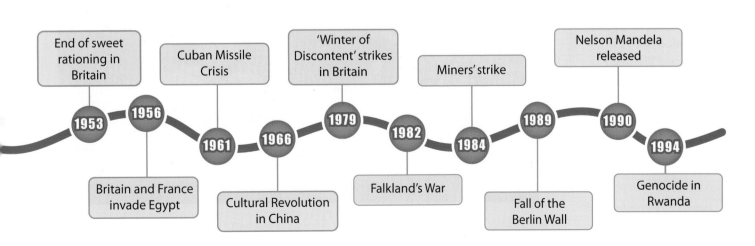

End of sweet rationing in Britain — 1953

Cuban Missile Crisis — 1956

Britain and France invade Egypt — 1956

1961

Cultural Revolution in China — 1966

'Winter of Discontent' strikes in Britain — 1979

Falkland's War — 1982

Miners' strike — 1984

Fall of the Berlin Wall — 1989

Nelson Mandela released — 1990

Genocide in Rwanda — 1994

Was there truly an Edwardian 'golden summer'?

What was life like in the pre-war years?

In this lesson you will:

■ find out what Britain was like in the years 1900–1914

■ work out whether this lesson gives you the whole picture.

? *Imagine your class has been chosen to select an 'Image of Britain' for the 2012 Olympics. What will you choose? The 'London Eye'? The 'Angel of the North'? Your local fish and chip shop? David Beckham? The choice is yours!*

Work with a partner to come up with one idea and then share your idea with the rest of your class. What is your final decision about the image that best represents Britain? Why?

A long summer afternoon?

Queen Victoria died on 22 January 1901, aged 82 years old. Most people living in Britain had known no other monarch and so in many ways her death, coming at the very start of a new century, marked not only the end of an era but the promise of a fresh beginning.

Agnes (**source a**) wasn't alone in her views. Many people, looking back on the pre-war years from the other side of the First World War, saw them as being full of optimism and a kind of innocence that was to be destroyed forever in the mud and death of the trenches in northern France. But was it a 'long summer afternoon' for everyone, as Agnes hints at? What was Britain really like in the years to 1914?

a

All in all, they were lovely, happy days. Of course there were sad times. My first baby, Leonard, died before he was a month old. But my daughters, Elsie and Constance, were fit and healthy. We lived in London – a great, bustling, busy city. In the summer holidays the girls went to stay with my sister Alice and her husband in the country and spent the time running wild over the fields with their cousins. In my memory it was all just like one long summer afternoon. And it ended, bang, just like that, in August 1914. Our lives were never the same again.

■ *Agnes Woolfe, born in 1883 and married in 1904, remembered when she was 80 years old what life had been like for her at the beginning of the century.*

Look and think

1 Look at **sources b–d**, all taken in Britain in the years before the First World War. With a partner, write down exactly what you can see in each source. What does this tell you about Britain in the early 1900s?

■ *Providence Place, Stepney, London, taken in 1912. This was one of the worst slums in London.*

c

■ *Beach at Rhyll, North Wales, in the summer of 1913.*

d

■ *Upper classes of the Edwardian era enjoying themselves.*

Asking questions

2 You are hoping to become an investigative journalist. Your editor has asked you to find out whether or not the years before the First World War really did resemble 'a long summer afternoon', as Agnes Woolfe (**source a**) believed.

You want to do well, but the editor has only given you three photographs (**sources b–d**). You've got to get the most out of them that you can.

For each photograph, think of at least five questions you could ask that will take your investigation further.

3 In pairs, compare questions, taking out those you think won't help your investigation or can never be answered.

4 Write a note to your editor, explaining how you think you can use the photographs.

Setting up an enquiry

5 Return to the questions you and your partner decided were the best ones to ask in task 3. Copy the table below and write the questions in it. Say what you hope to learn from the answers. One has been done for you. This will allow you to structure an enquiry, which is the basis of all good investigative work.

Your editor will be pleased with you!

Source	The question I would ask	What I hope to learn from the answer
c	How much did it cost to have a holiday in Rhyll?	Whether only rich and well-off people could afford holidays

Was there truly an Edwardian 'golden summer'?

In this lesson you will:

- find out about the issues that dominated the news in the summer of 1914

- investigate the significance of events in the summer of 1914.

Key words

Dockers
People who worked at the docks to load and unload ships.

Trade unions
Organisations set up to represent the interests of workers.

What were the threats to stability?

? *Think back to Lesson 2.1a. Which five words would you use to describe the years before the outbreak of war in 1914? Now look at source a. What can you see? How far does it support the impression of the long summer afternoon given in Lesson 2.1a?*

What were the issues?

The summer of 1914 was generally sunny and hot. However, as you discovered in Lessons 1.1a and 1.1b, all was not well. There were a number of issues and events that increased tension in Britain.

a

- Strikers at a cricket ball factory in the summer of 1914.

What are the issues?

1 Opposite are reports of six significant events from the summer of 1914. Imagine you are an investigative journalist. You have studied the evidence in Lesson 2.1a. Now you will try to expose the truth about the summer of 1914.

   a) Read through the reports carefully.

   b) Put the events into chronological order.

   c) In no more than 20 words per extract, say what each of the events is about.

Discussion point

There are three main issues raised in the six reports opposite:

- Ireland
- strikes
- votes for women.

2 Discuss with a partner (who is also an investigative journalist) how serious a threat each of these three issues poses to day-to-day life in Britain. For each you should discuss these questions.

   a) How is this issue a threat to day-to-day life?

   b) What are the limits to the threat?

   c) Who in society do these threats affect most? Think about different groups within society such as the working classes, middle classes, men, women, soldiers.

Daily News
22 May 1914

Shock raid on Palace

Fifty-seven protesters were arrested today after they attempted to reach Buckingham Palace to present a petition to the king. They were led by Emmeline Pankhurst. The demonstrators, some armed with clubs, attempted to break through the lines of some 1,000 policemen who were protecting the Palace. The petition was drawn up and signed in response to the defeat in Parliament earlier in the month of a bill to give 'Votes to Women'.

EVENING MAIL
4 April 1914

Demonstration in Hyde Park

Today saw a huge rally in Hyde Park in London which was protesting against the use of the British Army in Ulster in the north of Ireland. The Third Battle Squadron of the Royal Navy has already been stationed just off the coast of Ulster. The rally in Hyde Park was addressed by Sir Edward Carson, leader of the Ulster Unionists. The Unionists are bitterly opposed to the idea that Ireland is granted Home Rule. It is clear that many British Army officers are not happy with the idea of being sent to Ulster with the idea that they might have to confront the Unionists. Indeed, around 70 army officers have resigned over the issue.

DAILY SUN
4 June 1914

Strike escalates

A number of railway workers and miners from coalfields including Kent have gone out on strike in support of building workers who have been out on strike for some time. Two million workers are now on strike. This is another sign that the working people of Britain are restless and are increasingly going on strike for better pay and improved working conditions. Recently the most powerful **trade unions** (the miners, railway workers and transport workers – including the **dockers**) joined together in what is being called the Triple Alliance. Their aim is to act together to force employers to listen to their demands.

Liverpool Echo
25 April 1914

Guns landed in Ulster

It has been reported that the Unionist organisation, the Ulster Volunteer Force, has succeeded in bringing 20,000 rifles into Ulster. Last night the Ulster Volunteer Force supposedly took over the port of Larne where the rifles were landed. It is also reported that four million rounds of ammunition were brought ashore. If these reports are true, this is a worrying development for Ulster. It means that the Unionists will have weapons which they might use against the British Army to resist the introduction of Home Rule.

OXFORD POST
2 June 1914

Church destroyed

The Church in Wargrave Reading was set on fire in the early hours of yesterday morning. The police are not quite sure who is to blame but Suffragettes are suspected. The evening before the fire two women had been seen acting suspiciously near the church. At the scene of the fire some postcards were discovered on which were written pro-suffragette messages. The Suffragettes have made it clear recently that they do not like the Church of England because, in its wedding ceremony, women have to promise to obey their husbands. The church in Wargrave is totally destroyed; the roof has collapsed, the bells fell to the ground and the church glass is shattered.

Barnsley Gazette
2 April 1914

Miners out

At the end of the last month, 100,000 Yorkshire miners went on strike demanding a minimum wage. We can now report that 140,000 miners in the Yorkshire coalfield are on strike. It does not seem that the mine owners are willing to compromise and this strike could last for some time. This might have a big impact on the economy considering the fact that so much of Britain's industry transport relies on coal.

Write your article

3 Look back at task 2. You now need to write your article about 1914. First, make up a headline. Here is an example: 'The Summer of 1914: The terrible truth'.

In your article you need to explain to readers the reality of the summer 1914, commenting on all of the issues you have uncovered. Your article is probably going to shock its readers, so be careful to back up what you say with evidence.

Back to the start

Go back to the start of this enquiry. How accurate is it to describe the summer of 1914 as a 'golden summer'? Which aspect of the last two lessons have you found most interesting and why?

Next Lesson

How were the 'home fires' kept burning during the First World War?

In this lesson you will:

- find out how industry was kept going and how people were fed during the war
- use sources to show you understand why some people reacted as they did.

Key words

Munitions
Military weapons, ammunition and equipment.

U-boat
German submarine.

How did the country keep going?

While husbands, brothers, boyfriends and fathers were away fighting in the First World War, those left at home had to cope somehow with day-to-day living as well as supporting the war effort. Several songs were written to keep people's spirits high. **Source a** shows a chorus from one of them.

? *Is the chorus in source a really only about putting another lump of coal on the fire? What is the hidden message? Do you think the song was more likely to be sung at home or by soldiers at the Front?*

a

Keep the home fires burning,
While your hearts are yearning,
Though your lads are far away
They dream of home;
There's a silver lining
Through the dark clouds shining
Turn the dark cloud inside out,
Till the boys come home.

■ *Popular song entitled 'Keep the Home Fires Burning', written by Lena Ford (lyrics) and Ivor Novello (music) in 1914.*

How did British industry and agriculture keep going?

In the years 1914–18, more than 2 million men left Britain to fight in the First World War. The government had to be sure that the men at the Front had all the supplies they needed to win the war. Everything, from bullets to boots and from shells to sandbags, had to be made and sent out from Britain. This meant industry had to be geared up to support their needs.

But who would keep industries running now the men were away? It was the women who kept family businesses going and who worked as tram drivers and welders, ticket collectors and **munitions** workers. They worked on the land, milking and ploughing, foresting and harvesting. They did all this to keep the men at the Front supplied and to keep their homes running – to put food on the table, keep a roof over their heads and clothes on the backs of their children.

c

We had to pack the powder into shells with broom handles and mallets. You see, you'd have your own shell, broom handle and your tin of powder. And you'd put a bit in, pack it down, put a bit more in, pack it down. It took all your time to get it all in. It was very hard work.

■ *Memories of Elsie McIntyre of what it was like when she worked in a munitions factory during the First World War. This was particularly dangerous work. The powder was highly explosive.*

d

February 1916

Today, the men from Lang's on the Clyde are out on strike owing to the introduction of women into the works.

■ *Extract from Frances Stevenson's diary. She was secretary to the prime minister, David Lloyd George.*

b

■ *Women workers at Vickers Ltd, May 1917. They are working lathes, turning brass nose cones for shells. This was precision machine work.*

e
Some of the labourers on the Wolds [an area of Lincolnshire] who were not used to their wives going out said that the same standard of comfort and cleanliness was impossible in their homes under the new conditions.

■ *From a report entitled 'Wages and Conditions of Employment in Agriculture', published in 1919.*

How was the nation fed?

In 1914 there were about 45 million people living in Great Britain, and a lot of the food they ate came from abroad. War inevitably meant food shortages. Not only did German **U-boats** sink ships bringing food to Britain, but also the British government had to make sure that sufficient supplies went abroad to feed the troops.

f
Saturday, 24 February 1917

2.20pm: Afternoon's post brought me a circular from the Food Controller urging all ministers of religion to encourage a voluntary cutback in food consumption to avoid rationing. Suggested limits were four pounds of bread, two and a half pounds of meat and three-quarters of a pound of sugar per person per week.

■ *From the diary of the Reverend Andrew Clark, vicar of Great Leighs, Essex.*

g
My daughter went out at 7am to the Maypole Dairy Co shop and after waiting until 10.30am was turned away without any margarine. She came home chilled to the bone besides losing her education. If we could have a system of rationing I believe these hardships could be overcome.

■ *From a letter published in a newspaper entitled* The Workers' Dreadnought, *19 January 1917. Women who worked had to send their children to queue for food.*

h
It was a terrible time, terrible. We were starving. I can remember my mother going out and picking dandelion leaves and washing them and making sandwiches with them. My mother, my grandmother, my little brother and me used to go out into the fields and pick the green tops off the turnips and swedes. We took them home and cooked them with potatoes and mashed it up with margarine. That was our Sunday dinner.

■ *Memories of Ruth Armstrong, aged 96, of what it was like to go hungry as a child. She was born and brought up in the village of Tilshead, Wiltshire, where her father was an agricultural labourer. In 1917 she was 11.*

What shall we tell Fred?

Men fighting abroad relied on letters from home to keep their spirits up. Women at home needed to keep in touch with their husbands, brothers and sons who were miles away. While they wanted to tell them the truth about how they were coping, they didn't want to alarm them, either.

Women's work is never done!

History detective

How were the 'home fires' kept burning during the First World War?

What did people fear?

? *What frightens you? Quick – before you really have time to think. Spiders? Flying? Snakes? Now think again. If you were living in a country where people's husbands, fathers, sons, brothers and uncles had left to fight overseas, would you be afraid of the same things? Source a might give you a hint.*

In this lesson you will:

- find out how the Germans threatened mainland Britain
- explore the reactions of people and the government at home to the threats posed by the war.

a I can remember my mother going pale one afternoon as she saw the telegram boy coming towards the house. She turned to me and smiled as he cycled past, but she didn't say a word. My father and brother were in the navy and you never knew if the telegram was for you.

■ *A woman remembers what it was like in the war when she was 14 years old.*

Key words

Barrage balloon
Very large gas-filled balloon anchored to the ground in wartime to deter enemy aircraft.

Total war
War involving the civilian population as well as the military.

Zeppelin
German airship, sometimes called a dirigible.

■ *A **Zeppelin** aircraft, used by the Germans during the First World War.*

Why were Zeppelins frightening?

c I turned out of bed and saw just above us two Zepps. The searchlights were on them and they looked as if they were among the stars. They were very high and like cigar-shaped constellations. They kept pulling away from the searchlights only to be caught again. It was lovely.

■ *Mrs Holcombe Ingleby, wife of a Conservative MP, describes a Zeppelin raid on London in August 1915. She wrote this in a letter to her son who was an army officer in Cairo, Egypt.*

d To me it was what I would call an awful sight. All of the bag part that was full of hydrogen had caught fire. It was roaring flames: blue, red, purple. We knew that there were about 60 people in it and that they were being roasted to death. I was appalled to see the good-hearted British people dancing about in the streets at the sight of 60 people being burned alive.

■ *Sybil Morrison describes what she felt when she saw the first Zeppelin shot down in 1915.*

Zeppelins: beautiful or beastly?

1 Look at **source b**. What words would you use to describe this Zeppelin? Discuss this with a partner, then compare what you think with others in the class.

2 Read **sources c** and **d**. Why do you think these two women had such different reactions to seeing a Zeppelin?

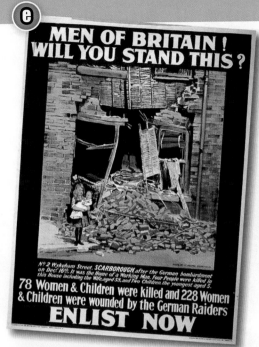

A poster trying to persuade men to enlist for war, issued by the government in 1915.

Putting disaster to good use?

3 Look at **source e**. It is a poster in which the government uses the shelling of Scarborough as part of a recruitment campaign.

   a) What might people have said in criticism of this?

   b) Do you think the government was justified in using the bombing and death of British people in this way?

   c) Compared to the total population of 45 million people, relatively few were killed by enemy bombs and shells. Why, then, were people so afraid of them?

Fear of shells and bombs

As the information boxes below show, the destruction, violence and death of war were brought to mainland Britain for the very first time. The result was that ordinary people were killed in their houses, shops, offices and schools. This was **total war**. No one had ever thought that Britain would have to be defended from air attacks. After the first raids, anti-aircraft guns were built, searchlights installed and **barrage balloons** set up.

> **Shelling from battleships.**
> In December 1914, German battleships in the North Sea shelled towns along the north-east coast of Britain. Most destruction happened in Scarborough, Whitby and Hartlepool, where 119 men, women and children were killed.

> **Bombing from Zeppelins.**
> In January 1915, Zeppelins began bombing British towns, starting with Kings Lynn and Great Yarmouth on the east coast. Altogether, Zeppelins made a total of 57 raids on British towns, killing 564 people and injuring 1,370.

> **Bombing from aeroplanes.** In May 1917, German Gotha bombers attacked Folkestone and killed 95 people. Then they raided London and killed 162 people – including 16 children who died when their school was hit. Altogether, the Germans made 27 bomber raids on British towns, killing 825 people and injuring 1990 others.

PROCLAMATION
DEFENCE OF THE REALM.
THE ENEMY HAVING INVADED THE COAST
OF LINCOLNSHIRE,
The Civil Population are Hereby Directed to Carry Out the Following Instructions :

1. No Motors, bicycles, horses, mules, donkeys, carts, carriages, or other vehicles will be moved, except under orders issued by the Military Authorities.

2. Failing other orders from the Military Authorities, live stock will be driven into fields off the roads and scattered as much as possible.

3. No attempt, except under orders from the Military Authorities or the Police acting under such orders, should be made to burn, cut, or destroy :—

   Bridges.   Waterworks.
   Railway Rolling Stock.   Sluices or Locks.
   Electric Light or Power Stations. Piers or Jetties.
   Telegraph or Telephone Wires. Ferries.
   Wireless Stations.

The arrangements already made with the Police should be carried out.

Twenty copies of this Proclamation were issued to all local military commanders along the east coast of Britain. It was not dated and was never issued to the public. When the invasion scare was over, all copies were recalled and destroyed, still in their unopened envelopes. All that is, except one. An extra copy was stuck to the back of the twentieth copy and kept back. This is it.

Invasion!

The shelling of the east coast of England frightened the authorities. Nothing like it had ever happened before. They prepared for what they believed was the inevitable invasion by German troops.

Be prepared!

4 Carefully read **source f**. How sensible are the instructions? Why do you think the Proclamation was not issued before an invasion so that people could prepare for it?

How were the 'home fires' kept burning during the First World War?

Did everyone in Britain hate the Germans?

In this lesson you will:

■ find out how British people reacted to Germans living in Britain

■ investigate whether everyone felt the same.

■ *A crowd attacking a German-owned shop in London in 1915.*

Key words

Intern
To take away from the home and workplace and put into a camp until the war was over.

Prisoner of war
Member of the enemy's armed forces who was captured and sent to Britain for the duration of the war.

German people had lived and worked in Britain for many years without any problems whatsoever. However, when war was declared, many British people became suspicious of foreigners living in their midst and turned on them.

● German shepherd dogs were renamed Alsatians.

● Dachshund dogs were kicked and stoned in the streets, and two were reportedly burned alive.

● German measles was renamed 'Belgian flush'.

● Boots the Chemist explained that eau de Cologne had nothing to do with the German city of Cologne.

● Perrier water advertised itself as the 'table water of the allies' and sales of Apollinaris water (made in Germany) slumped.

● The *Daily Mail* ran a campaign urging people to boycott restaurants employing German waiters.

● Prince Louis of Battenberg resigned as First Lord of the Admiralty and changed his surname to Mountbatten. Battenberg is the name of a town in Germany.

● The Royal family changed its name from Saxe-Coburg-Gotha to Windsor.

Rioting was going on quite near here. It is a mercy they have interned the Germans at last. It ought to have been done long ago. It is a pity that our folk descended to lawlessness, but it was the only way our people could show their feelings in the matter. We have a great camp of German prisoners of war not far from here. Would you believe that people were actually asking for cakes for them?

■ *From a letter written by Margaret Lilley, of Stroud Green, London, in May 1915.*

Think about it

1 Look at **source a** and read **source b**. How similar are the reactions to German people shown in the photograph and in Margaret Lilley's letter? Discuss this with a partner, then write down as many points of similarity and difference as you can.

? *What is your immediate reaction to these happenings? Were they silly? Serious? Sinister?*

How did the authorities treat Germans in Britain?

Early in the war, the government decided that all foreign nationals, including Germans, who were old enough to serve in the armed services, should be **interned**. They were taken away from their work, homes, friends and families and put in camps until the war ended.

All sides in the war took prisoners. The British sent their German **prisoners of war** (PoWs) to live in camps in various different parts of Britain. Sometimes the camps were in buildings that were no longer in use, like old schools and workhouses; sometimes they were purpose-built. Most prisoners worked, under guard, outside the camps during the day. They usually wore specially made uniforms so that they could be spotted if they tried to escape.

c

Monday 4 March 1918

The German prisoners are hard at work on the aerodrome at Chelmsford. They have quarters in the workhouse and are marched back there from their work about 4.30pm each day. They are said to be very happy, laughing and joking with each other as they pass along the street. Several girls have been taken before the magistrates for giving them stamps and chocolate.

Thursday 29 August 1918

Mrs Matthew has four German prisoners doing work on her farm. They are brought in a lorry at 8am. They have a meal in the workhouse before they start in the morning, and bring another meal with them. She does not think this is enough, because they work until 7 or 8pm. She is annoyed because the authorities forbid her giving them more food, but quietly ignores the prohibition. The men are excellent workers.

■ *From the diary of the Reverend Andrew Clark, vicar of Great Leighs, Essex.*

d

2 Read **source c**.

  a) Why do you think the authorities were so keen to stop British people getting friendly with the German PoWs?

  b) Does **source d** prove that they were unsuccessful?

3 Read **source c** again.

  a) What would one of the German PoWs have written in his diary?

  b) Rewrite the two entries from the point of view of a German PoW.

How good is the evidence?

Historians rely on sources to build up their picture of the past. The more reliable the source, the more accurate their picture of the past is likely to be.

4 Look again at **sources a–d**.

  a) Think about their reliability as evidence of the attitudes of British people to the Germans in Britain. Rank each one on a scale of 1–5 (where 1 = most reliable and 5 = least reliable).

  b) Explain why you have given your 'best' and 'worst' sources their ranking.

Back to the start

Look back over the work you have done in this enquiry. How successfully do you think the British people coped on the home front? Rank their success on a scale of 1–5, where 5 = very successful and 1= totally unsuccessful. Explain why you have given this ranking.

■ *German prisoners of war with women who worked at the tailoring factory. This factory made German uniforms for German PoWs and British uniforms to send to Germany for British PoWs.*

How did people in Britain survive the Second World War?

In this lesson you will:

■ find out how people at home tried to keep themselves safe

■ explore the differences in people's reactions to the threats posed by the war.

Key words

Blitz
Concentrated and focused bombing.

Identity cards
Everyone living in Britain, including newborn babies, had to carry an identity card to prove they were who they said they were.

Luftwaffe
The German air force.

What did people fear this time?

People living at home during the First World War were afraid of death. They were afraid of the death of loved ones at the battlefront. They were afraid of the shelling and bombing that could kill them, and their friends and family in their own homes. They were afraid, too, of invasion by the enemy. It was the same in the Second World War. However, by this time the ways of killing had become more sophisticated, so people tried different methods of protecting themselves against what they thought might happen.

? *Look at source a. What can you see? Write down three things. Compare these with the person next to you and the people next to them until you have a class list of what can be seen.*

a ■ *An Anderson shelter survives a bombing raid, 1940.*

How did people shelter from bombs?

You might think that no one survived the attack in **source a**. But they did. The reason for their survival lies in the remains of the corrugated iron structure you can see in the middle of the photograph. This was an Anderson shelter.

These shelters were designed to protect people from anything except a direct hit. The shelters were free to families where the husband earned less than £250 a year. Families with a bigger income could buy one for £7.

The government began distributing Anderson shelters at the beginning of 1939. By the time war broke out in September 1939, more than 2 million families had one in their garden. The government also built public shelters on street corners and in shopping centres that could be used by anyone passing. During the **Blitz**, Londoners felt safe in the deep Underground stations, where they slept on the platforms (and on the track once the electricity had been switched off).

In 1941 the government began issuing a different sort of shelter: the Morrison shelter. These were constructed from heavy steel and could be used as a table. One side was made from steel mesh and, when a bombing raid began, people could crawl underneath. Morrison shelters meant that people could stay inside their own homes when bombing began rather than rush to a shelter in their garden.

Your turn ...

1 Study **sources a–c**.

a) Imagine you are one of the children on the top bunks of **source b**. What are you thinking? What are you feeling?

b) What would you have written in your diary for the night of 8 September 1940? Begin 'Suddenly the sirens started wailing …'

Did you know?

Between September 1940 and May 1941, the German Luftwaffe made 127 large-scale bombing raids on London. The Luftwaffe also raided Belfast, Birmingham, Bristol, Cardiff, Coventry, Glasgow, Hull, London, Manchester, Newcastle, Nottingham, Plymouth, Portsmouth, Sheffield and Southampton.

b

Made from six curved sheets of corrugated iron bolted together at the top, with steel plates at either end.

Inside they measured 1.95m by 1.35m.

■ *This cut-away drawing shows how a family, including the dog, fitted into an Anderson shelter.*

Entrance would be protected by a steel shield and an earthen blast wall.

Shelter half buried in the ground and had earth heaped on top.

c

When air raids are threatened, warning will be given in towns by sirens, or hooters will be sounded in some places by short blasts and in others by a warbling note, changing every few seconds. The warnings may be given by the police or air-raid wardens blowing short blasts on whistles.

When you hear the warning, take cover at once. Remember that most of the injuries in an air raid are caused not by direct hits by bombs but by flying fragments of debris or by bits of shells. Stay under cover until you hear the sirens sounding continuously for 2 minutes on the same note, which is the signal 'Raiders passed.'

■ *British government circular, issued in 1939.*

Shelters: nasty or nice?

2 Study **sources b** and **d**.

   a) What does Barbara Castle say was wrong with Anderson shelters?

   b) How far does the drawing (**source b**) support what she says?

3 Now read **sources e** and **f**.

   a) Why are Evelyn Ross and Muriel Simkin criticising Underground stations when they doubled up as deep shelters?

   b) How far does Barbara Castle (**source d**) disagree with them?

d

In 1939, Sir John Anderson insisted that blast and splinter-proof protection was all that was needed. The shelters he approved consisted of nothing more than enlarged holes in the ground covered by thin steel. They had no lighting, no heating and no lavatories. People had to survive a winter night's bombardment in them as best they could. When the Blitz came, Londoners found their own deep shelters: the London Underground. Night after night, just before the sirens sounded, thousands of Londoners trooped in orderly fashion into the nearest Underground station, taking their bedding with them, flasks of hot tea, snacks, radios, packs of cards and magazines. People set up their own little communities where they could relax. I joined them one night to see what it was like. It was not a way of life I wanted for myself but I could see what an important safety-valve it was. Without it, London life could not have carried on in the way it did.

■ *From Barbara Castle's autobiography* Fighting All the Way, *published in 1993. Barbara Castle was a Labour Party politician and MP.*

e

If you were out and a bombing raid took place you would make for the nearest shelter. The Tube [Underground] stations were considered to be very safe. I did not like using them myself. The stench was unbearable. The smell was so bad I don't know how people did not die from suffocation. So many bodies and no fresh air coming in. People would go to the Tube stations long before it got dark because they wanted to make sure they had reserved their space. There were a lot of arguments among people over that. We did not have an Anderson shelter, so we used to hide under the stairs. You felt the next bang would be your lot and it was very frightening.

■ *Interview with Evelyn Ross, a teenager during the London Blitz, in 1987.*

f

Rosie, my Mum's sister, had to go to hospital to have a baby. Her mother-in-law looked after her 3-year-old son. There was a bombing raid, and Rosie's son and mother-in-law rushed to Bethnal Green Underground station. Going down the stairs somebody fell. People panicked and Rosie's son was trampled to death.

■ *Memories of a family tragedy from Muriel Simkin, who worked in a munitions factory in Dagenham, Essex, during the Second World War.*

g

We shall not flag or fail. We shall go on to the end. We shall defend our island, whatever the cost may be. We shall fight on the beaches, we shall fight on the landing grounds, we shall fight in the fields and on the streets, we shall fight in the hills; we shall never surrender.

■ *From a speech made in the House of Commons by Prime Minister Winston Churchill immediately after the evacuation from Dunkirk, 4 June 1940.*

h

The Home Guards' value to the defence of Great Britain was unquestionable. Apart from weapons and equipment, the regular army's greatest need throughout the summer was for training; and training was impossible while there were 5,000 miles of coast to watch, road blocks to man and bridges to protect. For all these duties the Home Guard was available. Had it not been, an almost intolerable strain would have been placed on the army.

■ *From Peter Fleming's book* Invasion, *published in 1958.*

i

Over a million men enrolled in the Home Guard by the summer of 1940. This provided a welcome activity for the veterans of the First World War. It had less value as a fighting force. There were few rifles to spare for it until the late summer, and even when these were issued, there was no ammunition. The Home Guards harassed innocent citizens for their **identity cards**, put up primitive road-blocks and sometimes made bombs out of petrol tins. In a serious invasion, its members would presumably have been massacred, if they had managed to assemble at all. Their spirit was willing though their equipment was scanty.

■ *From A. J. P. Taylor's book* English History 1914–45, *published in 1965.*

How were people preparing for invasion?

In the summer of 1940, there was a very real possibility that the Nazis would invade Britain. What was left of the British army had been evacuated from the beaches of Dunkirk. France had surrendered to the Nazis and German troops had occupied the French Channel ports. Would Britain be next?

The government ordered thousands of huge concrete blocks and millions of coils of barbed wire to be put on the beaches of the south and east coasts to deter invaders who would come by sea. Farmers parked old tractors and ploughs to stop gliders landing. Signposts were taken down and train station names blacked out so that any Nazi invaders would get lost. Vicars did not ring church bells on Sundays because it was agreed that ringing church bells would be a sign that an invasion had started.

Everyone got ready for an invasion, not just people living on or near the south and east coasts. Men who were not in the regular armed forces joined the new Local Defence Volunteers (LDV), which was soon renamed the Home Guard. Women, who were not allowed to join the LDV, formed the Women's Home Defence Corps (WHDC) and learned to fire rifles and pistols.

How effective was the Home Guard?

4 Read Churchill's speech (**source g**). Listening to it, Anthony Eden, a member of the government, muttered 'What with? Broken bottles?'
Most of the British army's equipment and tanks had been left behind on the beaches of Dunkirk. Look back to Lesson 1.5a to remind yourself what had happened. Was Churchill, then, talking rubbish? What was the point of him making a speech like that?

5 Read **sources h** and **i**. How different are the views of these two historians about the usefulness of the Home Guard?

6 Both the shelters and the Home Guard were there to protect the British people. How well do you think they did their job?

■ *Women of the Women's Home Defence Corps being drilled in the use of rifles, 1941.*

How did people in Britain survive the Second World War?

In this lesson you will:

- discover how the government hoped to keep children safe during the Second World War

- use sources to explore the reactions of some children and the families with whom they stayed.

Key words

Censor
Person who decides what can be published and what cannot.

Evacuation
Sending children away from the cities to the countryside or abroad to keep them safe from enemy bombs.

Women's Institute
National women's organisation that co-ordinated the evacuation of children.

How were children kept safe?

In order to keep children safe during the Second World War, the government organised their mass **evacuation** from the cities to the countryside. From 1–5 September 1939, more than 1 million children were sent to safety. But when the bombs didn't fall, their parents took them back home. There was another wave of evacuation in 1940 when the Blitz began, and again in 1944 when Germany launched V1 and V2 'flying bombs'.

? *What three questions would you like to ask about the photograph in source a? Swap questions with the person sitting next to you. Have you got six different questions? (You should find answers to all your questions as you work through this lesson.)*

a

■ *Children and teachers walking to Blackhouse Road station, north-east London, 1939.*

Did you know?

Some children were evacuated to safe parts of the Empire: Australia, Canada, New Zealand and South Africa. But in September 1940 the SS *Benares*, sailing from Liverpool to Canada, was torpedoed and 77 children were drowned.

Read and think

1 Read **source b**. Here, villagers chose the children they wanted.

Do you think this was the right way to decide which children went with which adults? Try to work out a better system. (Remember, though, this was wartime and decisions had to be made quickly.)

b

We were told to sit quietly on the floor while villagers and farmers' wives came to choose which children they wanted. Eventually, only my friend Nancy and myself were left. Two plain, straight-haired little girls wearing glasses, now rather tearful. A large, happy-looking, middle-aged lady rushed in asking, 'Is this all you have left?' A sad, slow nod of the head from our teacher. 'I'll take the poor bairns.' We were led out of the hall with this stranger and taken to a farm where we spent two years.

■ *Evacuee Beryl Hewitson describes what happened to her when she arrived in the country in 1939.*

Evacuation: a success or a failure?

2 Read **sources c–f**. Make a list of problems faced by:

- evacuees
- the families with whom they lived.

3 *'There would have been no problems if the evacuee children had tried harder to fit in with their new families.'* Explain whether you agree or disagree with this statement.

How did evacuation work?

Mothers usually went with children who were under school age. School-age children went with their teachers. Parents did not know where their children were going. They just had to believe government promises that their children would be well looked after.

Evacuation of children was not compulsory, but it was compulsory for people in the countryside to accept city children into their homes. The children were lodged with families and sometimes single people who had a spare room. The government paid families 10s 6d (52.5 pence) a week for the first evacuated child and 8s 6d (42.5 pence) a week each for any others. Not all families in the countryside wanted city children living with them, and not all children wanted to be there.

c The village didn't know what hit them when we first arrived. It was gang warfare between us and the local kids. There wasn't a fruit tree within miles around with a single item of fruit left on it. After a while, things settled down to an uneasy truce.

■ *Patricia Barton remembers life as an evacuee.*

f They would tie me to a chair and hold red-hot pokers in front of my eyes. I had terrible nightmares. I was sent away when the three of us took down the knickers of the girl next door. I ended up in a spick and span place. Every day I would come home from school to 'clean this, shine that'. So I started to save my milk money, a halfpenny a day. I came home one day and wrote across the list of things to do, 'Gone back to London'. My mother hid me in the attic for two days before telling my father. I wasn't sent back and stayed in London during the raids.

■ *Christopher Portinari had three evacuee homes. Two boys in the second home bullied him very badly.*

d There were six of us from my school. A distinguished, white-haired gentleman met us at Foston House. His warmth and genial hospitality gave us such comfort. The orchard bore fruit, we had a car to take us to school, a piano, a beautiful home, servants, typing lessons, mini-golf and a fine lawn. Most of all we had met warmth and understanding. But I became a snob. Each weekend I'd board the bus home. The street looked dingy, poor, and I hated it. I remember seeing my father cooking a pigeon on our kitchen fire and the repulsion stayed with me. Eventually, Mother called me home to help care for the others. Then my lovely world crumbled.

■ *Sheila Price, one of a family of eight children from Hammersmith, London, was evacuated when she was 12 years old.*

e
- The children were filthy.
- We have never seen so many children with lice and nits, and lacking any knowledge of clean and healthy habits.
- Some children had dirty, septic sores all over their bodies.
- Some of the children were sewn into their ragged little garments.
- There was hardly a child with a whole pair of shoes.
- Many of the mothers and children were bed-wetters.

■ *Extracts from reports sent to the* **Women's Institute** *headquarters in 1940.*

In conclusion ...

4 Look at **source g**. Why do you think the government **censor** banned the publication of this photograph?

5 The government was trying to persuade parents to send their children to the safety of the countryside. Why, then, wouldn't it use a photograph like this one to prove how dangerous it was to keep children with them in the cities?

g

■ *Children's bodies wrapped in sacking, recovered from a bombed-out school. The photograph is dated 21 January 1943.*

How did people in Britain survive the Second World War?

In this lesson you will:

■ find out how food and clothing were rationed during the Second World War

■ understand how the government tried to help all the people to be fed and clothed.

Key words

Allotment land
Usually owned by local councils and rented out in plots to people to grow fruit and vegetables.

Coupons
Printed in ration books, clipped out and then stamped by shopkeepers to show that rationed foods had been bought.

Making connections

1 Look again at **source a** and read about rationing in **source b**.

a) Why was the government urging people to 'Dig for victory'? Did you get it right when you talked about it at the beginning of the lesson?

b) Do you think the poster was an effective way of getting them to do this?

How were people fed?

These days, we have a huge variety of food and clothes in our shops. And what we can't buy there we can almost certainly have delivered by post. But things are very different during times of war.

? *Look at source a. Why would the government publish a poster like this? How do you think digging could lead to victory? Talk about this with the person sitting next to you and share your ideas with your class.*

■ *Government poster, released in 1939.*

Fair shares for all?

Much of Britain's food came from overseas, and enemy action could starve Britain into submission unless drastic action was taken. The government learned from the mistakes made on the First World War home front (see Enquiry 2.2) and quickly introduced food rationing.

By the end of January 1940, everyone had a ration book and had registered with their local shops to make sure they could get their weekly ration. **Coupons** from their ration book, as well as money, had to be handed over for rationed food. Pregnant women had green ration books; they had first choice of any fruit and twice the egg ration. Children had blue ration books, and were allowed fruit and half a pint of milk a week. Everyone else had buff-coloured books and the same entitlement.

Bread was never rationed. Neither were fruit and vegetables, but they were in desperately short supply. All fruit had to be home grown, so pineapples and bananas, for example, were not seen in the UK for years. Thousands of people grew their own fruit and vegetables in gardens and **allotments**. Many of them also kept hens and geese. Every available bit of land, from golf club fairways to railway embankments, seaside promenades and even the moat around the Tower of London, was used to grow cabbages and cauliflowers, peas and beans, parsnips, carrots, leeks and potatoes. Farmers were ordered to plough up grassland and grow oats, barley, wheat, potatoes and cattle fodder.

How did the Ministry of Food help?

The Ministry of Food produced a range of recipes and menus to ensure that, during each week, people ate as well as they could within the constraints of rationing. Children were introduced to 'Doctor Carrot' and 'Potato Pete' who would help keep them fit and healthy. The Minister of Food, Lord Woolton, gave regular talks on the radio encouraging people to grow their own food and eat healthily. A large chain of 'British Restaurants' was set up where people could get cheap, hot meals and 'Food Advice' centres opened.

Food	Amount
Bacon or ham	4oz
Meat	1s 10d worth
Cheese	4oz
Butter	4oz
Fresh eggs	1
Milk	3 pints
Tea	3oz
Sugar	12oz
Sweets	3oz
Dried milk	4 pints
Dried eggs	1 tin every eight weeks

■ *A typical weekly food ration for an adult. The amount varied during the war depending on the availability of supplies. (4oz = 115 grams; 1s 10d in 1940 would buy two lamb chops or a larger amount of cheaper meat for stewing, and families could combine their meat coupons to buy a joint of beef, lamb or pork.)*

c Woolton Pie

Ingredients

• 1lb potatoes • 1lb carrots
• 1lb swede • 1lb parsnips

Method

Boil vegetables together for a few minutes. Drain, then mix in with a good white sauce. Put vegetable sauce mix into a pie dish and cover with pastry. Cook in oven until pastry is golden brown.

■ *A Ministry of Food recipe, originally created at the Savoy Hotel in London.*

d

MONDAY
Breakfast (each day): Porridge or breakfast cereal. Fruit. Toast. Marmalade. Eggs occasionally. Milk or milky tea.
Dinner: Vegetable soup or Jacket sausages. Raisin dumplings with golden syrup.
Tea-Supper: Blackberry bake. Wholemeal bread and butter. Cocoa.

TUESDAY
Dinner: Mutton pie. Jacket potatoes. Baked apple.
Tea-Supper: Macaroni cheese. Bread and butter. Fruit. Milk or tea.

WEDNESDAY
Dinner: Braised beef (keeping bones for soup). Vegetables. Chocolate blancmange.
Tea-Supper: Scrambled eggs on toast. Stewed dried apricots. Milk drink.

THURSDAY
Dinner: Baked marrow with leftover beef. College pudding.
Tea-Supper: Vegetable casserole. Bread and jam. Tea or fruit-juice drink.

FRIDAY
Dinner: Bombay rice. Cabbage. Golden apples.
Tea-Supper: Vegetable salad on lettuce. Wholemeal bread and butter. Rice pudding.

SATURDAY
Dinner: Liver casserole. Mashed potatoes. Greens. Milk jelly.
Tea-Supper: Bread and butter pudding. Fruit.

SUNDAY
Dinner: Beef, carrots and dumplings. Greens. Sponge pudding.
Tea-Supper: Cheese and tomato sandwiches. Cake. Milk drink.

■ *A week's menus from a government information sheet.*

e

Item	Men	Women	Children
Raincoat	16	15	11
Overcoat	7	7	4
Jacket	13	12	8
Shirt/blouse	5	4	3
Jumper/cardigan	5	5	3
Trousers	8	8	6
Shorts	3	3	2
Skirt	–	8	6
Boots/shoes	7	5	3
Nightdress/pyjamas	8	6	6
Pants/knickers/vest	3	3	6
Socks/stockings	2	2	1

■ *Government allocation of points to clothes.*

… and clothing too

Clothes were rationed from June 1941 due to:

● a shortage of raw materials

● the need to turn clothes factories over to producing weapons, aircraft and ammunition for the war.

Everyone was given a book of clothes coupons and was allowed to 'spend' 66 coupons a year. This was cut to 48 in 1941 and 36 in 1943. Second-hand clothes were not rationed and were swapped and sold within families and between friends. 'Make do and mend' became a well-known government slogan.

Eat your greens!

2 Read **source d**.

a) What is your immediate impression of this as a weekly menu?

b) Would it stop people going hungry?

c) Why do you think the government felt it had to provide recipes like **source c** and menus like **source d**?

3 Think carefully about what you had to eat and drink yesterday. Write down everything from the moment you got up to the moment you went to bed. Now compare it with the same day on the government menu.

a) Which food is better balanced?

b) Which is healthier? Why?

c) How would you have felt if you had been alive in the 1940s and had to stick to the government menu?

In conclusion …

4 Food and clothes rationing might look grim and depressing to you. Use all the information in this lesson, including **sources a–e**, to show families how important it was to do what the government wanted, and that it could even be fun! You can present this as a poster, a leaflet or a five-minute sketch.

Back to the start

Towards the end of the Second World War, American servicemen arrived in Britain in great numbers. How would one of them have told his folks back home about the ways in which people in Britain survived the war? You could present this as a letter, a conversation or a short sketch.

How did people in Britain survive the Second World War?

Taking it further!

The end of the war in Europe

On 7 May 1945, German radio broadcast that General Alfred Jodl would sign the official surrender of Nazi Germany the following day. Prime Minister Winston Churchill immediately announced that 8 May 1945 would be a national holiday – Victory in Europe (VE) Day.

Did you know?

The Second World War wasn't finally over until the surrender of Japan on 15 August 1945. This was called VJ Day.

a

■ *Gunner Hector Murdoch is welcomed home on 15 October 1945.*

b

The same year that Patty started school, the war ended. It had lasted for six long weary years, and for those of us who had been young at the time, it was a big slice out of our lives. When it was finally all over, there was singing and dancing in the streets. Victory bells rang and people cried and laughed at the same time and hugged each other. We had street parties for the children, and though they were too young to know what it was all about, they caught the excitement of the moment, and with balloons and streamers they joined in the fun.

■ *Joyce Storey remembers the end of the war in her book* Joyce's War, *published in 1992.*

c

Sara and I sit quietly and watch the city [Birmingham] lights flicker below. 'It's over,' we say, 'it's over, it's over.' We say it again and again, trying to grasp the full meaning of the day. Inside me, though, there is a large, dark, numb presence which I dare not look at. The last I heard of my parents was the rumour that they had escaped to Yakutsk, Siberia. I refuse to contemplate the alternatives.

■ *Professor Joel Elkes writing about his memory of VE day in a letter dated 4 November 1994.*

What can we learn about the end of war?

1 Carefully study **sources a–d**, which give four different reactions to the ending of war in Europe.

2 For **sources a–c**, explain why the people concerned reacted as they did.

3 **Source d** is a bit different.

   a) What is its message?

   b) Why was it published in a national newspaper on VE day?

"Here you are! Don't lose it again!"

Cartoon published in the Daily Mirror, 8 May 1945.

In this lesson you will:

■ explore what happened to Jews under Nazi control

■ use pictorial information to investigate a problem.

○ Key words

Anti-Semitism
Hatred of Jews.

Deportation
Forced removal from your home or country.

Genocide
Deliberate attempt to murder an entire national or ethnic group of people.

Ghetto
Part of a town walled off from the rest where Jews were forced to live.

How did the Nazis try to kill all European Jews?

When they joined the German army, some officers might never have imagined they would order the shooting of defenceless women and children. But from 1941 to 1945 many did; they saw it as their duty to ensure that the German nation survived.

Sowing seeds of hatred

Source a is clear evidence of just one act of murder. The Nazis, and those who they got to help them, killed 6 million people, mostly Jewish men, women and children, between 1939 and 1945. In fact, the Nazis wanted to kill all 11 million Jews in Europe. It is very difficult to understand the reason for this. Germany was a modern country with an educated population. What caused some otherwise ordinary people to become killers?

There were a number of ways in which the Nazi government tried to encourage **anti-Semitism** between 1933 and 1945, including:

● propaganda

● use of laws to exclude Jews from public life

● threat of arrest for those who disagreed with Nazi views

● removing Jews from Germany and forcing them to live elsewhere in terrible conditions.

? *In pairs, look at source a. Why might this soldier have carried out this shooting? Try to list three possible reasons.*

(a)

■ *A German soldier in the Ukraine about to shoot a woman and child, 1942.*

Use your eyes!

1 Look at **sources b–e**. For each one:

a) decide which method of anti-Semitism this source best shows

b) explain your decision using details from the source.

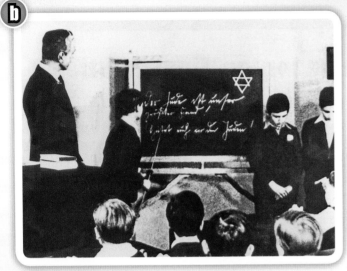

■ Anti-Semitism was taught at school, especially in history and biology lessons. Here, two Jewish children are forced to stand by a blackboard that reads 'The Jews are our greatest enemy! Beware of Jews.' Jewish children were eventually excluded from German schools in 1938.

■ Ninety-one Jews were killed and 30,000 Jews were sent to concentration camps in November 1938 after a Jew murdered a German diplomat in Paris. All German Jews had to wear a Star of David badge after 1 September 1941.

■ German Jews were **deported** to **ghettos** in Polish towns from October 1941. Living conditions in these ghettos were hellish.

■ The Nazi Party controlled the media – newspapers, radio and cinema. It produced lots of anti-Semitic propaganda like this film, The Eternal Jew.

Weigh the evidence!

2 Look again at **sources b–e**. Which two do you think give the best evidence that Nazis were trying to make ordinary Germans hate the Jews? As you make your decision remember to think about:

● the content of the source

● the nature, origin and purpose of the source.

Why did so few people help the Jews?

In Germany, the Nazis tried to control every single aspect of people's lives – the books they read, the music they listened to and who they could marry. If you did not fit in, you could become a victim of a powerful police state. Many people were arrested, imprisoned and even killed without a fair trial, because all the judges were Nazis.

Going undercover!

The Social Democrat Party (SPD) was banned in 1933, shortly after the Nazis came to power. The SPD leaders fled from Germany to Prague to escape arrest, but they kept spies in the country to send reports about what was going on.

3 Imagine you are an SPD spy in 1939. You are told to send a report about how the Nazis are trying to encourage anti-Semitic attitudes. In your report, use the evidence you have seen to make clear what you think are the most important pressures.

Give lots of details about these pressures.

In this lesson you will:

- investigate who was responsible for the 'Final Solution'

- use written sources to support an argument.

Who was to blame for the 'Final Solution'?

Between 1940 and 1942 the Nazis shot more than 1 million Jews in Poland and Russia. However, Nazi leaders worried that shooting was too slow and had a bad impact on the morale of soldiers. At some point in 1941, leaders began to talk about a 'Final Solution' to the 'Jewish problem', but it was not clear what this would be. There were plans to send the Jews to Siberia or Madagascar. Siberia is a huge, flat plain in central Russia where temperatures can plunge as low as minus 50 degrees Celsius in winter. Madagascar is a large island off the east coast of Africa where malaria is a common disease.

? *Why would the Nazis want to send the Jews to such places?*

Camps and killing

Failure to defeat Russia in the war meant that plans to send Jews to Siberia were not possible. So the Nazis experimented with quicker ways to kill Jews within the areas they controlled. Explosives and exhaust fumes from vans were tried before a gas called Zyklon B was found to be a quick killer. Between 1941 and 1944, **extermination** camps were built where all European Jews, gypsies and homosexuals could be murdered in huge gas chambers.

Read for yourself

1 Read **source a**.

   a) What images do you find the most powerful in this letter?

   b) Why do you think Zalmen Gradowski wrote this letter? Try to list three reasons.

■ The extermination camp at Auschwitz, Poland, 1944.

Dear reader

I am writing these words in the hour of my greatest despair. I hope that you will take revenge on the murderers! You must give my life some meaning! In the large room, deep underground, a sign tells the victims to undress because they are now in the 'showers'. They look terrified; they know, they understand: they will be wiped out. It will be as if they were never born. These are not real showers: not water but gas comes out of them. After the gassing, the dead bodies are dragged from the tangle to the **crematoria**. Children are piled up like logs at the side then added afterwards, thrown on top of each pair of adults on an iron stretcher. The furnace is opened and the stretcher pushed in. The hair catches light first. The skin swells and blisters, bursting open after a few seconds. Arms and legs twist, veins and nerves seize up and cause the limbs to jerk. By now the whole body is on fire, the skin splits open, fat spills out and you hear the fire sizzle. The stomach bursts. The intestines pour out and within a few minutes no trace remains. The whole process takes 20 minutes, a body, a world, is reduced to dust …

■ Letter found buried near the gas chambers in Auschwitz extermination camp in Poland. It was written by Zalmen Gradowski, a Polish Jew forced to work at the extermination camp.

Who was to blame?

Zalmen Gradowski wanted revenge on the murderers, but who was to blame? Almost 5 million people were taken from their homes to camps like Auschwitz where they were either murdered straight away or worked to death in what became known as the Holocaust. Many Germans who lived through the Second World War claimed they did not know what was happening to the Jews. Some historians doubt this claim and think that pressure for the 'Final Solution' came from ordinary people as much as from the Nazi leaders.

In 1996, an American historian called Daniel Goldhagen published a book called *Hitler's Willing Executioners*. In this book, he argued that most ordinary Germans wanted the Holocaust to happen because they hated Jews; the Nazi leaders just 'unleashed' this hatred. This caused lots of arguments in Germany: some thought that he unfairly insulted the German people; others thought he made true points that were difficult to accept. What will you think?

If the Jews start another world war, the result will be the destruction of the Jews in Europe!

■ *From a speech by Adolf Hitler in the German Parliament, 30 January 1939.*

The Jews were removed from the region without the local people noticing. The action went very smoothly.

■ *Extract from a letter between two leading Nazis who went on to run the 'Final Solution', 29 October 1940.*

Following the orders of 31 July 1941, it was agreed that work should be done to prepare for the 'Final Solution', but without upsetting the population. This work should begin in Poland because the ghettos are overcrowded.

■ *Extract from the record of a meeting of Nazi leaders in Wannsee, a small town near Berlin, on 20 January 1942.*

Your turn ...

2 Use **sources b–g** and the map to make a list of the people who helped to carry out the 'Final Solution'. For each, decide whether it suggests Nazi leaders or ordinary people were to blame for the 'Final Solution'.

What's the confusion?

Despite years of research, many historians still do not agree who was ultimately to blame for the Holocaust. This is partly because the sources are not very clear. There is no source that says: 'I order you to kill all the Jews.'

3 Look again at **sources b–g**. This time, for each source explain why the content and the nature, origin and purpose of the source might lead to different interpretations about who was to blame.

Online arguments ...

4 Below is the start of a thread in an online forum. Add your own longer comment, explaining which view you agree with the most. Make sure you use lots of detail from the sources (and other information) in this and the previous lesson to support your argument.

By Joe_247, 14 May 10.33am
It might be tough for the Germans to hear, but I think Goldhagen is right. The Germans hated the Jews before the Second World War started and they did nothing at all to stop the killing!

By Lisa_365, 14 May 11.45am
Goldhagen is wrong! The Nazi leaders tried their best to make ordinary Germans hate the Jews, but even then they had to keep the killing a secret. There were lots of other reasons why some people helped carry out the Holocaust – not just anti-Semitism!

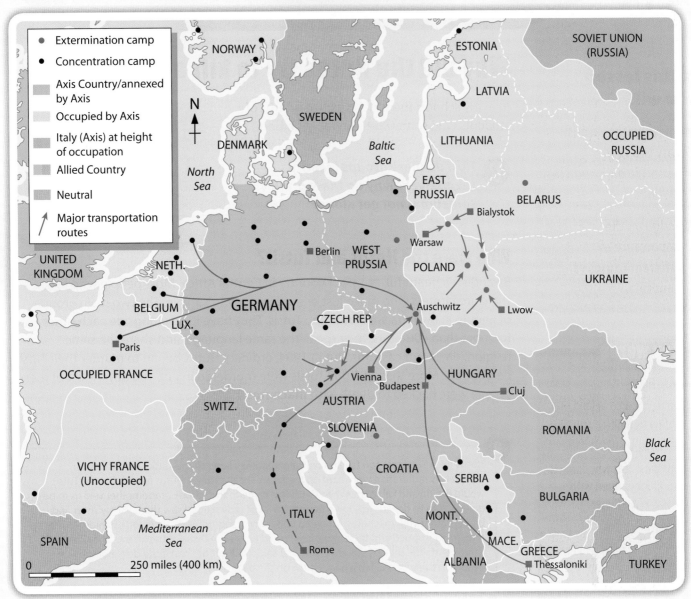

Legend:
- Extermination camp
- Concentration camp
- Axis Country/annexed by Axis
- Occupied by Axis
- Italy (Axis) at height of occupation
- Allied Country
- Neutral
- ↑ Major transportation routes

0 ——— 250 miles (400 km)

■ *Rail networks leading to prisons and extermination camps from the major cities.*

e

Q: *What was your job during the war?*

A: It was very similar to my job before the war. I organised the timetables for special trains.

Q: *Did you know that trains to Auschwitz meant death for the people on board?*

A: Of course not! I never went there. I stayed at my desk in Krakow.

Q: *Auschwitz to Krakow is 40 miles.*

A: That's not very far. And we knew nothing. Not a clue.

Q: *But you knew that the Nazis – that Hitler – didn't like the Jews.*

A: That we did. It was no secret. But as to their extermination, that was news to us.

Q: *But the Polish people knew everything.*

A: That's not surprising. They lived nearby, they heard, they talked. And they didn't have to keep quiet.

■ *From an interview with Walter Stier in 1985. He was one of 900,000 Germans who worked on the railways.*

f

I was present this afternoon at a 'special action' applied to female prisoners. All the men are keen to take part in these actions because they get special rations: alcohol, five cigarettes, sausage, bread.

■ *Extract from the diary of Dr Johann Kremer, a doctor at Auschwitz, 5 September 1942. Doctors who had developed ways to kill the mentally and physically handicapped in Germany in 1939 were sent to help with the 'Final Solution'.*

g

The builders can only finish the crematoria if they use wires and metal that are being kept for other buildings. If we can use these, 'special treatment' can begin on 15 February 1943.

■ *From a letter from architect Karl Bischoff to the commander of Auschwitz, 29 January 1943.*

Why do genocides happen?

In this lesson you will:

- investigate reasons why the 1994 genocide happened in Rwanda
- weigh up the importance of different causes of genocide.

Key words

Colony
Country or area of land that is ruled by another country.

Interahamwe
Extreme Hutus who formed into groups armed with guns and machetes.

Machete
Long heavy knife, usually used to hack through jungle or to clear plants.

Why did the Hutus try to kill all the Tutsis?

In many schools there are different groups of students who sometimes do not get along.

? *How do these groups identify themselves? Why do these groups sometimes not get along?*

Who were the Hutus and Tutsis?

Rwanda is a beautiful, but poor country in Central Africa. Most people who live there are farmers who make just enough money to survive. The two main groups of people in Rwanda are Hutus and Tutsis. They have lived alongside each other for more than 400 years; they speak the same language, and share the same religion, dress and customs. But in 1994, ordinary Hutus began to murder their Tutsi neighbours. More than 800,000 Tutsis were murdered in just 100 days. Most of these people were hacked to death with **machetes**.

Janet's story

1 Read **source a**. Try to pick out reasons why Janet thinks the Hutus wanted to murder her.

Hutus think Tutsis are too tall and delicate; that they keep all the cattle and money for themselves rather than work hard on the farms like the Hutus. Hutus feared that the Tutsis would rise up and kill them. When the Hutus came to the school, grandmother told us to be quiet and to lie down. I lay down between a lot of grown ups. I saw them kill my sister and grandmother with machetes. I crawled under my grandmother's dead body to hide. All the screaming stopped and the only voices I could hear were those of the killers. One killer said, 'I think that little thing is still alive.' Another said, 'I will cut her and if she does not move she is dead.' That was when I felt a heavy blow on the back of my neck.

■ *From an interview with Janet Uylsabye, in 2004. Janet is a Tutsi who managed to survive a horrific attack at her school by the Hutus.*

Card 1
The Belgians

Rwanda was a Belgian **colony** from 1919 until 1962. The Belgians believed that the Tutsis were racially superior. In 1931, they introduced identification cards that said whether a Rwandan was Hutu or Tutsi. Only the Tutsis could work for the Belgians, and the Hutus became jealous. When the Belgians left, the Hutus rose up and took power for themselves.

Card 2
President Habyarimana (Hutu)

President Habyarimana had ruled Rwanda since 1973. He did not let the Tutsis in neighbouring countries return home. He gave all the best jobs to Hutus. In 1993, he signed the Arusha Accords, an agreement to share power with the Tutsis, and to merge the Rwandan Patriotic Front (RPF) and the Rwandan army. He was killed on 6 April 1994 when his plane was shot down. The genocide started the next day.

Who was to blame?

There is still a lot of argument about who was to blame for the genocide in Rwanda. Cards 1–5 give information about a range of possible suspects.

2 **a)** In pairs, read the cards then place them in order of most to least responsible for the genocide.

b) Once you have agreed an order, compare your card order with a different pair. If your orders disagree, try to explain why you placed your cards in a different order.

c) Try to agree on a single order in your group of four, then in the whole class!

Card 5
The United Nations (UN)

Romeo Dallaire, the UN General in Rwanda, reported that Interahamwe members were making lists of Tutsis to murder. He asked for permission to seize their guns. Kofi Annan, his boss at the UN headquarters, told him to do nothing but keep watching. On 21 April 1994, the UN evacuated all white people, and reduced their number of troops in Rwanda from 2,568 to 270.

Card 3
The RPF (Tutsi)

In 1962, many Tutsis fled to neighbouring countries where they were forced to live in refugee camps. In 1988, when it became clear they would not be allowed home, the Tutsis formed their own army, the Rwandan Patriotic Front (RPF) to fight their way back home. In October 1990, the RPF started the attacks on Rwanda that eventually forced Habyarimana to sign the Arusha Accords. Many Hutus began to fear the return of Tutsi power.

Card 4
The Akazu (Hutu)

Akazu means 'little hut'. It was the name given to the small group of President Habyarimana's friends and relatives who controlled all the powerful jobs in Rwanda. In 1990 they started to organise the **Interahamwe**. Between 1992 and 1994, the Interahamwe leaders imported a huge number of machetes. They were handed out by local mayors in the villages. The mayors also drew up lists of local Tutsis. In 1993, the Akazu set up the RTLM radio station. On 7 April 1994, the DJ said, 'The cockroaches [Tutsis] have killed the president. You must take your spears, clubs, guns, swords, stones, everything – hack them, those cockroaches!'

Your decision!

3 Trials are still being held for the criminals who took part in the genocide in Rwanda. Imagine you are a judge. You have been asked to give your decision on the following.

a) Which group shot down President Habyarimana's plane on 6 April 1994: the Akazu or the RPF?

b) Which group was most responsible for the genocide in Rwanda?

You must explain your decision using evidence from the cards!

Back to the start

In this enquiry you have read about two different genocides. Now compare the Rwandan genocide with the Holocaust. Are there more similarities or more differences between them?

Taking it further!

Are genocides unique?

In this enquiry, you have explored two of the worst genocides in the twentieth century. But is it possible to compare them? Some historians argue that genocides are so different you cannot make useful comparisons. Other historians argue that, although there are some differences, it would be wrong to ignore the similarities. By looking at similarities we can improve our understanding of why genocides happen.

Draw conclusions

1 Using Lessons 2.4a–c, think of areas in which you might be able to compare the Holocaust with the 1994 genocide in Rwanda. Try to list at least three categories.

2 For each category you have come up with, are there more similarities or more differences between the Holocaust and the 1994 genocide in Rwanda? Use details from this enquiry to complete a table like the one below.

Area of comparison	Similar	Different
1 Causes of the genocide	Use of media to increase hate for the Jews and Tutsis	Death of the Rwandan president as a trigger for 1994 Genocide; but no single trigger for Holocaust

3 Many history teachers still argue about how the Holocaust should be taught in schools. Was it unique or can it be compared to other genocides? Imagine you have been asked to write an article for a magazine for teachers called *Teaching History*. The title of your article is: 'Were there more similarities or differences between the Holocaust and the 1994 genocide in Rwanda?' When you write your article:

- make your argument clear right from the start
- make clear the areas you have used to compare the genocides
- explain your argument using details from the previous enquiries.

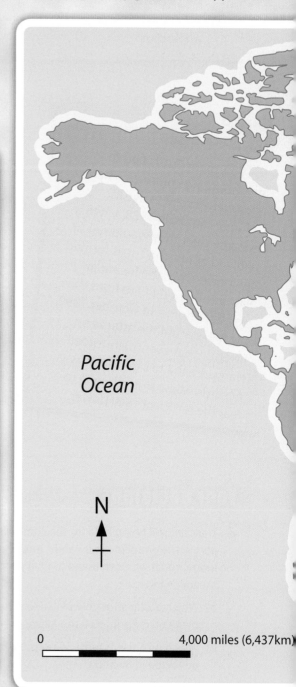

Pacific Ocean

N

0   4,000 miles (6,437km)

Some Germans have called the British and American bombing of Dresden from 15–17 February 1945 a 'Holocaust by bomb'. Is it fair to call the death of 40,000 Germans in Dresden a 'Holocaust'?

Many Ukrainians argue that a famine in 1932–33, which left 7 million people dead, was genocide. They argue that Josef Stalin, who ruled the Ukraine as part of the USSR, created the famine on purpose. Was this genocide?

In July 1995, 8,000 Bosnian Muslims from the city of Srebrenica were killed by Bosnian Serbs. Why did this genocide take place in Europe when the UN wanted the Holocaust to be the 'genocide that ended all genocides'?

Between 1975 and 1979 Pol Pot, leader of the Khmer Rouge, was responsible for the death of around 1.7 million people in Cambodia. He wanted to kill most of the people who lived in the cities to start a new 'pure' society. Why did his terrible ideas become reality for the people of Cambodia?

Dresden, Germany

Ukraine

Bosnia

Armenia

Atlantic Ocean

Darfur region, Southern Sudan

Cambodia

Indian Ocean

Pacific Ocean

History detective

There were many more genocides in the twentieth century than we have covered in this enquiry. Use your library and the Internet to explore one of the genocides shown on the map.

You can use the categories of comparison that you used in task 2 to help you approach these new genocides.

From 2003–2008, 400,000 people died and 2 million people were forced to leave their homes in the Darfur region in southern Sudan. Why has this happened? The US government says that this is genocide, but the UN does not agree. What will you think?

Most historians agree that the murder of around 1 million Armenians by Turks in 1915–17 was the first genocide of the twentieth century. The Turkish government disagrees. It argues that only 300,000 Armenians died, and that this was due to a civil war in which many Turks died as well. It is a very controversial topic. What will you think?

Next Lesson

Where was life better in the 1930s: communist Russia or capitalist America?

Key words

Depression
Time when there are not enough jobs and people have less money to spend.

Hoovervilles
Slum housing on the outskirts of cities, named after President Hoover, who many blamed for the Depression.

What was life like in the USA in the 1930s?

By 1929, America had become the richest country in the world. Americans boasted that they had achieved this through 'the American way': a government that allowed people to be free to work hard and keep their profit. However, for many people, 'the American way' had left them in great poverty in the 1930s: until 1935, there was no 'safety net' to help the sick, the old or the unemployed.

The Great Depression

The 1930s are remembered in America as the time of the Great **Depression**. In 1929, the value of shares in companies collapsed. Banks, which had lent money to people to buy shares, lost huge sums of money. People were scared that the banks would collapse so they withdrew their savings as fast as they could. Soon, there was no money to lend to businesses and many were forced to sack their workers and shut down.

As more people became unemployed, there was less money being spent in shops and even more businesses had to close – causing more unemployment! It was not just workers in towns and cities who were affected; the price of food collapsed and caused great poverty for farmers in the countryside. A large drought in the mid-1930s made things even worse. Many farmers were forced to abandon their farms and live in **Hoovervilles** to try to find work.

a

? **What does source a suggest about 'the American way'? Is it fair that some Americans could afford luxuries while others had to queue for bread in 1937?**

■ *People queuing for food in Kentucky in 1937.*

b I left New Jersey in 1937 as there was no work. In the CCC they'd take you out in trucks. We'd go out on different projects like building roads, reservoirs, and things like that. There were about 180 to 200 of us in camp. They (the government) paid you US$30 a month. US$25 went home and you kept US$5. You also got your food, clothing and medical treatment.

■ *From an interview with Civilian Conservation Corporation (CCC) worker Thomas 'Toddy' Wozniak, July 1987. The government set up the CCC in 1933 to employ 3 million men who had no work.*

c I'm a butcher on a production line. Been in the place 20 years, I believe. You got to have a certain amount of skill to do the job I'm doing. Long ago, I wanted to join the Butcher's Union. They wouldn't let me in the Union. Never said it to my face, but reason of it was plain. Negro. That's it. That's wrong. You know that's wrong.

■ *From an interview with slaughterhouse worker Jim Cole, May 1938.*

d The last ten years has seen the biggest change in farm life. The radio brought the world to the farm kitchen. The automobile and better roads brought the farmer more trade and social links. Farm men and women are poor, but they began to read about things they only thought were for city folk before.

■ *From The Vermont Farmer by Mrs Halley, a farmer's wife in 1938.*

Happy or unhappy?

1 Look at the stories of life in the 1930s in **sources b–d**. For each source, find examples of things that made their life in 1930s America:

a) happy

b) unhappy.

Why the long face?

2 Look again at **sources b–d**, and at **sources e–g** below.

a) Place the people in the sources in order of their suffering in the 1930s. Start with 1 for the happiest, and finish with 6 for the saddest.

b) Look at the happiest and saddest people in your list. What do these sources tell us about the reasons for happiness and sadness in America in the 1930s?

e Apart from US$2,000, the rest of my money was in the Merchant's Bank. Just a few days after I got a new job, the Merchants' Bank closed its doors and I lost every penny of my US$42,000 that was on deposit there.

■ *From I'm Planning to Make a Comeback, a book by Ada Radford from Georgia, February 1940.*

f I sit here on my wooden box and I wait for customers. I don't get too many. I only get a nickel for each shoe shine, but it's better than selling apples. You see, when you get a shine kit it's a permanent investment, and it doesn't cost as much as a box of apples anyway.

■ *From an interview with a New York shoeshine boy aged 16, reported in the New York Times, 5 June 1932.*

g I have to go the garbage dump to look for food, just like all the other poor wretches. I used to do housework and laundry, but now I have no work. I have to feed myself and my 14-year-old son on the leftovers. I take off my glasses before I pick up meat, so I can't see the maggots.

■ *From an interview with a widow in Chicago, printed in New Republic magazine, February 1933.*

A new deal

In January 1933, Franklin D. Roosevelt became president of the USA. He wanted to change the American way by taking more tax from the rich to pay for schemes to help the poor; he called it the 'New Deal'. This was very controversial and he needed lots of help to persuade powerful Americans to accept the changes.

3
a) Plan a billboard poster, like the one shown in **source a**, but one that shows the *real* results of 'the American way'.

b) If you want to, turn your plans into an actual poster, complete with lots of illustrations. Make sure you use lots of evidence from the sources to make your poster powerful and convincing.

Where was life better in the 1930s: communist Russia or capitalist America?

In this lesson you will:

- **explore what life was like for people in Russia in the 1930s**

- **compare and contrast people's memories with contemporary sources.**

Key words

Purge

Flush something out. In Russia in the 1930s, millions of people were purged from society and sent to prison camps for little or no reason.

What was life like in the USSR in the 1930s?

Communism was the idea of a German philosopher called Karl Marx. Here is what he said:

- *The workers should seize power from the wealthy.*
- *Everyone in society should be equal.*
- *All factories, shops and land should be owned by the government, not by individuals.*
- *The government should decide what should be made and how much it should cost.*
- *People should work for the good of the community, not for profit.*

■ *The ideas of Karl Marx.*

? *Which of Karl Marx's ideas do you agree with the most? Which of his ideas do you disagree with the most? Why?*

Use your eyes

1. a) Read **source b**. What reasons can you find to explain why Iraida thought life was good under Stalin?

   b) Now look at **sources c–g**. For each source explain whether it supports or goes against Iraida's memory of life in Russia in the 1930s. Use details from the sources to explain your answer!

From idea to reality

Before 1917 communism was just an idea. But in 1917 a great experiment with people's lives began when the Russian Tsar (emperor) was overthrown and communists seized power in the Russian Revolution. Before the Revolution, a small group of rich aristocrats owned most of the land, while 80 per cent of Russians were poor peasant farmers.

Clearly a great deal of change was needed to create a communist society. However, Josef Stalin, the communist ruler of Russia in the 1930s, wanted to make Russia a communist society in only ten years! To do this he:

- announced 'Five Year Plans' to build new cities and factories. By 1939, 33 per cent of Russians lived in cities

- introduced 'collectivisation', a plan to turn lots of small peasant farms into large farms owned by the community or the government (by 1937, 99 per cent of farm land had been collectivised)

- used propaganda to inspire people to work hard

- used '**purges**' to force people to accept these changes; 8 million innocent people were arrested by the secret police and sent to gulags (prison camps), and 1 million people were killed.

How would these great changes affect the lives of ordinary Russians in the 1930s? Take a look at **sources b–g** to find out!

b

Life under Stalin was more peaceful and happy. We were all poor, but we had lots of fun. Families shared everything they had. Today every family lives only for itself. We believed that life would get better if we worked hard. We took more pride in our work than we do today.

■ From an interview by historian Orlando Figes with Iraida Faivisovich in 2003. Iraida lived under Stalin's rule for 18 years after she was born in 1935.

c

■ Government poster from 1930. It says, 'Peasant women! Let us increase the harvest! Let us unite our houses into collective farms!'

d

The joys of everyday life. I wake up in the morning and think: thank God I was not arrested last night, they don't arrest people during the day, but what will happen tonight no one knows. Every single person has enough against him to be arrested and sent to the gulags. I'm lucky, I simply don't care, but most people are living in complete terror.

■ From the diary of Liubov Shaporina, a woman from Leningrad (now St Petersburg), 22 November 1937.

e

What are the people unhappy about? First, the worker is hungry, he has no fats and the fake bread is impossible to eat. The wife of the worker stands all day in queues for bread. In the queues there is shouting and fights, people curse the communists!

■ From a report for Communist Party leaders in August 1930.

f

The room had no running water; sheets marked off 'rooms' where grandparents, parents and children slept. Sinks, toilets, a stove and a tap were all in an unheated hallway.

■ From a description of a communal flat in Moscow in 1936.

g

■ Gulag prisoners forced to help build the White Sea Canal.

Is it reliable?

2 Look again at **sources b–g**.

a) Put the sources in order of which ones you think are the best for finding out what life was really like in Russia in the 1930s. Start with 1 for the most reliable source and end with 6 for the least reliable.

b) Explain your order of reliability. Remember to think carefully about:

● the type of source it is

● when and why it was created

● the question you are using the source to find out about!

Dear Mr Figes ...

Orlando Figes wanted to find out what life was really like in Russia in the 1930s when he wrote his book *The Whisperers*. A lot of his book is based on diaries and interviews with people who were alive in the 1930s.

3 Imagine Figes has employed you as a researcher on the next edition of *The Whisperers*. Write a letter to him that explains:

a) how far you think people's memories are a useful way of finding out what life was like in 1930s Russia

b) the best contemporary sources you have found to show what life was really like.

 Back to the start

Think about everything you have covered in this enquiry. Would you rather have lived in the USSR or the USA in the 1930s?

2.6a

In this lesson you will:

- discover what life was like in China under Chairman Mao

- use sources to identify the key features of a different society.

Key words

Commune
Group of people who live together and share goods and chores.

Economy
Organisation of a country's resources.

Factfile

Mao Zedong

Born: 26 December 1893 in Hunan Province, south China.

Work: Ran a book shop in Hunan before working for the Chinese Communist Party (CCP).

Leadership

- He became the most powerful member of the CCP during a civil war between 1927 and 1936.

- He was made Chairman of the CCP in 1945. This was the most powerful position in the Party.

- The CCP took power in China on 1 October 1949 and Mao became the most powerful man in China.

- He ruled China until his death from a heart attack on 2 September 1976.

What was the Great Leap Forward?

In 1957, enormous changes began to take place in China, affecting the ordinary lives of many hard-working people.

? *Look at source a. What can you see? What is going on?*

Suggest a possible English translation for the Chinese words at the top.

China before Mao

In the 1950s and 1960s, China had a very different society from Western countries like Britain. The Chinese had a rich culture that had developed separately from the West for over 2,000 years. The Chinese had great respect for their traditions and for their elders and, compared to Europe, things had changed very little between 1500 and 1900. All of that was about to change due to the ideas and leadership of one man: Mao Zedong, or Chairman Mao as he liked to be called. In 1958, Mao argued that China needed to make a 'Great Leap Forward' to catch up with the West.

a

■ *Poster put up in towns and villages across China in 1958.*

b

China's **economy** is weak and we do not make enough goods. This is why we are not yet free from foreign control. We must make more goods. After fifteen years, we shall catch up and then make more goods than Britain. Then we will have plenty of food, iron and steel, and we will be free to act as we please. The peasants are the future, not the 'experts'! We must ignore old learning and use the revolutionary power of the poor people to make these changes for China.

■ *From a speech by Mao Zedong, 12 January 1958.*

Mao Zedong thought …?

Chairman Mao wrote several articles for newspapers and gave many speeches to convince the Chinese people of the need for change.

1 Read Mao's speech (**source b**) and pick out the phrases that sum up:

    a) why change is needed

    b) what needs to be changed.

Read and think

2 Read **sources c–e**. List how Mao tried to change traditional Chinese farming.

How did Mao make changes?

Mao used propaganda and terror to make the Chinese people carry out his wishes. Lots of posters, like **source a**, were made to tell people what to do and what to think. Huge rallies were held to celebrate the new ideas and to punish those who did not help.

c

We could no longer farm our own strip of land. All our tools had to be given to the big new **communes**. We were ordered to plant lots of rice seedlings very close together in a system called 'Sky full of stars'. We knew the plants would die but we could not oppose. We were ordered to smash our water jars to make fertiliser. We knew this was stupid but we had to smash the jars. No grain was stored. People became so hungry that they could not sleep.

■ *From an interview with a villager in Chen Village, south of Beijing, in 1992.*

d

In many places, people who did not boast of huge increases in food production were beaten up. The commune boss in Yibin asked a team leader, 'How much wheat can you produce per acre?' '400 jin [about 950kg],' he said. They beat him and asked the same question, 'How much can you produce?' 800 jin he said. This was an unrealistic amount but they beat him until he said, '10,000 jin.'

■ *From Jung Chang's book* Wild Swans. *Jung Chang wrote the book in 1991 after she escaped from China to Britain.*

e

Your commune is a great treasure. You must hand over your land, houses and trees. You must live in dormitories and eat in canteens to help with production and control.

■ *From the orders Mao gave to set up Chayashan Commune, July 1958.*

■ *The Communist leader Chairman Mao.*

Did you know?

Source a shows a poster from the mass campaign to kill the 'Four Pests': sparrows, rats, mosquitoes, flies. So many sparrows were killed that few were left to eat the insect pests. Mao had to secretly buy 200,000 sparrows from Russia to replace them! Mao exported nearly 5 million tonnes of grain in 1959. In the same year a famine started in which more than 30 million Chinese people died – the greatest famine in history.

... and ACTION!

3 Imagine you have been asked to write a script for a film about the Peng family who lived in Chen Village near Beijing.

The father, Xu Peng, and his wife, Jun Ying, worked hard on a local farm. Their daughter Shinney and son Wing Hang both went to school, which pleased Xu and Jun Ying. Then, in 1957, their life began to change.

The film-makers want you to capture the experiences of ordinary people who lived through this period of change. In the first half of your script focus on the parents. What will happen to them?

Use details from the sources to make your script realistic and believable. Leave the story on a cliffhanger! You will finish your script after the next enquiry.

2.6b

In this lesson you will:

■ **discover what happened during the Cultural Revolution**

■ **use sources to explore the effects of an event on people.**

Key words

Culture (cultural)
Way of life of a group or of society.

Revolution
Large and sometimes sudden change in the way things are done.

What was the Cultural Revolution?

By autumn 1966, things in China were quite different to how they had been before the leadership of Chairman Mao.

? *What is happening to the teacher in source a? Why do you think the students are doing this to him?*

a

■ *Teacher in the painful jet-plane position, his hair being shaved off by some of his students.*

The Revolution begins

Mao had changed the way people lived; now he wanted to change the way they thought. Mao wanted to make sure there could be no return to the old ways of living. The only way to do this was to get rid of all the old ideas: to start a '**Cultural Revolution**'. In 1966, he began by encouraging students to attack those who spread old ideas: their teachers! Anti-teacher articles appeared in student newspapers; huge posters were put up that accused teachers of crimes. Finally, students formed gangs called 'Red Guards' and started to attack their teachers. Between August and November 1966, 12 million students took advantage of the free train tickets to Beijing to see their idol, Chairman Mao. At eight huge meetings he told them to 'be violent!' Red Guard violence soon spread all over China. Things got out of control and Mao finally had to use the army to restore order in July 1968.

Did you know?

During the Cultural Revolution 4,922 of the 6,843 temples in Beijing were destroyed. Mao wanted to replace them with factories.

What happened next?

Mao wanted to change the arts (painting, music, theatre) and education above all else.

1 Study **sources a–e** and, for each source, explain how old ideas are being changed.

b

Teacher Li and teacher Shen were dragged from the Teachers' Building. 'What's the matter?' they said. Little Bawang yelled, 'We're here to sweep you ox ghosts and snake spirits away!' He hung boards on the teachers' necks that said 'Enemy running dog' and 'Horrible spy'. I liked teacher Li, but I tried to focus on his crimes. The teachers were forced into the jet-plane position and Little Bawang shaved half teacher Shen's hair off. Following our class revolution other classes organised struggle meetings and parades. Any teacher who argued back was certainly a liar.

■ *From Gao Yuan's* Born Red, *published in 1987. Gao was a reluctant Red Guard and later felt ashamed.*

d

I was not forced to join the Red Guards. I wanted to. It never occurred to me to question Chairman Mao. One of our slogans was 'We vow to fight anyone who resists the Cultural Revolution, or Chairman Mao!'

■ *From Jung Chang's book* Wild Swans.

■ *Scene from* The Red Detachment of Women. *This was one of the eight 'Model Plays' that celebrated Mao's ideas. All older plays and operas were banned.*

c

e

■ *Buddhist statues being burned in Tibet. Lots of temples and statues were smashed by the Red Guards.*

Who was to blame?

Many Chinese people look back on the Cultural Revolution with shame.

2 Look again at the sources in this lesson. This time, use them to decide who was more to blame for the violence and destruction: Chairman Mao or the student Red Guards. To plan your answer, use a Venn diagram like the one below to organise the key details from the sources.

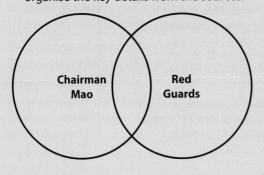

Chairman Mao   Red Guards

... and ACTION!

3 Use the information in **sources a–e** to finish the film script about the Peng family, which you began in Lesson 2.6a. This time, focus on the children, Wing Hang and Shinney. Before you continue you have some choices to make: *Will your characters support the Cultural Revolution or suffer from the changes?*

a) Make clear what your characters think of the Cultural Revolution and why.

b) Make sure you use lots of detailed evidence from the sources to make the script realistic!

Back to the start

Look back through this enquiry. Which do you think caused the greater change in the life of the Chinese: the Great Leap Forward or the Cultural Revolution?

Next Lesson

In this lesson you will:

- learn about the extent and dangers of the Cold War

- recognise the significance of events that contributed to the tensions during this period.

Key words

Democratic
System of government that elects its leaders by allowing the people to vote for candidates.

Non-aligned
Countries not part of the NATO or Warsaw Pact alliances.

Superpower
World power: a state powerful enough to influence events throughout the world.

What was the Cold War?

WAR OVER

? *Imagine it's 1945 and this headline is on the front page of today's newspaper. What sorts of emotions would you and your family be feeling? What do you think will happen in this new peaceful world?*

What was the 'Cold War'?

Most wars are fought by one country physically attacking another, but for 45 years after the Second World War the two **superpowers**, the USA and the USSR, struggled with each other over ideas and influence. Their differences become known as the 'Cold War'.

On 7 May 1945 Germany surrendered to the Allied forces led by the USA, the USSR, France and Britain. You might have expected that there would be a time of peace but, very quickly, Europe was divided into two parts:

- Eastern Europe fell under the control of communists led by the USSR

- Western European countries were supported by Britain, France and the USA.

The USSR and the USA had very different ways of running countries. The USSR wanted to use its power to spread communism across land it controlled, while the USA wanted to support the **democratic** states in the West. This battle of ideas became known as the 'Cold War' as the two superpowers tried to avoid fighting each other in a real 'Hot War'.

Read and think

1 Read **sources a** and **b**. Make a list of Churchill's concerns about what would happen to Europe after the Second World War had ended in 1945.

2 Look at the map of Europe in 1955. How far do you think Churchill was right to be worried?

a
What is to happen about Russia? I feel deep anxiety because of the combination of Russian power and the territories under their control or occupied, coupled with the communist technique in so many other countries, and above all their power to maintain very large armies in the field for a long time.

■ *From a telegram from Prime Minister Winston Churchill to US President Truman, 12 May 1945. It refers to Russian influence in Europe after the war.*

b
From Stettin in the Baltic to Trieste in the Adriatic an iron curtain has descended across the Continent.

■ *From a speech by Winston Churchill at Westminster College in Fulton, Missouri on 5 March 1946.*

■ *Europe in 1955.*

What happened to wartime trust?

It disappeared! Both superpowers had developed the atomic bomb by 1950, so they knew that they could destroy each other at the push of a button. Instead, to try to 'win' the Cold War they supported countries and actions that they felt would help their side. These included getting involved in foreign wars, the space race and the use of spies to find out information.

What's the temperature?

3 The table below shows some events that happened during the 'Cold War'.

a) Look at each description and make a 'snap' decision as to whether you think the event would have made relations between the West and the East warmer (better) or colder (worse).

b) Compare your answers with a partner and explain why you made your decisions to them.

In conclusion ...

4 A local newspaper, seeking to stimulate a debate among its readers, has posed the question: *Was the 'Cold War' more frightening than a conventional war?*

Write a reply to the editor, setting out your reasons for and against the statement.

How would each of these events affect the relationship between the East and West?	Warmer	Colder	Not sure
1945: USA drops the first atomic bomb on Hiroshima, Japan.			
1946: Former Prime Minister Winston Churchill describes USSR occupation of Eastern Europe as an 'iron curtain' beginning to separate Europe.			
1948–49: Western access to Berlin is restricted by USSR; in response the West flies in supplies for nearly a year.			
1949: Russia develops the nuclear bomb.			
1949: The West forms a military alliance – NATO (North Atlantic Treaty Organization) – to protect itself from the threat of attack from Eastern Europe.			
1950–53: Korean War pitches communists in the north against the Western-supported forces in the south.			
1955: USSR and Eastern European states form a military alliance in response to NATO: the Warsaw Pact.			
1961: Communist troops build the Berlin Wall to seal off West Berlin from the rest of the city and communist East Germany.			
1962: Cuban Missile Crisis – nuclear missiles installed in communist Cuba.			
1965–73: USA becomes involved in fighting communists in Vietnam.			
1968: USSR crushes an uprising against the communist government in Czechoslovakia.			
1988: New leader of USSR, Gorbachev, calls for '*glasnost*' (openness) with the West.			
1989: Berlin Wall is torn down.			

In this lesson you will:

- learn about what happened during the Cuban Missile Crisis

- explain why President Kennedy made his decisions in the crisis.

Living in the shadow of the bomb: Cuba

? *Look at the 'key players' table below. Which of these three men do you think is the odd one out?*

Key players

Fidel Castro President of Cuba	John F. Kennedy President of the United States	Nikita Khrushchev General Secretary of the USSR
Came to power in 1959.	Came to power in 1960.	Came to power in 1953.
Led a forcible government takeover of many US companies in Cuba.	Opposed communism in Cuba.	Developed missile-based defences.
Fought off US invasion of the island in 1961.	Authorised the failed **'Bay of Pigs'** invasion of Cuba in 1961.	Gave support to Cuba after the attempted invasion by the USA.
Close ally of USSR.	Concerned about the growing strength of the USSR.	Concerned about US weapons that could strike the USSR.
Was suspicious of anti-Castro Cubans who lived in the USA.	Sold missile defences to Turkey.	

Nuclear missiles

The first atomic bomb was dropped from a plane over Hiroshima in Japan at the end of the Second World War (see Lesson 1.5e). Although it was successful, the military on both sides realised that if they could put a warhead on a missile, it would allow targets at greater distances to be reached more quickly.

By the end of 1958 both the USSR and the USA had succeeded in building and test firing nuclear ICBMs – intercontinental ballistic missiles, capable of travelling from one continent to another.

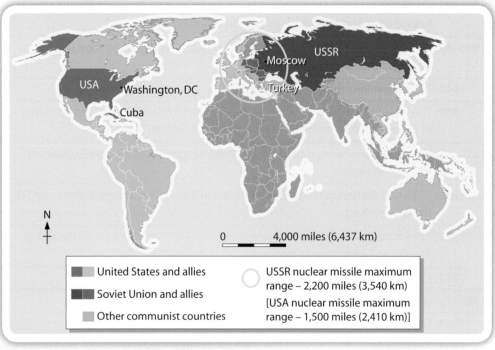

■ *World map showing range of Soviet missiles.*

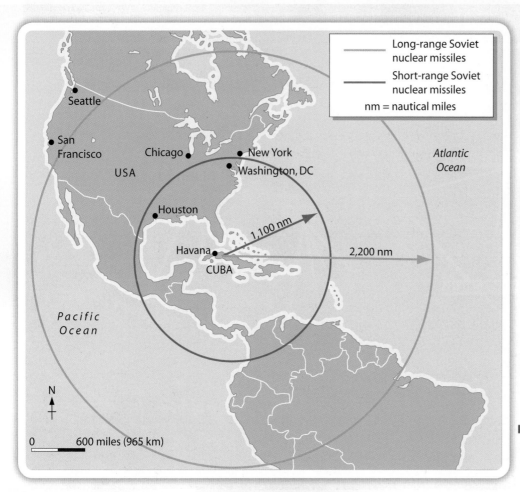

Key words

Bay of Pigs

Failed attempt by Cuban exiles supported by the USA to overthrow the government of Fidel Castro.

DEFCON

DEFense readiness CONdition is a measure of how ready the USA is for war.

White House

Place in Washington, DC, USA, in which the president and his team work and make decisions.

Map of North America showing the distances that short-range and long-range Soviet nuclear missiles could reach from Havana, Cuba.

Crisis!

A revolution brought the dictator Fidel Castro to power in the Caribbean state of Cuba – 45 km (90 miles) south of the US state of Florida. By 1961 the country had adopted communism. In order to know what was going on, spy plane photographs were used by the USA to spot military movements on the island. However, on 15 October 1962 an American spy plane spotted something that shocked everyone in the **White House**. The photographs showed newly installed Soviet-built nuclear missiles.

Look and think

1 Look at the world map on page 118.

  a) Who do you think would feel most threatened by nuclear missile attack in 1960?

  b) What problems can you see from the map of this being so?

2 The USA made an agreement with Turkey in 1960 to place short-range nuclear missiles in Turkey.

  a) Why would Turkey want this?

  b) Looking at the map, what effect would this have?

  c) Who would feel threatened by nuclear missile attack now?

3 Now look at the map of North America above. In 1961 the USSR wanted to set up a Soviet missile base in Cuba.

  a) What effect would this have in the USA?

  b) How might they respond if they found out the bases were there?

ERECTOR/LAUNCHER EQUIPMENT

TENT AREAS

EQUIPMENT

ERECTOR/LAUNCHER EQUIPMENT

8 MISSILE TRAILERS

■ *One of the reconnaissance photographs shown to President Kennedy. It shows one of the Soviet missile sites in Cuba.*

Decision time!

The photographs that the President of the United States, John F. Kennedy, received on 16 October 1962 were going to lead to him making the biggest decision of his life. As Kennedy studied the photos with his government and military advisers, he had to choose – to allow the missiles to stay in Cuba or to risk nuclear war against the USSR.

Over to you ...

4 With a partner, discuss how you think newspapers in the USA will have reacted to the developments in the crisis.

5 Imagine you are a newspaper reporter.

a) Create a headline and an opening paragraph of a news story from the brief pieces of information that you have been given opposite.

b) You have also been asked to find a source (a person) close to President Kennedy who will leak you some secret inside information from time to time that you can use in your articles.

Any headline and story will need to:

● be interesting to your readers and help them to understand the importance of the daily events by building on what has happened in previous days

● give an indication of whether the day's events are helping or deepening the crisis

● give some suggestions as to the possible consequences of the event

● possibly give advice on how ordinary people may want to cope with the news.

Monday, 15 October 1962

A US spy plane spots several SS-4 nuclear missiles in Cuba.

Tuesday, 16 October

The crisis begins: President Kennedy calls on trusted advisers to consider America's options.

Wednesday, 17 October

An SS-5 missile site is detected in Cuba.

Thursday, 18 October

President Kennedy meets with the Soviet foreign minister to tell him that America will not tolerate Soviet missiles in Cuba.

Monday, 22 October

President Kennedy addresses the American public and announces his plan to introduce a naval blockade (quarantine) of Cuba to stop new missiles arriving from the USSR.

US military alert is set at **DEFCON 3** and Castro mobilises all of Cuba's military forces.

Tuesay, 23 October

US Spy plane photos reveal that Soviet missiles in Cuba are ready for launch.

Wednesday, 24 October

Soviet ships reach the quarantine line, but … receive radio orders from Moscow to hold their positions.

President Kennedy concludes that if the USA invade Cuba it is likely that at least some of the missiles will be fired at US targets.

Thursday, 25 October

American military forces are instructed to set DEFCON 2 – the highest ever in US history.

Friday, 26 October

Khrushchev receives a cable from Castro urging a nuclear first strike against the US in the event of an invasion of Cuba.

Kennedy receives a letter from Khrushchev stating that the Soviets will remove their missiles if President Kennedy publicly guarantees the US will not invade Cuba.

Saturday, 27 October

While one U-2 spy plane accidentally flies into the USSR, another is shot down over Cuba.

Kennedy receives a second letter from Khrushchev stating that, in addition to a public promise not to invade Cuba, the US should promise to remove its missiles from Turkey.

Sunday, 28 October

The crisis is over. In a speech aired on Radio Moscow, Khrushchev announces the dismantling of Soviet missiles in Cuba and does not insist on his demands concerning the removal of US missiles from Turkey.

After a few months President Kennedy issued an order to start to remove the US missiles from Turkey. His agreement with Khrushchev about the Turkish missiles was not made public for many years. However, following the crisis it was decided to set up a dedicated telephone 'hotline' between the two presidents for use in case of any further 'emergencies' involving the two countries.

The crisis is over!

6 Imagine you are President Kennedy. Write a diary entry explaining the decisions you took and why. Make sure you mention anything that helped you to achieve a successful conclusion.

7 a) Who do you think 'won' the Cuban Missile Crisis in 1962?

b) Who do you think 'won' in the long run?

Did you know?

The USA and USSR agreed not to test nuclear weapons from 1958 to September 1961. During the two weeks of the crisis, the USA tested four nuclear weapons, and the USSR tested two.

2.7c

In this lesson you will:

■ learn about how people were encouraged to treat the threats of nuclear war

■ develop a perspective on how people saw events at the time.

How to survive a nuclear attack

? *Can you think of five weapons that have been used in wars? Who or what do these weapons target? Are there any weapons or targets that should be banned? Why?*

During the period of the 'Cold War' ordinary people felt that nuclear war was a real possibility, and they looked to their governments to provide them with answers. But what were the dangers of being caught up in a nuclear attack?

Immediate effects on people	After-effects on people	Effect on buildings
Within 500m of blast – fatal	Scar tissue	Tiles and glass melt 1km from blast
Burns up to 35km from blast	Cataracts	Blast of wind 440m per second destroys many buildings
Wounds	Blood cancer	Communications disrupted or destroyed
Loss of eyesight if you look at the blast	Cancers	Fire
Loss of hair	Radiation sickness	Broken water and sewage systems

■ *Effects of the first atomic bomb to be used – against the Japanese city of Hiroshima in 1945.*

The atomic age

After Hiroshima, governments and people realised there was little defence against such a weapon. During the 1950s and the 1980s there were two occasions when governments in the West, fearing the threat of nuclear war, issued advice to their populations on how to protect themselves.

The USA

In the early 1950s the US Civil Defense Office issued advice to both children and adults. For children 'Bert the turtle' became the most recognisable symbol for what people should do (see **source a**).

a

OH MY! DANGER

BERT DUCKS and COVERS

HE'S SMART, BUT *HE* HAS HIS SHELTER ON HIS BACK.

YOU MUST LEARN TO FIND SHELTER

■ *Bert the turtle was used to help children understand what they should do in a nuclear attack.*

Look and think

1 Look at the table above. Imagine that you are a Red Cross worker in Hiroshima a few weeks after the bomb. (See Lesson 1.5e for more details.) Write a brief report on what you have seen and create a list of the priorities as to what help people need.

■ *US schoolchildren practising to 'duck and cover' during an air raid drill in the 1950s. These drills were part of everyday life.*

Britain

In the early 1980s as tension grew between the West and the communist East, the British government reissued the leaflet 'Protect and Survive' across the country.

■ *Suggestions on how to build your 'inner refuge' inside your fall-out room. From 'Protect and Survive', republished in 1986.*

e

Have you blocked up the windows and other openings (e.g. vents, chimney) of your fall-out room?

Have you made your inner refuge, inside the fall-out room?

Have you put the following items in your fall-out room?

- Enough water, in sealed or covered containers, to last you and your family for fourteen days?

- Enough food to last you and your family for fourteen days, including tinned or powdered milk for the children, and food for the baby – and a closed cupboard or cabinet in which to store these supplies?

- A portable radio (two if possible) and spare batteries?

- A portable stove and fuel for it?

- Improvised lavatory seat, polythene buckets fitted with covers, polythene bag linings, for emptying the containers, strong disinfectant and toilet paper?

- A first-aid kit?

■ *Part of the preparation checklist for householders from 'Protect and Survive'.*

c

Know your own home

- Know which is the safest part of your cellar, learn how to turn off your oil burner and what to do about water and electricity.

Have emergency equipment and supplies handy

- Always have a good flashlight, a radio, first-aid equipment and a supply of canned goods in the house.

Close all windows and doors and draw the blinds

- If you have time when an alert sounds, close the house up tight in order to keep out fire sparks and radioactive dusts and to lessen the chances of being cut by flying glass.

Use the telephone only for true emergencies

- Do not use the phone unless absolutely necessary.

■ *Advice from Survival Under Atomic Attack, published by the US Civil Defense Office in 1950.*

Over to you ...

2 In pairs look at the advice given to people in 1950 and the 1980s (**sources c–e**).

  a) Draw up a table with two columns: 'Advice that is similar'; and 'Advice that is different'.

  b) Complete the columns with information from the sources.

  c) Now try to identify the reasons why some of the advice is similar and some different.

3 Try to answer this question: *To what extent was this advice 'common sense' to people at the time?*

4 While living in the 1980s a TV presenter announces that there is a real threat of nuclear war. It's time to prepare. Imagine you have grandparents in the USA who lived through this in the 1950s. When you ring them, they tell you what advice they were given in the 1950s and compare it to what you have been told. What would you do and what advice would you ignore? Why?

In conclusion ...

5 How do you think that ordinary people would behave if they believed there were only a few days to prepare for a nuclear attack?

6 The crisis passes. Write an email to your grandparents explaining to them how differently people in your area reacted to the threat of nuclear war.

Did the Cold War lead to an age of fear?

Life behind the wall

At the end of the Second World War Berlin was divided among the four allies. This meant that families wanting to pass into the Soviet sector had to pass through closely guarded checkpoints. So many people fled across the barbed wire divide to West Berlin that the Soviets came up with a solution.

? *How would you feel if you were on the other side of the wall from the rest of your family? Would you try to escape to be with them? What do you think would be the dangers?*

Key words

Stasi

Secret police of communist East Germany.

a ■ *Construction of the Berlin Wall in August 1961.*

Look and think

1 Study **sources a** and **b**.

   a) What reasons can you find for why the wall was built?

   b) What emotions do you think the people on each side would have been feeling on seeing the wall go up?

b We no longer wanted to stand by passively and see how doctors, engineers, and skilled workers were induced … to give up their secure existence in the GDR and work in West Germany or West Berlin.

■ *From an East German propaganda leaflet, February 1962.*

c Travel was greatly restricted into and out of East Germany. The **Stasi** spied at length on the citizens to suppress opponents through its network of 175,000 informants and 90,000 agents.

■ *Adapted from a description of the building of the Berlin Wall from the UK National Cold War Exhibition website.*

What was life like behind the wall?

The wall completely surrounded democratic West Berlin. However, with Britain, France and America's support it became a wealthy 'island' inside Soviet-controlled East Germany. In East Germany, the way that ordinary people lived and worked was very different.

d A thousand soldiers! They would come from Moscow, Warsaw, and Prague. Of course soldiers would come from Berlin and Erfurt too; they were all coming to Brenbach. They should feel content and at home.

■ *From Dietrich Herfurth's book* Britt and Bert and Bärenbach, *an East German storybook produced for children in 1985.*

e East Germans had government health insurance, welfare services, and pensions … men could retire as early as 60; the retirement age for women was generally a few years earlier. The rate of violent crime was low. The streets were safe. But crimes of corruption, such as bribery, flourished.

■ *From a United States Constitutional Rights website, giving a modern US view of East Germany.*

f We were terribly anxious when we entered the police station. The door opened and they snapped at us: 'You can't just come and knock on the door here. What do you want?' And the following words errupted from our throats: 'We want to leave the country!'

■ *Frau Wedekind, describing her life in East Germany in the 1980s.*

Think about it

2 Would you have liked to live in East Berlin? With a partner, justify your answer by using **sources c–f** to construct a spider diagram that identifies the advantages and disadvantages of living in the city.

The end of the wall

For the next 28 years the wall divided the city of Berlin. Politicians such as President Kennedy and President Reagan of the USA called for it to be torn down, but when it finally fell there were extraordinary scenes.

Did you know?

The entire length of the Berlin Wall was 154 kilometres (96 miles). More than 900 people were shot attempting to cross the wall, causing 200 injuries and 239 deaths.

g Everything was out of control. Police on horses watched. There was nothing they could do. The crowd had swollen … The final slab was moved away. A stream of East Germans began to pour through. People applauded and slapped their backs. A woman handed me a giant bottle of wine, which I opened, and she and I began to pour cups of wine and hand them to the East Germans.

■ *From Andreas Ramos's* A Personal Account of The Fall of the Berlin Wall, *11 and 12 November 1989.*

h

■ *Crowds gathering by the Berlin Wall near to the Brandenburg Gate in 1989.*

In conclusion ...

3 Think about everything you have read in this enquiry.

a) How important do you think the fall of the Berlin Wall was in 'Cold War' history?

b) Did it matter more to people at the time or now?

Back to the start

The Second World War was fought to end the fear of Nazism across the world. Look back to the start of this enquiry and answer this question:

Do you think the world is a safer and freer place to live than it was during the war years?

Next Lesson

How did healthcare change in the twentieth century?

In this lesson you will:

■ learn about the impact of individuals in changes in healthcare

■ develop and apply criteria in order to reach a conclusion.

Key words

Culture
Material used to grow germs or bacteria in a controlled way.

DNA
Deoxyribonucleic acid; the material that contains the genetic code needed to build new living cells.

Nobel Prize
International award given to people who have made important advances in areas such as science and medicine.

Which was the greatest breakthrough in healthcare?

Over the last 100 years the way in which people have been treated for their illnesses has changed a great deal. Advances in science and medicine have meant that, in many cases, medics today can easily treat diseases and accidents that would have been fatal in 1901. But what was the biggest development?

? *In what areas of healthcare do you think the greatest changes over the years have been? Discuss your answer with a partner and explain why you believe your answer to be true.*

a

Sick man given new hope after unique operation

Mr Louis Washkansky, a 56-year-old businessman, was making satisfactory progress in Groote Schuur Hospital, Cape Town, today 12 hours after receiving the transplant of a complete heart. The head of the surgical team was Professor Christiaan Barnard.

■ *From The Times newspaper, 4 December 1967.*

Factfile 1

Christiaan Barnard, 1922–2001

Nobel Prize: None

Area of research: Transplant surgery

Background: Barnard was a highly respected surgeon who developed the techniques he used by experimenting on animals' hearts without lasting success. However, in 1967 he successfully transplanted a human heart to a man suffering from incurable heart disease. He became an overnight superstar with the world media for his achievement.

Legacy: Today transplant surgery of all types is a routine way of extending people's lives.

Achievement					
Recognition					
Fame					
Impact					

Your turn...

1 Read **source a** and the factfile for Christiaan Barnard.

Transplants of all sorts today are seen as a common surgical solution, but before 1967 no one had transplanted a heart before.

Why do you think Barnard's achievement was of such interest at the time?

2 Imagine you are a journalist at the press conference after the first heart transplant operation. What questions would you ask and why?

3 Some people opposed the whole idea of transplant surgery. Why might they have objected to what Christiaan Barnard was doing?

Surgery was just one area in which there were advances that would benefit people's health. Opposite are the factfiles of three who won the prestigious **Nobel Prize** for their work in medicine and science.

Read and think

4 Look at factfiles 1–4. How would you rate each of these medical pioneers in the following four categories?

Achievement: How 'groundbreaking' their discoveries were.
Recognition: The extent to which their fellow scientists officially recognised the importance of their work.
Fame: How well recognised they were by scientists and media alike.
Impact: The extent to which their methods have improved life for people.

Use the table in the factfiles to help you make your judgements.

Here is an example for Christiaan Barnard.

Achievement					
Recognition					
Fame					
Impact					

Top trumps

5 In pairs agree on the ratings you would give to each of the people in the four categories on factfiles 1–4. Compare your answers with those of another pair. How do their answers differ from yours, and why do you think this might be?

6 With your original partner decide on an order for these pioneers, placing the person you believe had the most impact on medicine today at the top.

7 How would you re-order these pioneers if you chose a different category instead of who had the most impact? Why?

Make a judgement

8 Imagine you are a junior science reporter. Your editor has asked you to write a 100-word article on the twentieth century's 'Giant of Medicine'. Using the ratings you have already completed, decide who to write about, then construct your article based on their factfile. Be careful to explain to your readers the criteria you have used to make your judgement.

Factfile 2

Marie Curie, 1867–1934

Nobel Prize: Physics 1903, Chemistry 1911

Area of research: Development of X-rays

Background: Recognised as a pioneer in her field, Marie Curie's research was crucial in the development of X-rays in surgery. She discovered and was able to use radioactive radium to reduce suffering among patients. Ambulances equipped with X-ray machines were used on the front lines during the First World War. Later she received many honorary science, medicine and law degrees for her work.

Legacy: Today X-rays are widely used in the treatment of cancers and are used to 'see' inside the body.

Achievement					
Recognition					
Fame					
Impact					

Factfile 3

Alexander Fleming, 1881–1955

Nobel Prize: Medicine 1945

Area of research: Bacteriology

Background: In 1928, while conducting an experiment Fleming discovered that a mould that had accidentally infected a **culture** dish growing skin disease germs had created a bacteria-free circle around itself that killed the germs. After more experiments, Fleming named the active substance penicillin. His discovery brought him a wide range of honours.

Legacy: Today penicillin is widely used to combat bacterial infections and disease around the world.

Achievement				
Recognition				
Fame				
Impact				

Factfile 4

James Watson, 1928–
Francis Crick, 1916–2004

Nobel Prize: Medicine 1962

Area of research: DNA

Background: In 1951, these two Cambridge scientists began work on trying to understand how the body is able to recreate itself and how human genes transmit their information to the next generation. In 1953 they were able to explain to the world how **DNA** works. Since then they have received many honours in recognition of one of the discoveries of the twentieth century.

Legacy: The ability to understand how DNA works has helped in the development of better drugs and cures for a range of diseases and has revolutionised forensic science.

Achievement				
Recognition				
Fame				
Impact				

How did healthcare change in the twentieth century?

In this lesson you will:

- learn about the impact of the National Health Service on people's health

- assess the value of the National Health Service.

Out with the old; in with the new

In Britain today, if you were not feeling well you would probably go to see a doctor without thinking too much about it. However, if you had lived before 1948 you would probably have thought twice about such a trip.

? *What services and treatments do you know that the modern National Health Service provides? In pairs construct either a spider diagram or list of those things you both know.*

Look and think

1 Study **sources a** and **b**. What surprises you about the way people received medical treatment before the National Health Service?

Key words

Dispensary
Place where drugs and medical treatments are handed out.

GP
General practitioner; doctor who provides a range of medical services at a local level.

a When somebody came to the surgery you saw them, and made a diagnosis. Then after the surgery you would go into the **dispensary** and make up the medicines. Then you would send a bill out at the end of the month. Some would pay and some wouldn't, so we had a 'doctor man' who used to go round and collect the money.

■ *GP Alan Merson, in 2008, recalling the days before the NHS.*

b

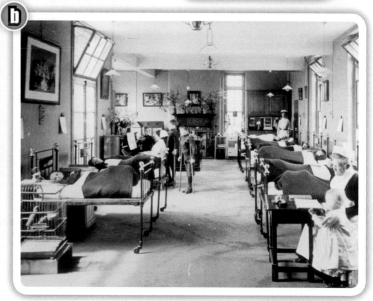

■ *Children's hospital during the 1930s.*

Timeline of key events

1948 — NHS founded. Care is free at the point of need for the first time

Prescription charges introduced at 1 shilling (equivalent of £1 today) — **1952**

1958 — Mass vaccination for under 15s begins

Contraceptive pill becomes available to all women — **1961**

1962 — General hospital building started – one for every 125,000 of the population

Abortion Act makes abortion legal up to 28 weeks into a pregnancy — **1967**

Changes to healthcare

The sacrifices that Britons made during the Second World War changed most people's expectations of the conditions they lived in and the care they should receive throughout their lives. After the war ended, the Labour government's health minister, Aneurin Bevan, established the National Health Service (NHS) in 1948. The NHS began the idea that in exchange for a contribution from wages, medical diagnosis and treatment became free at the point of use.

For most working people this was a revolutionary change. The fear that most people had, of falling ill and not being able to afford treatment, disappeared, and over the years the health of the nation began to improve.

The NHS: then and now

	1948	2008
UK male life expectancy (years)	65.8	76.9
UK female life expectancy (years)	70.1	81.3
Diseases immunised against	Smallpox Diphtheria Tetanus	Diphtheria Polio Influenza Meningitis C Whooping cough Rubella Measles Mumps Tetanus
Infant mortality (deaths) in England and Wales (%)	34	0.5
NHS Budget	£240,000,000 (£240 million)	£105,000,000,000 (£105 billion)
Prescription charges – England	Nil	£7.10
Number of nurses	93,591	510,777

Track the history

2 Imagine you have friends visiting you in Britain from the USA. They have sent an email asking you about the sort of healthcare they might expect in case of an accident. They have heard about the NHS, but are anxious to know more about what it has done for the typical Briton. Use the table and the timeline to reply, explaining the differences the NHS has made to someone living today compared with someone in 1948.

Make a judgement

In Britain the government pays for the NHS by money raised through tax and everyone has access to it. In America people have to pay for healthcare themselves to get treatment.

3 Write a second email to your American friends explaining which system you feel is better and why.

Back to the start

What do you think has been more important in medicine?

● The discoveries of famous individuals.
● The establishment of organisations like the NHS.

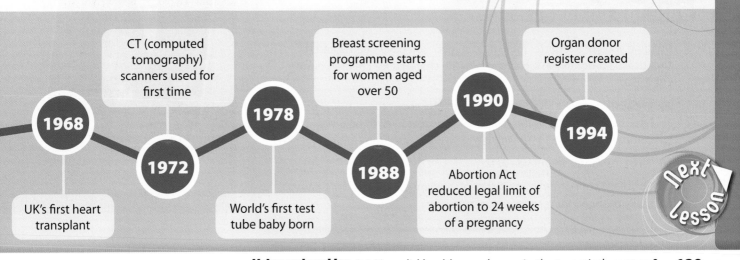

1968 — UK's first heart transplant

1972 — CT (computed tomography) scanners used for first time

1978 — World's first test tube baby born

1988 — Breast screening programme starts for women aged over 50

1990 — Abortion Act reduced legal limit of abortion to 24 weeks of a pregnancy

1994 — Organ donor register created

In this lesson you will:

- investigate the influences on young people in Britain growing up in the 1950s

- use sources to reach conclusions about a historical period.

You've never had it so good: Britain in the 1950s

Even in the last five years, you can probably think of events that have been important in your life.

? *What five events can you quickly think of? Make a list and share with a partner. Explain to them what made the event so memorable. How many of your events are the same as your partner's? What does this say about why you chose to include them?*

Have you ever kept a scrapbook of all of the really important times in your life? Mel did from the age of 10 in 1950. Some of the events that happened over the years have been included in this book.

Your turn ...

1 Look at **source a**.

a) Describe what these children felt, smelt and saw as they rushed into this sweet shop.

b) Why would Mel have included this moment in the scrapbook?

Note the changes

2 Imagine you are a reporter for a radio station. You have been asked to broadcast a programme looking at how life changed for children during the 1950s.

a) In pairs, conduct a short interview with Mel about the cuttings that have been included in the scrapbook (**sources a–h**) to help you compare life in the 1950s with life now. What questions might you ask?

b) What responses might you get?

c) Conclude your programme by saying how much you think life has really changed for teenagers over the years.

In 1953 sweet rationing ended. Children were now able to buy as many as they could afford.

d

'As I turned into Bramley Road I saw a mob of over 700 men, women and children stretching 200 yards along the road. Young children of ten were treating the whole affair as a great joke and shouting, "Come on, let's get the blacks and the coppers. Let's get on with it." Groups of policemen stood at strategic points carefully watching the "meeting" while police cars and **Black Marias** waited around the corner.'

*Description of the violence faced by black **immigrants** during the Notting Hill riots, Kensington News and West London Times, 5 September 1958.*

Magazine cover published during rock and roll sensation Bill Haley and His Comets' first UK tour, 1957.

b

Street party in Plumstead, London, for Queen Elizabeth II's coronation, 1953.

c

In most parts of the country, in the towns and cities, streets were deserted on the morning of Coronation Day, 2 June 1953. In the residential quarters, and in the suburbs, groups of cars were parked, here and there, in the silent roads. They stood outside houses where the 'H' aerial of TV had drawn neighbours and friends inside. More than half the viewers all over the country watched in the homes of friends. About a million and a half watched big-screen relays in cinemas and other public places.

Written by the Alexandra Palace Television Society.

e

Bannister runs mile in four minutes

Britain's jolly Roger Bannister has done it. Last night he ran the fabulous 4-minute mile, a feat which the world's athletes have been trying to achieve for years. His time was 3 minutes 59.4 seconds. As he passed the post at Oxford's Iffley Road track he was swept up in a mass of cheering and shouting spectators.

From the Daily Mail, 7 May 1954.

f

Knots of youths were standing about, on the steps, inside the vestibule, on the pavement outside. The ones in blue or brown suits had their hair swept into shiny quaffs, stiff with grease, above the forehead. Those who had violent coloured shirts on, stood with their jackets unbuttoned and hanging a long way open.

Description of Teddy Boys from John Wain's book Hurry on Down, *published in 1953.*

h

Manchester United in air crash – seven players among 21 dead

Twenty-one people, including the captain and six other players of the Manchester United football team and eight British sports journalists, were killed yesterday when a BEA Elizabethan airliner bringing the team home from Belgrade crashed just after taking off from Riem Airport, Munich, in a heavy snowstorm. The airliner caught fire after hitting buildings on the edge of the airport.

From The Times, 7 February 1958.

What's your view?

On 20 July 1957, Prime Minister Harold Macmillan described life for people in Britain at the time by saying: 'Most of our people have never had it so good.'

3 Looking at all of the cuttings in Mel's scrapbook with a partner, decide which of the following phrases you would agree with and why.

- *The Prime Minister's view is very accurate about life in the 1950s.*
- *The Prime Minster's view is not at all accurate about life in the 1950s.*
- *It's not easy to know whether the Prime Minister's view was right or not.*

4 Use evidence from Mel's scrapbook to produce a short presentation supporting your decision.

What was it like 'back in my day ...'?

In this lesson you will:

- learn about key moments in the life of a person living in the 1960s

- evaluate the motivation and purpose of collecting historical sources.

Growing up in the 1960s

Draw a vertical line 30cm in length on a piece of paper. Divide the line from 1 to 30. Now think about all the key moments in your life so far and mark them on the line at the age you were when they happened. Consider what you think will be the key moments for you between now and when you are 30, and add them to the timeline.

(?) *Compare your timeline with a partner's. What events are roughly the same and why?*

Life through the 60s

It is January 1970 and Mel is 30 years old. The scrapbook you looked at in Lesson 2.9a had been started when Mel was 10.

Mel now decides to have a look at what happened during the 1960s. But the clippings have become unstuck and scatter all over the floor.

Getting the order

1 Look at the clippings (**sources a–h**) and suggest ways or methods in which Mel could re-order them.

a) In pairs, discuss what clippings you would group together and why.

b) In a class discussion, decide what you think might be Mel's way of ordering the clippings and why?

a

It's 5, 4, 3, 2 – RADIO 1

'Get tuned to Radio 1 or 2: five, four, three, Radio 2, Radio 1 – go.' With these words, Robin Scott, head of Radios 1 and 2, put the BBC's new pop programme Radio 1 on the air at seven in the morning.

■ *From the Observer, 1 October 1967.*

b

Nothing to lose but our men
by Sasti Brata

A group calling itself the New York Radical Women staged a protest at the 1968 Miss America contest. The most dramatic feature of which was the 'Freedom Trash Can' into which fearless females threw bras, girdles, curlers, false eyelashes, wigs and issues of women's magazines.

■ *From the Guardian, 16 May 1969.*

c

Ramsey proved right in World Cup
ENGLAND 4, WEST GERMANY 2

England, the pioneers of organised football and the home of the game, are the new World Champions for the first time.

■ *From The Times, 1 August 1966.*

Look and think

2 Working on your own, look at all the sources you can see on these pages. Which of them do you think fits with each of the statements below?

- *This is the most important one; it's the most serious.*
- *This is least important; I cannot see why this is here.*
- *This has been included because of how they felt at the time.*
- *It's a sign Mel is getting older, because it wouldn't have been included otherwise.*

3 a) Now working in pairs, explain to your partner how you came to your decisions.

b) Compare your answers with your partner, and then with the pair next to you. How different are other people's answers, and why do you think they have reached their conclusions?

d In the distant future, when our descendants study the history books, they will see one word printed against the year 1963 – Beatles! – just as convincingly as 1066 marked the Battle of Hastings.

■ *From the New Musical Express, 6 December 1963.*

f

KENNEDY ASSASSINATED

■ *Clipping from the Daily Mail, 23 November 1963.*

e ## Speech that has raised a storm

In a speech at Birmingham on Saturday, Mr Enoch Powell said Britain must be mad to allow the inflow of some 50,000 dependants of immigrants every year. It was like watching a nation 'busily engaged in heaping up its own funeral pyre', he told the annual meeting of the West Midlands Conservative Political Centre.

Tory leader rules Powell out of Shadow Cabinet

Mr Edward Heath said last night, 'I consider the speech Powell made in Birmingham yesterday to be racialist in tone, and liable to exacerbate racial tensions. The Conservative Party is opposed to racialism and discrimination of a racial or religious kind.'

■ *Clippings from the Birmingham Post, 22 April 1968.*

Time to reflect

4 a) Many years later, one of Mel's children has found the scrapbook and asked about the significance of all the cuttings. Mel quickly scribbled down a word and handed the paper to the child to stick on the front as a title. From the list below which of these words do you think it was?

● Technology

● Famous people

● Change

● Achievement

b) In no more than 100 words explain why this title summarises the cuttings to be found in Mel's scrapbook.

c) If you could choose another word to describe the theme, what would it be and why?

g ## Students and the Pill

Research among young people and in particular my recent visits to university have confirmed that the great majority of students come eventually to sexual intercourse as part of a loving and responsible relationship and that in an age when the Pill makes contraception almost 100 per cent safe, they should demand the right to have this made available under proper medical supervision. A year's supply can be obtained for less than £5.

■ *From the Observer, 12 February 1968.*

h ## Suddenly, happiness is flower shaped.

The 'in' things [today are] Indian jackets and dresses, kimonos, Victorian dresses, elaborately patterned, beaded and flowing twenties and thirties dresses, bell-bottomed trousers and brocade waistcoats. Plus of course, those beads, bells – and flowers.

■ *From the Daily Sketch, 22 July 1967.*

Back to the start

Look back at the scrapbook of the 1950s and 1960s set out for you in this and the previous lesson. Of all the items, which would you select as being a real turning point for Mel?

Next Lesson

What role did trade unions play in people's lives?

In this lesson you will:

- find out what trade unions are, and how they have tried to improve things for workers

- use a case study to make general conclusions about a historical issue.

Key words

Blackleg
Person who continues to work even though a strike has been called by the trade union.

General strike
Refusal to work by those in many different industries.

Infer
Draw a conclusion from information without it telling you the answer directly.

Why join a union?

? *If you thought the students at your school were being treated unfairly, what could you do to try and change things? Think about the strengths and weaknesses of each method you come up with.*

A trade union is an organisation of workers that uses a number of methods to try to improve pay and working conditions for its members.

The Jenkins family

The men in this photo are all members of the same family. John is the oldest, born in 1882. He is the father of David, born in 1904, and the grandfather of Anthony, born in 1931. It is May 1950 and John has just finished his last ever shift at the coal mine. All three men sit down in the local pub to celebrate John's retirement. Their conversation soon turns to stories of life working at the pit, and their memories of the trade unions.

How can unions help workers?

Collective bargaining Union leaders represent the workers in talks with the boss to improve pay or conditions. The more workers represented, the better the chance of success!

Work to rule Workers do the minimum work possible while obeying all the rules.

Strikes Refusal to do any work until workers' demands are met.

Picket line Group of workers who stand at the entrance to the factory or mine to make sure it stays closed.

Propaganda The Trades Union Congress (TUC) printed a newspaper called the *British Worker* to encourage workers on strike to keep going.

Fundraising Many unions raise money to help the families of workers on strike. For most of the twentieth century, they also gave money to support the British Labour Party, so that the Party could pass laws in Parliament to help workers.

■ *Photo of three generations of Welsh miners, taken in 1950.*

John

You boys have it easy today! We used to do ten-hour shifts, and that was on top of the hours it took to get to and from the coal face underground! We didn't get the eight-hour day until the trade union got more powerful. My dad used to tell me to stay away from the unions, that they just caused trouble: pit closures, men losing their jobs and income. But I'm glad I joined in 1908 and helped get the eight-hour day for us miners. Those were great days, before the Great War: with the unions on our side we were strong. We even got a minimum wage in 1912!

David

Well, the union hasn't done much for me over the years! I still remember the terrible accident at the Senghenydd pit in 1913: 439 men died and nothing was done to make things safer for us! The unions didn't stop the mine owners cutting our pay in 1921: do you remember 'Black Friday', when we had to go on strike without the help of the railway or transport unions? Things got worse in 1925, just after I got married and had my first daughter. The union said we had to go on strike to get better wages and the mine owners just shut the mines! I had a wife and child to feed and no income! Even when the other unions did go on strike with us in 1926 it didn't help. Six months without work I was, and then I had to take a pay cut and work longer hours anyway!

Anthony

*It must have been hard, Dad, but you survived. The whole town rallied round to support the miners! Things are much better now, and I don't think we'd have the better pay, safer conditions and new machines without the trade unions. We wouldn't have the Labour Party! Until the 1926 **General Strike**, the unions gave Labour almost all the money it needed to get started, and now , after the war, the Labour government has bought the pit from the old mine owner and improved things.*

David

*The unions are only strong during wars, when everyone is needed at work! As soon as there's any unemployment, the unions are useless: there will always be **blackleg** workers who need the money, will ignore the strikes and keep the pits going! You mark my words, the unions will fail to help workers in the long run!*

John

You might be right, but without the strength of the unions to support the worker, you can be sure that things would be much worse!

Your turn ...

1 Use the conversation between John, David and Anthony to complete a timeline. Copy the dates below, and next to each one explain the significance of that year to this family.

1904:	
1908:	
1912:	
1914–18:	
1921:	
1925:	
1926:	
1931:	
1945:	
1950:	

Decisions! Decisions!

2 a) For each date on your timeline, decide which of the following categories it best belongs with.

● *It shows that trade unions helped the Jenkins family.*

● *You can **infer** that the trade unions helped the Jenkins family.*

● *It does not tell us anything about whether the trade unions helped the Jenkins family.*

● *You can infer that the trade unions did not help the Jenkins family.*

● *It shows that the trade unions did not help the Jenkins family.*

b) What other questions would you ask the men to find out in more depth whether the trade unions helped their family? Think of at least three questions.

A mine of information?

3 How useful do you think conversations are to historians who want to find out whether trade unions helped British workers in the twentieth century?

Try to think of ways in which such a conversation is useful and limits to its use. You could use the questions you came up with for task 2b to consider some limits to the source.

What role did trade unions play in people's lives?

Why did miners strike?

If you ask relatives who lived through the 1980s what they remember about the news in those years, most people will remember a clash (which turned violent) between two groups: the trade unions and the Conservative government under Prime Minister Margaret Thatcher.

? *Look at source a. What words do you think best describe Margaret Thatcher in this picture?*

■ *Cover of* Time *magazine, 14 July 1979.*

What happened?

Just as in 1926, the trouble began with the miners. The mines, owned by the government since 1947, were old and could not produce coal as cheaply as foreign mines. Thatcher wanted to close 20 mines and sack 20,000 miners to save money. The miners wanted to keep their jobs: whole communities depended on wages earned in the mines.

On 12 March 1984, Arthur Scargill, leader of the National Union of Miners (NUM), called for a national miners' strike. He used **flying pickets** to spread the strikes. On the 18 June 1984, there was a running battle between strikers and the police at a steel factory that used coal in Orgreave, South Yorkshire: 93 strikers were arrested; 51 strikers and 72 policemen were injured!

b The strike is not about pit closures. This is an attempt to bring down a democratically elected government with mob tactics. Most miners did not want this strike, but Arthur Scargill has forced it on them with his flying pickets. Margaret Thatcher is doing a great service to the British people by standing up to this challenge.

■ *From a letter to* The Times *newspaper, October 1984.*

c The strike affected whole families. There was no money to pay bills and things got very hard coming up to winter. We helped to raise money and get food parcels for the families of striking miners. We used to believe everything we were told by the media and the state but after all that we couldn't. It was terrible when police on horseback attacked the pickets with their truncheons. All the men wanted was their jobs and a decent wage.

■ *From an interview with Anne Suddick, March 2004. In 1984, Anne worked for the National Union of Miners.*

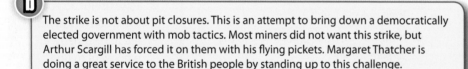

Oral history project: stage 1

You are about to carry out some oral history to find out what people thought of the trade unions in the 1980s. Oral history is a record of what people say or remember about the past. It can be very useful for historians who want to understand more about a period of recent history.

1 Write a list of questions that you would use to interview a relative who remembers the 1980s. Aim for a minimum of seven questions to ask on a range of different topics.

Oral history project: stage 2

The clash divided the nation: some people thought the miners were being treated very unfairly and supported the National Union of Miners (NUM) strikes. Others thought the miners were causing a lot of trouble and supported the government.

2 Study **sources b–f** about the clashes between the trade unions and the government.

a) For each one, decide how far, and how reliably, it suggests the miners' strike was popular. Remember to refer to the content, nature, origin and purpose of each source in your answer!

b) Use the sources to list at least three more questions to use in your interview with a relative. Try to make the questions focus on the tension between the unions and the government.

d

Area	Number of miners	% on strike 19 Nov 1984	% on strike 1 Mar 1985
Kent	3,000	96	93
North-East	23,000	95	60
Nottinghamshire	30,000	20	22
Scotland	13,100	94	69
South Derbyshire	3,000	11	11
South Wales	21,500	99	93
Yorkshire	56,000	97	83
NATIONAL	196,000	74	60

■ *From A. J. Richards's book called* Miners on Strike, *published in 1996.*

e

You saw the scenes that went on in television last night. This is an attempt to change the rule of law for mob rule. It will not succeed because the overwhelming majority of people in this country are honourable, decent and want the law to be upheld. I praise those workers who have crossed the pickets to work for their families and their futures.

■ *From a speech by Margaret Thatcher, 19 June 1984.*

Oral history project: stage 3

You now have a list of 15–20 questions to help you find out about trade unions in the 1980s. First of all you'll need to practise your interview technique.

3 Working in pairs, practise interviewing your partner by asking them your questions. Your partner should pretend to be one of the people from **sources b–f**.

4 Now write up the interview, or perhaps video or record it.

5 If possible, use your questions to interview a friend, relative or teacher who remembers the 1980s. Keep a record of the interview using any of the methods in task 4.

6 When you have finished the interview, consider how useful you found the person's memories to find out about life, and views of the trade unions, in the 1980s.

f

■ *Policeman hitting a striker at Orgreave, near Scunthorpe, 18 June 1984.*

Back to the start

How similar were the 1926 General Strike and the 1984 Miners' Strike? Try to make overall judgements about the popularity of trade unions in twentieth-century Britain from these two case studies.

Next Lesson

Making connections

In this unit you have examined a number of different lifestyles and have considered events that had an impact on the ways in which people lived and worked.

A question of image

Look at the images below. What sort of an impact would they have had on the lives of ordinary people? Would the impact have been positive or negative? Why?

■ *Street party in London for Queen Elizabeth II's coronation, 1953.*

■ *Roger Bannister running the 4-minute mile in Oxford, 1954.*

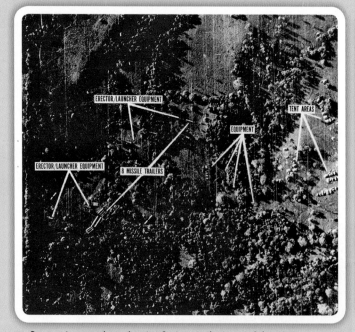

■ *Reconnaissance photo showing Soviet missile sites on Cuba, 1962.*

■ *People queuing for food in Kentucky, USA, 1937.*

'Now, in my day ...'

Has an adult ever said to you: 'Now, in my day things were so much better than they are today'? If no one has said it to you, they have certainly said it to a lot of young people! Your task here is to investigate whether or not this sort of statement is likely to be true. Was it really good to have lived and worked in the twentieth century?

Your turn ...

1 Look back at all the enquiries in this unit.

a) Work with the person next to you. Think and talk about the positive and negative sides of living and working in the twentieth century. Copy the table, then find as many examples as you can to complete it. One for each side has been done as an example for you.

It was good to live and work in the twentieth century because ...	It was awful to live and work in the twentieth century because ...
1 *Advances in medicine*	1 *Fear of nuclear war*
2	2
3	3

2 Share your ideas with others in your class. Do you have more positives than negatives, or is it the other way round?

Setting it up

3 Your local primary school has heard of your expertise in all things to do with the twentieth century. The headteacher has asked you to set up an exhibition that will show the children what it was like to live and work during this period. Unfortunately there is only room for ten items on the display boards.

a) Work with a partner to select what you think are the best items to show what living and working in the twentieth century were really like.

b) Write a brief explanation for each item. Remember, you are writing for young children so don't make it too complicated!

You could create this exhibition on large sheets of paper, on display boards or using your IT skills.

What's right? What's wrong?

4 Now turn yourself into a critic.

a) Study the exhibition created by another pair of students.

b) Write a review of it for your local community magazine. Remember to praise as well as give constructive criticism!

Assessment 1

Was it better to be a child in 1918, 1955 or 2005?

Imagine you have a penfriend who lives in another country. And imagine they have never been to your country. They have asked you what your country is like. What would you tell them? With a partner make a list of things you would tell them that:

● impress you about your country

● worry you about your country

● make you proud of your country

● you would change about your country.

As you have worked through Unit 2, you will have noticed that for most people there will have been some things that have remained the same. However, other people will have lived through major changes which will have made their lives quite different.

List your thoughts ...

1 Imagine three teenagers your age, but from different eras, are able to meet. There is a person from 1918, one from 1955 and one from 2005. They all want to discuss things about the world they live in. For each person develop a spider diagram like the one below that identifies key words about:

● what they feel pride in from their era

● how important they feel their country is in their era

● what they feel has changed recently about their era

● what they consider is a danger to the way they live.

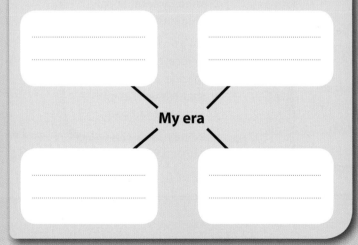

Share your thoughts ...

2 With a partner use your answers from your spider diagrams to add words to the Venn diagram below. Where you feel the same word can be used for two or more of the people from different eras, place that word in the overlapping sections. For each word that you place, explain to your partner the reason why you have located it in that section of the diagram.

3 Compare your answers with two other students from your class.

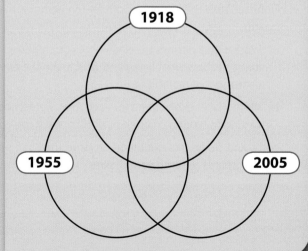

In conclusion ...

4 Having finished their discussion, the teenagers from different eras now have to return to their own time. Imagine they want to write a letter to a friend explaining what they have found out about the other time periods.

On your own, and using the information from the spider diagrams and the Venn diagram, choose one of the time periods and explain to the friend:

a) what you feel was similar

b) what you feel was different

c) the conclusions you have reached about how people lived and worked in comparison to life today.

How might you complete this letter?

● The first thing is to make sure you are clear about what the three people think about the years they come from.

● Look back at the work you have completed in the unit on living and working. For each of the years think about key words that describe what life was like. Try to find some evidence of an event that supports your choice of words.

● The Venn diagram helps you to sort your words and make connections between the three years. Think carefully as you complete this task.

● Some of the key words will be unique to a particular year, and these should appear in that year's circle.

● Some of the key words will be shared across the years. Place these words in the overlapping sections to show you feel that they apply to more than one of the years. Some words might apply to all three, in which case place them in the centre.

● In order to write your letter, choose two circles from the Venn diagram and think about how they intersect. What words and events are common to the two years? Does this mean the two teenagers had the same reasons for their similar feelings about the world they lived in?

● You also need to have a conclusion – your opinion – based on what you have found out, as to whether life was very different for teenagers who lived in different times.

How will your work be marked? Have you:

Level 5

Described some of the main features of the period?

Recognised and described how some things have changed while others have stayed the same?

Suggested relationships between causes?

Evaluated sources to establish evidence?

Selected and used information and used the correct historical words to support your work?

Level 6

Explained the type of change and continuity (things staying the same) and how these changed?

Begun to explain relationships between causes?

Evaluated sources to establish evidence important to your enquiry?

Selected, organised and used information, including the correct historical words, to produce structured work?

Level 7

Explained how change and continuity differed over time and between places and peoples?

Begun to explain why the significance of events, people and changes has differed according to different viewpoints?

Selected, organised and used the right information and the correct historical words to produce well-structured work?

What was life like in the twentieth century?

Imagine you have been asked to write an article for a new magazine called *The Young Historian*. The audience for this magazine is students between the ages of 11 and 14.

For the first issue the editor wants to focus on explaining what life was like in the twentieth century. You have been given **sources a–e** and a strict word limit of 300 words.

To help you with your article, you need to do the following.

1 Explain what each source says about twentieth-century life.

2 List the questions historians might have about using these sources.

3 Say how far you can accurately describe life in the twentieth century from these sources and what more you might need to form a better informed opinion.

a

■ *Anti-Semitism was taught in German schools, especially in history and biology lessons. Here, two Jewish children are forced to stand by a blackboard that reads 'The Jews are our greatest enemy! Beware of Jews.' Jewish children were eventually excluded from German schools in 1938.*

b

Life under Stalin was more peaceful and happy. We were all poor, but we had lots of fun. Families shared everything they had. Today every family lives only for itself. We believed that life would get better if we worked hard. We took more pride in our work than we do today.

■ *From an interview by historian Orlando Figes with Iraida Faivisovich in 2003. Iraida lived under Stalin's rule for 18 years after she was born in 1935.*

c

■ *Teacher being humiliated by some of his students during the Cultural Revolution of China in 1966.*

d The same year that Patty started school, the war ended. It had lasted for six long weary years, and for those of us who had been young at the time, it was a big slice out of our lives. When it was finally all over, there was singing and dancing in the streets. Victory bells rang and people cried and laughed at the same time and hugged each other. We had street parties for the children, and though they were too young to know what it was all about, they caught the excitement of the moment, and with balloons and streamers they joined in the fun.

■ *Joyce Storey remembers the end of the Second World War in her book* Joyce's War, *published in 1992.*

e

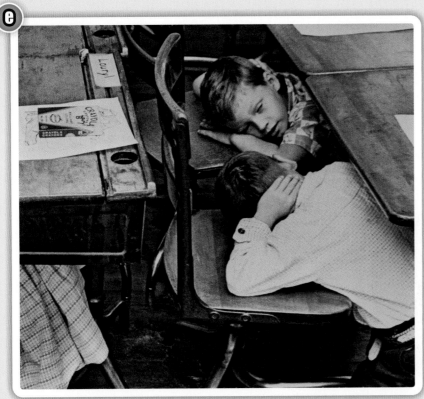

■ *US schoolchildren practising to 'duck and cover' during an air raid drill in the 1950s. These drills were part of everyday life.*

How should you write your article?

● Look back over all the work you have done for this unit to get an impression of what life was like in the twentieth century. Write down a few words that, for you, seem to sum up the period.

● Now look at each of the sources that you have been provided with. For each write down what you think it tells you about the century.

● Take a closer look at each of the sources and start to ask yourself whether there are any issues with that source. You need to consider who produced it, when and why, and whether this affects how and what you are able to write about twentieth-century life.

● Finally, you need to look back at the few words you started with. In what ways do these sources help you to explain a viewpoint to your readers, and what do they need to be aware of?

How will your work be marked? Have you:

Level 5

Suggested reasons for different interpretations of the past?

Investigated historical problems and begun to ask your own questions?

Evaluated sources to establish evidence?

Selected and used information and used the correct historical words to support and structure your work?

Level 6

Begun to explain how and why different interpretations of the past have been made?

Investigated historical problems and begun to ask your own questions as part of the enquiry?

Evaluated sources to establish evidence important to your enquiry?

Selected, organised and used information to produce structured work?

Level 7

Explained how and why different interpretations of the past have been made?

Investigated historical problems and issues by asking your own questions, refining them and reflecting on what you have done?

Selected, organised and used the right information to produce well-structured work?

Unit 3
Moving and travelling

Introduction

There had never been a time like the twentieth century for the movement of people across the world. Never before had it been possible for so many people with such different backgrounds, from nations all over the world, to travel such great distances in order to take advantage of new opportunities and to take part in the great challenges the century offered them.

■ British orphans arrive in Australia in the 1950s.

■ Some of the first West Indian immigrants arriving in Britain, 22 June 1948.

Timeline 1901–Present day

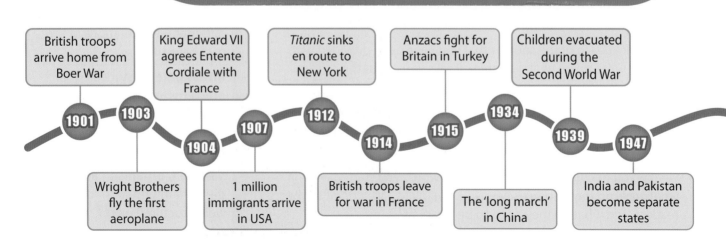

British troops arrive home from Boer War — **1901**

1903 — Wright Brothers fly the first aeroplane

King Edward VII agrees Entente Cordiale with France — **1904**

1907 — 1 million immigrants arrive in USA

Titanic sinks en route to New York — **1912**

1914 — British troops leave for war in France

Anzacs fight for Britain in Turkey — **1915**

1934 — The 'long march' in China

Children evacuated during the Second World War — **1939**

1947 — India and Pakistan become separate states

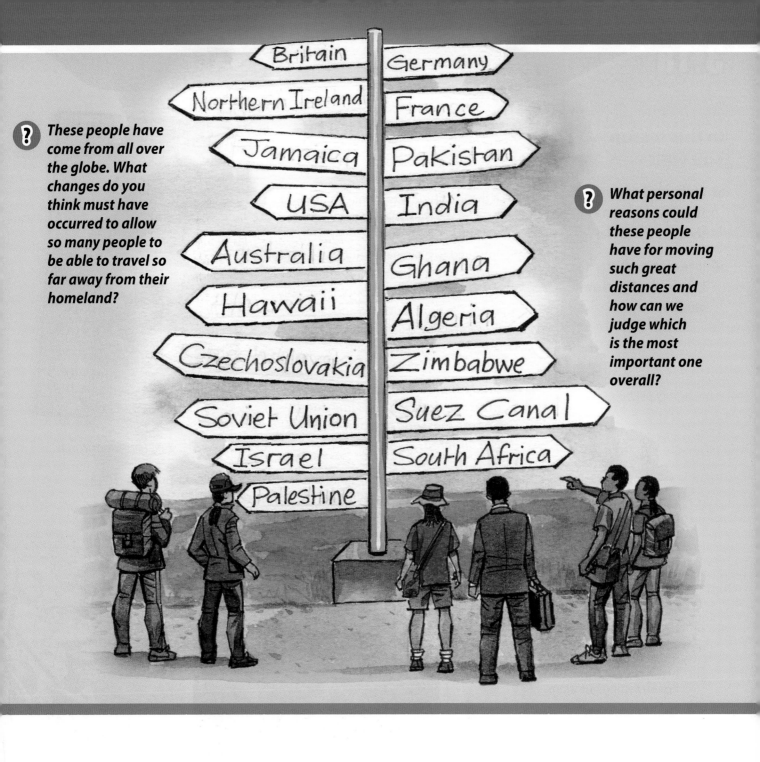

These people have come from all over the globe. What changes do you think must have occurred to allow so many people to be able to travel so far away from their homeland?

Britain
Germany
Northern Ireland
France
Jamaica
Pakistan
USA
India
Australia
Ghana
Hawaii
Algeria
Czechoslovakia
Zimbabwe
Soviet Union
Suez Canal
Israel
South Africa
Palestine

What personal reasons could these people have for moving such great distances and how can we judge which is the most important one overall?

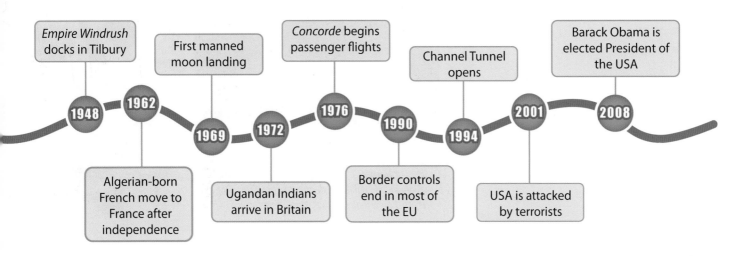

Empire Windrush docks in Tilbury

First manned moon landing

Concorde begins passenger flights

Channel Tunnel opens

Barack Obama is elected President of the USA

1948
1962
1969
1972
1976
1990
1994
2001
2008

Algerian-born French move to France after independence

Ugandan Indians arrive in Britain

Border controls end in most of the EU

USA is attacked by terrorists

In this lesson you will:

- find out who travelled to support Britain in the First World War

- investigate a historical issue and set your own questions.

For king and country, 1914–18?

In 1914 the British government declared war against Germany on behalf of the Empire. As the fighting during the First World War continued to claim large numbers of casualties, so the British government turned to its colonies for support. It not only needed men to fight, but men and women to work in Britain's war industries as well as raw materials from food to coal.

? *Study source a carefully. What message does it give? How does it put the message across? At whom is it directed?*

■ Poster entitled 'The Empire Needs Men', 1915.

Throughout this enquiry you will be shown evidence of the support given to Britain from across the Empire, along with the reaction to that support. You will undertake your own enquiry, part of which is to decide which questions you want to answer. You will try to weigh up the evidence and decide which has been most useful in helping you in your enquiry.

Set the questions

1 Study **sources b–e**. Then set three questions about support for Britain that you will answer. Here are some tips on setting questions.

Choose the stem

First, decide on the nature of the question. Here are some examples for you to chose from:

- *What?*
- *How?*
- *Why?*

Content

Now choose the focus of your question. Here are some examples of areas which you might consider:

- *Recruitment*
- *Employment.*

■ Drawing of Naik Darwan Singh Negi, the first Indian soldier to win the VC, by Allan Stewart. This picture was drawn and published during the First World War. The artist drew many famous scenes from the war.

c

■ *The crew of HM messenger ship* Trent *from the magazine* British Seafarer, *published in April 1916.*

e ■ *The British West Indies Regiment in camp on the Albert–Amiens road in the Somme, France, in September 1916.*

d

The rush to join the armed forces in Britain in 1914 was matched by a similar surge in Australia, Canada, New Zealand, South Africa and other colonies. In all 1.3 million men joined up from the four countries listed, of which 144,000 were killed. These troops are known by their role in various military operations. The Australian and New Zealand troops are best known for their involvement in the Gallipoli campaign in which 10,000 of them died. The colonies not only contributed men, they sent equipment, food and money.

■ *Adapted from historian Jay Winter's book* Remembering War, *published in 2006.*

Refine your questions

2 Share your questions with another student in your class.

a) First, ask them to advise you on how you might improve your questions.

b) Then comment on their questions.

You should both keep the following points in mind.

- *Does the question make sense?*
- *Can the sources be used to answer the question?*
- *Can the question be answered quite easily?*

Answer your questions

3 Write your answers to your questions. You can do this in note form. Your partner can then ask you your questions. You should use your notes to answer the questions verbally.

In this lesson you will:

- find out the reaction in Britain to help from abroad

- evaluate the use of newspapers as part of this enquiry.

What was the reaction in Britain to the arrival of Empire troops?

Historians often find newspapers very useful. They help us to understand a range of different viewpoints. For example, they contain editorials that show us some opinions from the time.

Read all about it

The First World War ended in 1918. People from across the British Empire who travelled huge distances to support Britain in time of need had made a real difference to the war effort. At the end of the war many troops returned to Britain before travelling home. There was a mixed response in Britain to the troops from the Empire.

? *Do you read newspapers? Discuss with a partner three aspects of newspapers in general that a historian might find useful when finding out about the past.*

a

Part of the Colonies

Without fear and tirelessly they accomplished their purpose. Thousands of strong men from Canada, Australia and New Zealand laid down their lives. The Colonies have always shared our history, now they have a history of their own. People will remember Gallipoli or Vimy Ridge for the skill and devotion of the men of Canada, Australia, New Zealand, South Africa and Newfoundland [which is now part of Canada].

- *Adapted from* The Times, *26 May 1919. The* Times *was probably the most important national newspaper of the day.*

What do they say?

1 Here are four extracts from newspapers (**sources a–d**) published after the end of the First World War. Your task is to find out the response in Britain to soldiers from abroad. You will also weigh up how useful newspapers are to historians in finding out about the past. Read through each extract carefully.

a) What useful points of information can you take from each source to tell us about reactions to the troops from the Empire?

b) Try to write down two or three points from each source.

- *Adapted from the* East London Observer, *16 August 1919. The* East London Observer *was a local newspaper.*

b

Serious rioting in Canning Town

A story of riots in Canning Town on Saturday afternoon and involving blacks and whites was told in the West Ham police court on Monday. The whole affair arose out of an unprovoked attack by a drunk dock labourer William James Grant on a black man who hit back. The magistrate pointed out that during the war the black people of the Empire had done splendid things and it was a shabby thing for those people who had lazed around at home during the war to turn on them.

c

Black and white at Liverpool

Further trouble between whites and blacks took place in the Upper Stanhope Street district of Liverpool late on Monday night. The district was in uproar and a number of black men were attacked. Some of the black men stated that during the war they obtained work without any problem. However, now the war is over there is more unemployment and a greater bitterness shown towards them and they are gradually being discharged from their work.

■ *Adapted from* The Times, *11 June 1919.*

d

Empire Day in Winchester

At the Empire Day celebrations at the Pitt Corner camp, the Reverend Canon Braithwaite spoke to the troops from Bermuda and the West Indies. 'Here in view of the ancient capital of England, we meet our brothers drawn from far-distant parts of the Empire. You needed no conscription but came forward voluntarily and I come here today as a British person to thank you most heartily for all that you have done for the Empire in this world war.'

■ *Adapted from the* Hampshire Observer, *31 May 1919.*

How useful is each newspaper?

2 Some newspapers are more useful than others. When judging how useful **sources a–d** are, ask yourself these questions.

- *What information does the extract give?*
- *What might have been left out?*
- *Is the focus local or national?*
- *What is the purpose of the article?*

3 After asking these questions for each source, choose the newspaper extract you think is most useful and explain why.

History detective

It has often been claimed that those people from around the world who fought for Britain were 'forgotten by history'. Now is your chance to put this right. Go to www.heinemann.co.uk/hotlinks (express code 9014P) for a list of websites containing information about soldiers from across the globe who travelled to contribute to the British war effort. In your research you might focus on individual soldiers or soldiers from specific countries. Your teacher will give you guidance on how your research is to be presented.

How useful are newspapers?

4 You have weighed up how useful each newspaper extract has been in your enquiry.

a) In summary, explain in 250 words your answer to the following question:

How useful are newspapers to historians when trying to find out about the reaction of the British public to the contribution of people from the Empire to the war effort in the First World War?

Back to the start

a) Look back over this enquiry and make a list of the areas where people from the British Empire had an influence. Now put each area into one of three categories:

- social
- economic
- military.

b) Which category has most entries in it? Do you think this shows where people from the Empire had the greatest impact?

Next lesson

How can moving make you safe?

What was Kindertransport?

? *Have you spent any length of time away from home? Perhaps you have had a sleepover with friends or spent a week with relatives? What did you feel about leaving home?*

Did you know?
Approximately 1.5 million children did not make it to safety and perished in the Holocaust.

Look and think

1 Look at **source a**. The children are clearly starting out on, or coming to the end of, some kind of journey.

a) What questions would you want to ask in order to find out why the sculpture is there and what it is all about?

b) Talk about this with the person next to you and draw up a list.

c) Compare your list with the questions others in your class would want to ask and draw up a class list of questions.

- *This sculpture is outside Liverpool Street station, London, and was unveiled in September 2006.*

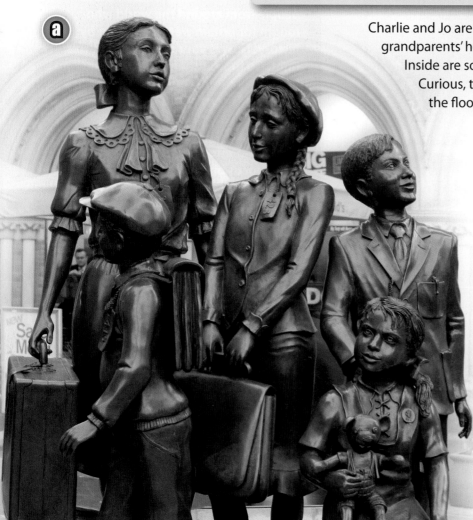

a

Charlie and Jo are exploring the attic in their grandparents' house. They find an old, dusty backpack. Inside are some photographs and yellowing papers. Curious, they pull them out and spread them over the floor. This is what they find:

- photograph of a wrecked synagogue as a result of Kristallnacht (November 1938)

- Hitler Youth membership card

- piece of fabric with a yellow Star of David and the word *Jude* embroidered across it

- child's passport/exit visa from Germany dated 1939

- photograph of Jewish children arriving at Harwich

- letters tied in a bundle with a slip of paper 'Killed in Auschwitz' tucked inside

- front cover of an exercise book from an English school with a German child's name on it

- pages from a diary, as opposite.

10 June 1939

Today I was chosen by a young couple with no children. At last I will leave the Dovercourt camp and have a home again.

20 June 1939

I hate the food. Porridge for breakfast instead of warm rolls and butter. My school packed lunch was fish paste sandwiches. I'm hungry.

20 August 1939

We've been away on holiday. I dug sandcastles with some English children and swam in the sea with them. They were nice.

10 September 1939

England is at war with Germany. Mummy and Daddy sent me here to be safe but I want them so much. Are English planes going to drop bombs on them? Where do I belong?

Jo rushes downstairs to find a photograph (**source b**) of a plaque she has seen her grandfather look at many times. They have asked him about it many times, but he clearly finds it too emotional to talk about.

'Does this', Jo asks Charlie, 'have anything to do with the backpack and its contents?'

b

In deep gratitude
to the people and Parliament
of the United Kingdom
for saving the lives of
10,000 Jewish and other children
who fled to this country
from Nazi persecution
on the Kindertransport
1938 – 1939

■ *A plaque in the Palace of Westminster, unveiled in June 1999.*

Answering questions

2 How would you answer Jo's question? Was there a connection between this plaque and what they had found in the dusty old backpack? And if there was, what was it? Can you sort it out?

3 Look back at the questions you wanted to ask about the sculpture outside Liverpool Street station. Which questions have still not been answered? How would you set about finding answers to them?

Telling the world

4 Imagine you are a local journalist and have heard of Charlie and Jo's discovery. You need to write up the story for your local paper.

   a) Think about the headline. How will you make it eye-catching?

   b) Think about what approach you are going to take to tell the story. How will you make your article dramatic, truthful and interesting?

In this lesson you will:

- find out what Oskar Schindler did to keep Jews safe

- reflect on Schindler's motives.

Key words

Black market
Illegal buying and selling of officially rationed goods.

Gestapo
The Nazi secret police.

Liquidated
Wiped out.

What motivated Oskar Schindler?

Think of people at school, at home or in the wider world who have, individually, made a difference. This difference can be for good or bad.

? *Think of three people. What difference has each one made? Compare these differences with a partner. Go round the class until you have a complete list of differences.*

a

First they came for the Jews
And I did not speak out because I was not a Jew.

Then they came for the communists
And I did not speak out because I was not a communist.

Then they came for the trade unionists
And I did not speak out because I was not a trade unionist.

Then they came for me
And there was no one left to speak out for me.

■ *Written by Pastor Martin Niemöller after the Second World War. He was a German minister of religion. During the war he stood up to the Nazis and, as a result, was imprisoned in the concentration camps of Sachsenhausen (outside Berlin) and Dachau (outside Munich).*

Read and think

1 Read **source a**.

a) What reasons does Pastor Niemöller give for keeping silent when others were persecuted?

b) According to the source, why does the pastor think he should have spoken out?

c) Do you think this was the only reason that he, and others, did not defend those who were persecuted by the Nazis?

d) What other reasons were there?

e) Is Pastor Niemöller really only writing about his own experiences?

Factfile

Oskar Schindler (1908–1994)

- Schindler was a German industrialist. Throughout his life he was a fast-talking, fast-living man; he gambled and drank, took and gave bribes and, although married, had many mistresses.

- When the war broke out in 1939 and the Nazis invaded Poland, Schindler quickly moved there and became involved in the **black market**, making connections and friendships with **Gestapo** officials. He supplied them with women, alcohol and anything else they wanted.

- These connections enabled him to set up a factory making enamel goods and munitions with the cheapest labour around – Jews from the Krakow Ghetto.

- As Nazi persecution of Jews intensified, Schindler became increasingly worried about the safety of his workers. He convinced the Nazis that his factory and his workers were vital to the German war effort. In doing so he saved them from deportation to the death camps.

- Schindler was making money, but everyone in his factory was fed, no one was beaten and no one was killed.

- However, in March 1943 the Krakow Ghetto was **liquidated** and Schindler's Jewish workers were moved to a forced labour camp at Plaszow, which was controlled by the brutal Kommandant Amon Göth.

- Swiftly, Schindler befriended and bribed Göth. As a result, he was permitted to set up his works, again with Jewish labour.

- He compiled lists of the Jews he wanted in his factory and Göth, heavily bribed, agreed to let Schindler have those workers.

- In 1944, Göth was ordered to liquidate the Plaszow labour camp. Always one step ahead, Schindler persuaded Göth to let him move his Jewish workers to Brunnlitz, Schindler's home town.

- There, they were eventually liberated by the Soviet army. By this time, Schindler was bankrupt but he had saved about 1,300 Jews from certain death.

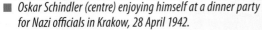

■ *Oskar Schindler (centre) enjoying himself at a dinner party for Nazi officials in Krakow, 28 April 1942.*

■ *Oskar Schindler (second from right) with a group of Jews he rescued, taken in 1946.*

d

Oskar suggested that they play one more hand. If Amon won, Oskar would pay him 7,400 zloty [Polish currency]. 'But if I win,' said Oskar, 'then you give me Helen Hirsch for my list.' Oskar won. Out in the kitchen, Helen Hirsch did not know that she had been saved by a game of cards. Rumours of Oskar's plan were heard all over the camp. There was a Schindler list. It was worth everything to be on it.

■ *From Thomas Keneally's book* Schindler's Ark, *published in 1982. Here he describes a game of cards between Amon Göth and Oskar Schindler. Helen Hirsch was Göth's Jewish maid, whom he abused.*

e

The women arrived at Brunnlitz haggard and shaved. My mother was very sick with pneumonia; they were not ready for us – there were no bunks – and we slept on the floor. But it was warm, on top of the factory, and there was such an overwhelming feeling of relief that we were reunited. That was the thing about Schindler: he saved families.

■ *From Elinor J. Brecher's book* Schindler's Legacy, *published in 1994. This book tells the stories of some of the survivors from Schindler's list. This extract is from Celina Karp Biniaz's story.*

What would Schindler have said?

2 Read the factfile and look at **sources b** and **c**.

a) How would Oskar Schindler have explained what was happening in **source b** to the Jews in **source c**?

b) Now turn the question round. How would Oskar Schindler have explained **source c** to Nazi sympathisers who remained in Germany after the war?

Time to reflect

3 Look again at **sources b** and **c**, and read **sources d** and **e**. Now look at these two views.

- *Schindler was out to make money. The Jews were simply cheap labour for him. He only saved them because he could make a good profit from them.*
- *Schindler was a brave man who worked at the heart of the Nazi state to save Jews.*

Which view do you agree with? Use **sources b–e** and the factfile in your answer.

4 Do motives matter as long as the result is good?

In this lesson you will:

- **find out how the Second World War affected Adam Rybczynski**

- **identify and explain the gaps in Adam's story.**

○ Key words

Alien Registration Certificate

Certificate issued to all non-British people with permission to live in Britain after the Second World War. They had to show it to the police every time they moved house or changed jobs.

Adam Rybczynski's story

The Second World War had ended. The fighting was over and peace had been declared. However, millions of people were on the move.

? *Why do you think people moved around after the Second World War. List at least two reasons, and share them with the class to build up a class list.*

Work it out

1 Read **source a**. What can you find out about Adam Rybczynski from this certificate? Make a list, and put it in chronological order.

a

Registration Certificate No. A.576023
Issued at Ramsgate, Kent
on 25th May, 1954.
Name (Surname first in Roman Capitals)
RYBCZYNSKI, Adam
Alias
Left Thumb Print (if unable to sign name in English Characters).
Signature of Holder } Adam Rybczynski

Nationality Polish
Born on 10.11.09 in Kudryn Buderaz
Previous Nationality (if any) Russian
Profession or Occupation { Labourer
Single or Married Married
Address of Residence { 13, Fairlight Avenue, Ramsgate.
Arrival in United Kingdom on
Address of last Residence outside U.K.
Polish Forces in Italy.
Government Service Served in Polish Army from Sept., 1942 until 3.3.47.
Passport or other papers as to Nationality and Identity.
Army Form X204 (Polish)

■ The **Alien Registration Certificate** issued to Adam Rybczynski in May 1954.

Who is Adam Rybczynski?

Adam Rybczynski grew up in a part of Europe where national boundaries were constantly shifting and where violence was commonplace. However, it was the Second World War that took him away from his family and friends, and which changed his life forever.

Along with thousands of other Poles, Adam decided to stay in Britain. He died in 1980.

In September 1941 Adam joined a new Polish army led by General Anders. It was made up of Poles who had been prisoners of the Russians and who wanted to fight for their country.

Adam, his wife and all his family, along with 1 million other Poles, were sent to labour camps deep inside the Soviet Union. Thousands died from exhaustion and starvation.

Adam was born in 1909 in a village of the Wolyn region of Eastern Europe in what was then the Russian Empire.

In September 1939 the Russian army invaded Poland and Adam's village became part of the Soviet Union.

At the end of the Second World War, national boundaries in Europe were redrawn. Adam's village was now in communist Ukraine. Adam was afraid to go home.

By 1920 the Wolyn region was part of independent Poland.

In 1942 Adam left the Soviet Union to train alongside the British army. He served as a driver in the 'Anders Army' and fought at the Battle of Monte Cassino in 1944.

In June 1941 Nazi Germany attacked Soviet Russia. Britain and the Soviet Union became allies. The Russians could no longer treat the Poles as enemies.

What happened in Adam's life?

2 Read the facts about Adam Rybczynski on page 154. Now look back to the information about him in **source a**, which you listed in task 1. Plot a time line of Adam's life, using your list and the facts. Each time Adam moved, create a 'break-out' explaining why.

3 There are a lot of gaps and silences in Adam's story.

    a) What questions would you ask about what happened to him after the end of the war?

    b) How would you set about finding the answers?

■ A photograph sent to Adam. On the back is written 'My dear brother-in-law, we send you our photograph for you to remember us by.' It is dated 1955.

THE BRITISH RED CROSS SOCIETY
14 & 15, GROSVENOR CRESCENT, LONDON, S.W.1.

Cables: BRITREDCROSS, LONDON
Telegrams: REDCROS, KNIGHTS, LONDON

Telephone: SLOANE 5191

Patron & President: HER MAJESTY THE QUEEN
Vice-President: HER MAJESTY QUEEN ELIZABETH THE QUEEN MOTHER.

Executive Committee
Chairman: THE RIGHT HON. VISCOUNT WOOLTON, P.C., C.H., D.L.
Vice-Chairman: THE COUNTESS OF LIMERICK, D.B.E. LL.D.
Deputy Chairman: MRS. A. M. BRYANS, C.B.E.
Secretary General: F. H. D. PRITCHARD, ESQ.

29th November, 1954.

MEW/VG/Polish

Mr. Adam Rybczynski.

Mr. Jozef RYBCZYNSKI

Dear Sir,

    We have received an enquiry from the Comite International de la Croix-Rouge in Geneva on behalf of your father, Mr. Jozef Rybczynski, Plawna Gorna, pta Plawna, pow. Lwowek Slaski, woj. Wroclaw, Poland, who is anxious to hear from you.

    We should be grateful if you would let us know whether you will be writing to your father and whether we may give the Comite International de la Croix-Rouge your address for onward transmission to him.

    We shall be glad if you will acknowledge this letter so that we may know it has reached you safely. We would not send your address to Mr. Rybczynski without first having received your permission to do so.

Yours faithfully,

(Mrs.) M. E. Wetherall
International Welfare Section
International Relations and Relief Department.

■ A letter to Adam from the British Red Cross, dated 29 November 1954.

Time to reflect

4 Look at **sources b** and **c**. How do these help you to fill the gaps in Adam's life after 1945?

5 Many terrible things happened as a result of the war. On a scale of 1–5 (where 1 = least effect and 5 = worst effect), where would you put the breaking up of families, perhaps never to meet again? Why?

In this lesson you will:

- find out about the journey made by *Exodus 1947* in July 1947

- conduct an investigation into the purpose of the voyage of the *Exodus 1947*.

Key words

Mossad Le'aliya Bet
Agency for Illegal Immigration.

British Mandate
Power given to Britain by the League of Nations to run Palestine.

What was Exodus 1947?

? *What does the word 'exodus' mean? Any ideas? What do you think was the significance of 1947? Source a may give you a clue.*

Your investigation

The *Exodus 1947* was an illegal immigrant ship carrying 4,500 Jewish refugees from Europe to Palestine during the final year of the **British Mandate**. It became the symbol of the struggle for the right to unrestricted Jewish immigration into Palestine and the need for a Jewish homeland. But everything was not necessarily as it seemed. Were the refugees genuinely trying to get into Israel, or was it all one vast propaganda stunt? This is what you are about to investigate. But first, you need to read the questions and answers on page 157, which will give you some background information.

Your turn ...

1. Look at **source a** and read the answers to the four questions opposite.

   a) What conclusions can you draw about the state of the ship shown in **source a**?

   b) What clues, so far, can you find that might lead you to think this wasn't a genuine attempt to get Jewish refugees to Israel?

   c) Discuss these questions with the person sitting next to you.

2. Are there any further questions you would like to ask as part of your investigation to the question: *Was the voyage of the* Exodus 1947 *simply a propaganda stunt?*

(a) ■ *The ship* Exodus 1947 *berthed at Haifa in the Middle East, 1947.*

(b) In the battle lasting two hours, our ship was rammed, constantly bombed with tear gas, sprayed with water from high-pressure hoses and fired at with pistols and sub-machine guns. Our resistance continued without let-up. Only when the ship's commander was informed that the wounded were coming into the ship's hospital at a rate too great to be treated, did he give the order to cease resistance and avoid a large loss of life.

■ *Part of the crew's statement printed in the New York Herald Tribune, 21 July 1947.*

Question 1: *What was the political situation in Palestine in 1947?*

Answer: In 1945, the Labour Party won the British general election. The new Labour government said it would work for a single, independent Palestine where Arabs would remain in the majority because the British government would limit the immigration of Jews into Palestine. The British allowed 1,500 Jews a month into Palestine. If any tried to enter illegally, they were turned away and usually ended up in refugee camps. This angered the Jews who had hoped for a separate Jewish homeland within the borders of Palestine.

Question 2: *How did the refugees get hold of a ship?*

Answer: In November 1946 the **Mossad Le'aliya Bet** bought an old American troop ship. It was anchored off Baltimore and destined for the scrap yard. The Mossad Le'aliya Bet fitted out the ship so that it would carry as many refugees as possible. A volunteer crew of 40 American Jews sailed the ship across the Atlantic to the south of France. There, 4,500 Jewish men, women and children, who had been moved from refugee camps in Germany, embarked on the ship.

Question 3: *Did the refugees get to Israel?*

Answer: In July 1947 the ship set sail. Once at sea, it was renamed *Exodus 1947*. Five British warships shadowed the *Exodus* as it made its way across the Mediterranean Sea. When it became clear that the ship was heading for Palestine, the Royal Navy rammed the *Exodus 1947* and sent boarding parties aboard. They fought with the refugees and crew, killing three and seriously wounding many. Then the British Navy towed the *Exodus 1947* to the port of Haifa. The world's press photographed the ship and interviewed the refugees.

Question 4: *Was there any particular significance in the choice of July 1947?*

Answer: Members of the United Nations Special Committee on Palestine were visiting Palestine on a fact-finding mission.

c

Mossad Le'aliya Bet not only suggested, they gave us orders that this ship was to be used as a big demonstration with banners to show how poor and weak and helpless we were, and how cruel the British were. I was told to make as much of a demonstration as possible, but not to let the fight go too far.

■ *Part of an interview with the captain of the* Exodus 1947 *given in 1970.*

d

■ *The* Exodus 1947 *and its refugee passengers were sent back to Europe. This photograph shows the flag flown on the ship by the refugees as they returned.*

Was it all a propaganda stunt?

3 Read **sources b** and **c**.

   a) How far do these sources agree about what happened when the British navy boarded the *Exodus 1947*?

   b) Which source is likely to be the more reliable?

4 Look at **source d**. What do you think was the significance of the flag hoisted by the Jewish refugees?

5 You should now be in a position to conclude your investigation to this question: *Was the voyage of the* Exodus 1947 *simply a propaganda stunt?*

Write a paragraph, remembering to back up what you say with evidence.

Reporting back

6 Imagine you have been asked by both a Jewish and a Palestinian newspaper to write an article about the *Exodus 1947*. Which one will you write for? You'll have to slant your article in different ways depending on which you choose. Remember, make your piece as eye-catching and dramatic as you can.

Back to the start

You have read about different people and groups of people who all made journeys to what they thought was safety. Did they, in fact, find safety? Discuss this in your class and work out which were the most successful, which were the least successful, and why.

Next Lesson

How did the British rule in India come to an end?

In this lesson you will:

■ consider the significance of Gandhi to the end of British rule in India

■ make a judgement using a range of information.

Key words

Untouchables
People who did the dirty jobs in India. Many Hindus believed you could be 'polluted' by their dirt if you touched them.

Why did the British leave India in 1947?

Mohandas K. Gandhi (1869–1948) was an extraordinary man who spent the last 27 years of his life trying to force the British rulers to leave his country, India.

? *Look at sources a and b. Why do you think Gandhi might have changed the way he dressed?*

■ *Mohandas K. Gandhi, 1906.*

■ *Mohandas K. Gandhi, circa 1935.*

Why wouldn't the British leave India?

Getting the British to leave India was easier said than done! The British had:

● invested a great deal of money in India

● made lots of money by trading with India

● controlled all the important jobs in the Indian government

● the support of a large Indian police force

● the loyalty of Indian soldiers.

At the same time, the Indians:

● were divided into many different groups by religion, caste and language

● had no army of their own

● were mostly peasants and had no time for protests or politics.

So how exactly did Gandhi hope to get rid of the British?

A cunning plan?

1 Try to come up with two methods you might have used to try and force the British to leave India.

2 In 1909 Gandhi wrote a book called *Hind Swaraj*. In this book he set out his plan to free India from British rule. Read **source c** and pick out the different methods Gandhi planned to use. Were your methods similar to Gandhi's?

c The British have not taken India: we have given it to them! We strengthen their hold by arguing among ourselves. We were one nation before the British came to India; they have divided Hindus and Muslims, but we must stand together once more. We must say to the British 'you can only rule us as long as we wished to be ruled; soon we shall no longer have any dealings with you'. We must boycott British tax, schools, law courts, and trade. We must spin our own cloth and refuse to buy British machine-made clothes. But we must not use violence. Violence only leads to more misery and is not natural to the Indian soil. We must defeat the British with passive resistance; we must win our freedom by showing the world that we are brave enough to suffer British anger.

■ *From Gandhi's book,* Hind Swaraj, *written in 1909.*

SEVEN STEPS TO INDEPENDENCE

20 August 1917: THE MONTAGU SPEECH

The British were grateful for Indian help in the First World War. The government in London promised 'to gradually allow the Indians, when they were ready, a greater share of power as part of the British Empire'.

13 April 1919: MASSACRE AT AMRITSAR

On 6 April Gandhi had organised a successful boycott in the Punjab supported by a peaceful crowd of Hindus and Muslims. The world was shocked when troops under British officer, General Dyer, shot and killed 379 of them.

September 1920–February 1922: NON-COOPERATION

Gandhi launched a non-cooperation movement across all India. While many people stopped paying tax or sending their children to school, many lawyers and politicians still worked for the British. Gandhi ended the movement after some of his supporters used violence.

March–April 1930: THE SALT MARCH

Gandhi walked 322 kilometres (200 miles) from his home to the seaside to make salt. Only the government was allowed to make and sell salt, so Gandhi and over 60,000 other Indians were arrested. Headlines around the world said the British were being unfair.

1930–31: THE ROUND TABLE CONFERENCE

In 1929 a new government came to power in Britain and set up talks with Indian leaders in London. Gandhi wanted to speak for all Indians at these talks. But the Indian princes, Muslims and **untouchables** wanted some power and all opposed Gandhi's ideas on how India should be run.

September 1939: SECOND WORLD WAR

As part of the British Empire, India had no choice but to join Britain in war with Germany. Gandhi organised a non-cooperation campaign called 'Quit India' to protest. 23,000 Indians were imprisoned for supporting Gandhi, but 'Quit India' was defeated.

15 August 1947: INDEPENDENCE DAY

India was divided into two countries: India (mostly Hindu); and Pakistan (mostly Muslim). Gandhi had opposed the division. He started a fast to try to end the violence that had broken out in many Indian cities between Hindus and Muslims. It worked for a while in Calcutta and Delhi.

Did the plan work?

3 a) For each event above decide how far it shows that the methods Gandhi used that you identified from **source c** were successful.

Write each event in a table like the one below and give each method a mark out of 5 (where 5 shows that Gandhi's method worked well and 1 that this method completely failed).

b) Explain your marks using details from the event boxes.

Event	Method 1	Method 2	Method 3
The Montagu Speech			
Massacre at Amritsar			

c) What mark would you give Gandhi's methods overall? Explain your answer.

Did the British really leave because of just one man?

Some historians argue that Gandhi's role in the British leaving India was very important. He is still widely known as the Mahatma (Great Soul). Others say his role has been exaggerated; the British wanted to leave India because it no longer created as much profit for Britain. The British handed more power to Indians to prepare for when they left India.

Stop press!

4 Imagine you are a journalist. You have been asked to create a front page that explains to readers why the British are leaving India. You need to explain how important Gandhi is in all this. You can choose to write for either *The Times* (British) or *The Hindu* (Indian). Remember to:

● create a catchy headline and introduction that grabs readers' attention

● use subheadings to make your explanation clear to the readers

● use lots of detail from the event boxes to back up your story.

In this lesson you will:

- explore reasons for the refugee crisis of 1947–48

- extract information from different types of source to explain a problem.

Key words

Partition

Division – in this case of India and Pakistan.

Refugee

Person driven from their home.

Why did 12 million Indians leave their homes in 1947?

Three months before the British left, three leaders – Nehru, Jinnah and Mountbatten – all agreed that the areas where mainly Muslims lived should be split from India to form a new country, Pakistan. None of the leaders guessed how tragic the results of this decision would be, but one British cartoonist did.

a

■ *A cartoon by L. G. Illingworth, May 1947.*

? *Look at source a. What can you see? For each detail you pick out, explain what you think the cartoonist means.*

When the British made it clear they would soon leave India, ordinary people began to panic. They did not know who was going to be in control. In some parts of the country they did not even know which country they would be living in – India or Pakistan. Hindus and Muslims began to attack each other, at first because of fear, but later out of revenge. In the two months after independence, the violence exploded into a mass slaughter in which one million people died. Twelve million people left their homes and became **refugees** – the largest movement of people in the history of the world. But why?

Why?

1 Look at the map and **sources a–d**. What reasons can you find to explain why violence broke out on such a large scale between Hindus, Sikhs and Muslims?

Make the links!

2 Look again at **sources a–d**. This time, give examples of where information in one source supports that in another source. Try to find at least three such links.

b

One night our Hindu neighbour banged on our door and warned us that angry Hindu mobs were coming towards this area, wanting to kill Muslims. A few hours later my dad decided that we should leave for Pakistan. The journey was by bus. It was one of the most terrifying and heart-aching moments of my entire life. We left everything behind in a blink of an eye: all our friends, our house, our belongings.

■ *From an interview with a Muslim woman in 2007. She was aged seven in 1947.*

c

We were lied to by our politicians. We were told that Pakistan would be a Muslim country; Hindus and Sikhs had to be killed or kicked out of Pakistan. It was 13 August when we stormed the Hindu temple. We were shouting 'Long live Pakistan' and challenging the Hindus to come out. Suddenly one of them appeared with a sword in his hand. I managed to grab the sword from his hand and killed him. The temple was burned with about 30 Hindu men and women inside.

■ *From an interview with Mujahid Tajdin in February 2000. He was 33 in 1947.*

d

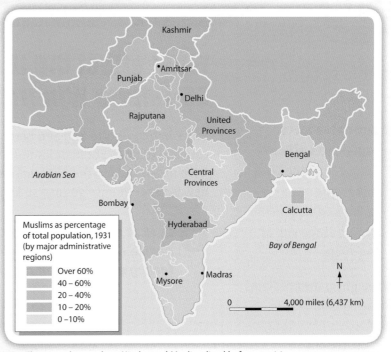

■ Dead bodies lie in the street in the Punjab after Hindu–Muslim clashes, August 1947.

■ This map shows where Hindus and Muslims lived before partition.

Muslims as percentage of total population, 1931 (by major administrative regions)

Over 60%
40 – 60%
20 – 40%
10 – 20%
0 – 10%

0   4,000 miles (6,437 km)

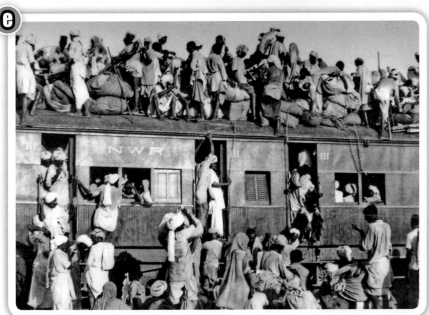

e

■ The Punjab in 1947. Trains like this ran alongside roads that were also full of refugees.

One new message ...

3 Imagine you have been sent an email from a student from the Punjab. He wants to understand why there was so much suffering during **partition**. He can only download one source. You can choose to send the map, the written memories or the photos. Which will you choose? Make sure he can use the sources to answer his question. Give suggestions of how he could use it. Explain why you think this type of source is more helpful than other available sources.

Did you know?

Hindus and Muslims have lived peacefully together in India but there are many reasons for tension.

• Hindus believe the cow is a holy animal. Muslims slaughter cows during the festival of Id. Some Hindus formed 'cow protection squads' to try to stop cow killing!

• Hindus believe there are thousands of forms in which God can appear. Hindu temples have statues of these Gods. Muslims believe there is only one God and that it is wrong to make images of God.

• Some historians argue that the British stirred up tension between Hindus and Muslims to make it easier to control India: 'divide and rule'.

Next Lesson

What effect did the arrival of the SS *Empire Windrush* have?

In this lesson you will:

■ find out about the experiences of black people from the West Indies who came to live and work in Britain at the end of the 1940s

■ weigh up the problems facing immigrants.

Some immigrants to England had never left their home countries before. But in order to move to the UK, they gave up everything that was familiar to them to make new lives for themselves in a strange country.

? *Look at source a. What are these people thinking? What are they feeling as they get off the ship?*

Did you know?

• More than 10,000 servicemen and women from the West Indies fought in the Second World War and many more served as merchant seamen.

• Today, 1 per cent of the British population is of Caribbean background.

a ■ *Some of the first West Indian immigrants arriving in Britain, 22 June 1948.*

b

Passenger opportunity

TO UNITED KINGDOM
TROOPSHIP
EMPIRE WINDRUSH
sailing about 23 May

Fares: Cabin class £48 Troop deck £28

Royal Mail Lines Limited
8 Port Royal Street

■ *This advertisement was put in a Jamaican newspaper, the Daily Gleaner, on 13 April 1948.*

What was the importance of *Empire Windrush*?

On 22 June 1948, the ship *Empire Windrush* docked at Tilbury, on the River Thames. On board were 492 passengers who had left their homes in the Caribbean to start a new life in Britain. It was the *Empire Windrush* that brought the first wave of West Indian immigrants to Britain after the Second World War. Few of them had jobs to come to, and even fewer had anywhere to live.

Why did the West Indians come to Britain?

People uproot themselves and their families for many reasons. Sometimes it is because conditions in their 'old' homelands are bad; sometimes because opportunities in their 'new' homelands seem good; and sometimes because of a combination of both these 'push' and 'pull' factors.

Many of the 492 passengers on the *Empire Windrush* were ex-servicemen who had fought for Britain and the Empire in the Second World War. Most of them had served in the RAF and some of them hoped to rejoin; others wanted to take up the promise of work and the chance of a better life in England.

However, many British people were not happy at the thought of immigrant workers coming to Britain. Indeed, even as the *Empire Windrush* was crossing the Atlantic, Parliament was debating the matter. But as all the passengers held British passports, there was nothing legally that could be done.

Key words

London Transport
Company that ran the underground trains and the buses in London.

Prejudice
Judging people or events unfairly without considering the facts.

Racism
Treating people badly because they are of a different race from your own.

Word went round that this boat was taking passengers for a cheap fare: £28 to go to Britain. It was common knowledge that there was work in Britain, just after the war. I had no ties. I wasn't married or anything like that. I knew no one in England. I had no idea what I was coming to.

■ *Mr Oswald 'Columbus' Denniston explains why he decided to come to Britain on the* Empire Windrush.

I came to England first in 1944 in the air force. I returned to Jamaica in 1946, but somehow it was too small for me. After you reach a certain time in life, you think you want to get away from the control of your parents. When the Windrush *came in 1948 I returned to England and greater freedom.*

■ *Arthur Curling explains why he decided to embark on the* Empire Windrush.

I came here in 1948 because my husband sent for me. He and his brother came up a year before. I was very anxious to come over because when he left we were just married. We got married and he left the following day. Jamaica in 1948 was all right to me. If my husband had not sent for me, I would not have come at that point, maybe later.

■ *Lucille Harris gives her reasons for sailing to Britain on the* Empire Windrush.

Why make the voyage?

1 Study **sources b–e**.

  a) Make a list of the reasons why these people decided to go to Britain on the *Empire Windrush*. Compare your list with the person sitting next to you.

  b) Together, label each reason 'push' or 'pull'. Are there more of one than the other? Why do you think this is? How could you check this out?

How successfully did the West Indians settle in Britain?

Britain was desperately short of workers at a time when reconstruction after the Second World War was badly needed. About 200 of the *Empire Windrush* passengers found work immediately, mostly with the newly set up NHS and with **London Transport**. There was work to be had in all the major cities, too.

However, it was a different matter when it came to housing. Thousands of houses had been destroyed during the war and some white people already living in Britain thought they should have priority when it came to being housed. In Liverpool, violence broke out as early as August 1948, with mobs of white youths attacking the hostels where black people were living. There were much more serious riots in Nottingham and Notting Hill, London, in 1958 and the white ringleaders were sent to prison for long periods of time.

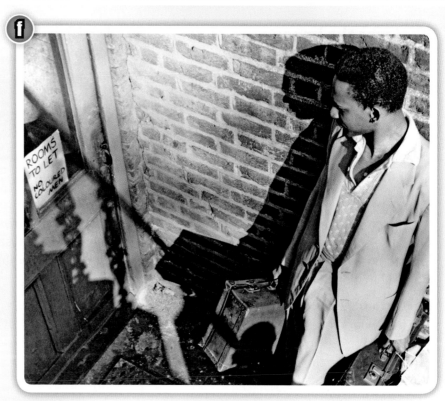

f

■ *A West Indian immigrant looking for a place to live, 1953.*

g

I went to school in King's Cross, London. I was the only black child in the school. I never associated with white people in any significant degree. At school I came across real hostility. I had no friends for several years.

■ *Vince Reid came over to Britain on the* Empire Windrush *when he was 13 years old.*

h

I was a welder, but instead of doing welding they gave me a wheelbarrow and a shovel. After a couple of weeks I packed it in and re-enlisted in the RAF. I knew what to expect there. After eight years I was demobbed [released from military duty] and got a job with the British Oxygen company as a laboratory technician doing welding of aluminium and various metals.

■ *Clinton Edwards came over on the* Empire Windrush *in 1948.*

i

The second day in England I went to Balham Labour Exchange and I was offered five jobs. Sad to say, the Right Honourable Creech Jones, he was the Minister of the Colonies, stated that we would not stay longer than one year. We are still here and I and my people are here to stay.

■ *Mr Oswald 'Columbus' Denniston describes how he found work.*

Link it together

2 Draw a spider diagram. In the middle put 'Windrush Immigration'. On the 'legs' of the spider, write as many consequences of the immigration that you can find in **sources b–i**.

3 Consequences don't usually exist in little boxes by themselves. Many are linked together. Link as many of these consequences as you can.

4 Very few of the consequences for West Indian immigrants in the late 1940s and early 1950s were good ones. Suggest why this was the case. Talk about it with the person sitting next to you. Have you any ideas as to what could be done to make things better?

How can racism and prejudice be ended?

Many people, black and white, worked hard and are still working hard to get rid of **racism** and **prejudice**. But what is the best way to do this?

1 Legislation

1965: Racial discrimination in public places prohibited.

1968: Racial discrimination in areas such as housing and employment illegal.

1976: Illegal to encourage racial hatred.

2010: ???

2 Community projects

Working together as a community to, for example, decorate an old people's day centre, tidy up a graveyard or organise a carnival.

3 Sport

Support mixed-race national teams.

4 Entertainment

Listen to and enjoy West Indian performers.

5 Education

Teach about the history of black people and make sure that every school has a proportion of black children in it.

Which is best?

5 Look at cards 1–5, which are in no particular order. Think about the advantages and disadvantages of following each course of action and talk about it to a partner. Give each approach a score out of 5 (where 5 = likely to work well and 1 = useless) and put the cards in order. Make sure you give a reason for each of your ratings.

6 Think about everything you have covered in this lesson. How can we best stamp out racism and prejudice today? Using your ratings and the examples you have studied, create a short speech to be performed as part of an anti-racism campaign.

In this lesson you will:

- weigh up how far South Asian culture has clashed with British culture since the 1960s

- research and prepare a script using a range of sources.

Key words

Fusion
Blending together the food, dress and ideas of different cultures.

Hijab
Head covering worn in public by some Muslim women.

British and Asian: a clash of cultures?

In Lesson 3.4a you looked at why people from the former British colonies came to live in Britain, and what the journey was like for some of them. But what was life like for the new South Asian immigrants, people from modern India, Pakistan and Bangladesh? How similar were their experiences to those of West Indian immigrants? Did the British like the new music, dress and ideas that immigrants brought with them? Do the immigrants and their children now feel British?

? *Look at source a. Does this look like a fusion of cultures or a clash of cultures? Apart from music and dress, what other areas of life would you look at to see whether there has been a fusion or clash between British and Asian culture?*

■ *Producer Ronnie Screwvala, actress Shilpa Shetty and director Anurag Basu at the film premiere of* Life in a… Metro, *8 May 2007.*

Asian immigration to Britain

In the 1960s and 1970s, many South Asians came to Britain to work in factories in cities like London and Birmingham, or in textile mills in towns such as Bradford, Bolton and Oldham. More recent immigrants moved to these towns because they already had friends and family connections there. Today, there are many second- and third-generation South Asian-Britons, who have Asian families but were born in Britain.

Some people think that there has been an exciting **fusion** of British and Asian cultures since the 1960s. Other people worry that there has been a clash of cultures that has caused tension in areas with a large Asian population.

Use your eyes!

1 Study **sources b–g**. For each one, decide whether it suggests more of a fusion or a clash of British and Asian cultures. Use a table like the one below and details from the source to support your answer.

Source	Fusion or clash?	Details that support this

b In 1967, I moved to Bolton and worked in a mill repairing machines. I enjoyed work: pay was good enough; you could take Indian food to the canteen and warm it up; I had many Indian friends there I could talk to. People here are very nice, very friendly.

■ *From an interview with Mr Ayub Adia in Bolton, 2005, for the 'Moving Here' project.*

c I spent the daytime speaking English at the local school, my evenings five days a week at Islamic school and Sunday afternoons learning Bengali. My mum and dad listened to Hindi film music, but rock music was my favourite.

■ *From an interview in Bradford, 2005, with Usman Ali, born in England in 1968 – 'Moving Here' project.*

d **Commentator:** David Beckham gets the ball again for Manchester United. It's a decent cross from Beckham, and there is Jess Bhamra. It's a fine header, and she's scored! Have we discovered a new star here? We're joined now by Jess's mother. You must be proud of your daughter.

Mrs Bhamra: Not at all! She shouldn't be showing her bare legs to people! She's bringing shame on the family. Don't encourage her! Jesminder Bhamra, you get back home now!

■ *Adapted from the film* Bend it like Beckham, *made in 2002.*

e
1 Spaghetti bolognese
2 Chicken tikka masala
3 Fish and chips

■ *From a list of Britain's favourite dinners, as given in The Sun, 7 September 2008.*

f

Ward	All minority origins	Pakistani	Bangladeshi	Black	Indian
Coldhurst	36.7	1.7	31.3	1.7	1.2
Werneth	38.0	27.0	4.3	1.1	3.4
Alexandra	20.7	14.1	3.4	1.8	0.7
St Mary's	31.2	23.9	2.5	3.1	0.6
Hollinwood	1.9	0.6	0	0.5	0.3
St James'	2.1	0.1	0	1.4	0.1
Lees	1.8	0.3	0	0.8	0.2
Oldham	**8.7**	**4.1**	**2.4**	**0.8**	**0.7**

■ *A table showing the percentage of people living in different areas of Oldham in 1991. The table is from the Richie Report published in December 2001. The report tried to find out why race riots took place in Oldham in May 2001.*

Over to you ...

2 Weigh up the evidence and make a decision about whether there has been either a fusion or a clash between British and Asian culture.

a) Use the table you made in task 1 to decide whether you think that the sources, on balance, better support a clash or fusion.

b) Explain how you used your table to make your decision.

c) Pick the one source that most influenced your decision. Explain what makes this source so important to your decision.

Tuning in!

3 The BBC wants to make a radio documentary about how far there has been a fusion of British and Asian cultures since the 1960s. You have been employed as a scriptwriter for one section of the programme. The director wants you to: come up with a name for the programme; write a script that explains whether there has been more of a clash or a fusion between British and Asian cultures.

Your section should last no longer than five minutes – about 400 words of script. If you want, you could record the programme using a cassette or digital recorder!

g

■ *Tanveer Ahmed, who won a fashion award in 2008 for his modern version of the traditional **hijab**.*

Back to the start

In this enquiry you have read about West Indian and South Asian immigrants to Britain. Look back over these two lessons and decide whether you think there are more similarities or differences between their experiences of life in Britain.

3.4c

Taking it further!

Why were British children sent to Australia?

Between 1950 and 1967 about 150,000 children were taken to Australia to begin new lives there. These children were not travelling with their families. They went alone. Many were from children's homes and some were orphans. However, in thousands of cases the children's parents had put their children temporarily into care because of sudden and unexpected difficulties, and had no idea that their children would be taken from them forever. Many parents believed their children had been adopted in Britain; many children were told their parents were dead; their birth certificates were destroyed and they were expected to begin their new lives afresh.

a ■ British orphans arrive in Australia in the 1950s.

b

There are two principal aims in child migration, which I wish to bring before the House this evening. The first, which is common to all migration projects, is to increase the British population in the empty spaces of the Commonwealth, where there are unrivalled resources of fine farmland and mineral and industrial wealth, which remain relatively undeveloped.

The second aim, certainly not less important, is to rescue the children of broken homes and a bad environment in the United Kingdom and to open for them the door of opportunity to a happy and hopeful future in our great overseas Commonwealth. Instead of a cheerless, back-street existence, often unloved and unwanted, these children, if they go to Australia, are given the fresh air, sunshine and beauty of the countryside, a new start in a new country and the prospect of a full and useful life.

■ *From a report in* Hansard, *which records debates in Parliament, 9 February 1959.*

d

The federal government is again defending its refusal to say sorry to British child migrants and to give them compensation. The federal government says that, while a database is to be established to help the former child migrants trace relatives back in the UK and other places, there will be no financial assistance for reunifications.

■ *From a transcript from* The World Today, *an Australian programme broadcast throughout Australia, on 28 January 2000.*

The stories of these migrant children only came to light because of the work of Margaret Humphreys, a social worker living in Nottingham with her husband and two children. **Source c** contains extracts from conversations she had with men and women who had been taken to Australia as child migrants.

c

A When we were on the boat, somebody told me that we would be going to families. I knew it wasn't a holiday then. They said there was a family specially chosen for me who were waiting for me in Australia. But it wasn't to be. No one was waiting.

B I've never forgotten England. It's my home. It's my birthplace but they just didn't want me.

C We were supposed to consider ourselves very lucky that they had found us a roof over our heads; a home where we could become part of a family. Only, these people didn't love me, they treated me like dirt, like a slave. They weren't my family. I feel I'm a nobody, a nothing, without any roots at all.

■ *Extracts from Margaret Humphreys' book* Empty Cradles, *published in 1996.*

Think about it!

1 What is the link between **sources a** and **b**?

2 Now read **source c**. What do you think went wrong?

3 Why do you think the British government was encouraging people from the West Indies to come and live and work in Britain (Lesson 3.4a) while at the same time sending British children to Australia?

4 Now think about **source d**. Is it ever right for a government to apologise for something that happened in the past and over which it had no control?

History detective

Australia wasn't the only country that took unaccompanied children. Use the Internet to find out where else children were sent and what happened to them.

In this lesson you will:

- find out about the life and career of Kwame Nkrumah

- consider how far Nkrumah deserves to be remembered positively by Ghanaians.

Does Kwame Nkrumah deserve to be remembered as the 'Osagyefo' of Ghana?

Kwame Nkrumah was born in September 1909 in Nkroful, a small village in the British colony of the Gold Coast. Europeans called it this because of the large gold deposits found there. In 1957 Nkrumah became the first leader of a new, free country called Ghana, which replaced the Gold Coast, and he became known as 'Osagyefo'.

a

■ Image of Kwame Nkrumah.

? *Look at source a. Based on this image, how would you describe Kwame Nkrumah's character? Think of three words that you think sum him up. What do you think the word 'Osagyefo' might mean in English?*

Nkrumah's early life

1909
Nkrumah born

1930
Graduated from the Achimota School in the capital, Accra.

1935
Got a place as a student at a university in America.

1935–40
Had to work washing dishes, selling fish and making soap to pay his university fees.

1945
Moved to England to study and helped to organise an All-Africa Meeting to protest against the British Empire.

1949
Returned to Ghana and made very popular speeches against the British. He said, 'We need self-rule now!'

1950
Sent to prison for his anti-British speeches. Was called 'our local Hitler' by the British Governor.

1951
In a general election, Nkrumah's party, the Convention People's Party, won 34 out of 38 seats, despite him being in prison! Nkrumah became prime minister.

1954
To make more profit from the sale of cocoa abroad, Nkrumah cut the amount of money that the government paid the native cocoa farmers for their crop. This caused anti-Nkrumah violence from the farmers. In June Nkrumah won the general election with 57% of the vote. Newspapers called him 'Man of Destiny, Star of Africa, Iron Boy!'

By 1957
Nine new hospitals had been built in Ghana and there were twice as many primary schools as there were in 1951.

From Gold Coast to Ghana

1874–1901
The British fought and won a series of wars against the native Ashanti people. The whole of the Gold Coast was put under British control. Few British people lived there due to the tropical climate and the threat of malaria, so many Africans were relied on to help British rule.

By 1945
The Gold Coast had become one of the wealthiest countries in Africa with one of the best-educated populations.

By 1947
Many people in the Gold Coast had heard that India had won independence. A number of politicians saw freedom as a goal for the Gold Coast.

By 1951
The British agreed to gradually hand over some power to rich, western-educated, African men. The British hoped to avoid a violent struggle for power.

6 March 1957
The British were satisfied that Ghana could cope without British rule and announced Independence Day. There were six days of celebrations!

What happened next?

Nkrumah was very popular when he became the first leader of independent Ghana.
However, in 1966 he was forced by the army to leave Ghana, never to return.

Nkrumah in power

1960	1959–64	1964	1965	1966
Nkrumah passed laws that made him a dictator. He could make laws without Parliament, arrest enemies without courts and spend government money how he wanted.	Ghana spent £430 million on lots of expensive, and mostly useless, projects. One example was the building of huge concrete storehouses to hold cocoa beans; the stores were not good enough and were never used.	Nkrumah declared himself president for life despite lots of criticism about him wasting money.	He wanted to be the leader of a 'United States of Africa'. £10 million was spent to host a meeting of African leaders. Many leaders refused to attend.	The army removed Nkrumah from power. Crowds gathered to cheer the soldiers. He left Ghana and never returned. (He died in 1972.)

b ■ *Bronze statue of Kwame Nkrumah, at the Kwame Nkrumah Memorial Park in Accra, the capital of Ghana.*

Read all about it!

1 Read the timelines for Nkrumah's early life and Ghana. Pick out details that suggest:

   a) Kwame Nkrumah was very important in winning independence for Ghana in 1957

   b) there were other reasons that explain Ghana's independence – not Nkrumah!

Look and think

2 Look at **sources a** and **b**. If you were to design a webpage about Nkrumah, which image would you choose? Support your answer by explaining:

   ● how Nkrumah is shown in the source

   ● how this image is supported by the information in the timelines.

In conclusion ...

3 The translation of 'Osagfeyo' is 'saviour'. Do you think Nkrumah should be remembered like this?

4 People in Ghana still argue about whether Nkrumah deserves to have a national holiday named after him or not. Imagine you are at a meeting in Accra to decide whether to make 21 September a national holiday in honour of Nkrumah. Write a speech to make it clear what your opinion is. Remember to use lots of the details from Nkrumah's life!

In this lesson you will:

- explain why the Algerian struggle for independence led to war

- devise categories to organise lots of information.

Why did the Algerians fight for their freedom?

 Look at source a. What might cause this situation? Try to think of three possible reasons.

Almost 1 million people died in a war between France and Algeria that lasted from 1954 to 1962. It was a particularly cruel conflict: both sides killed civilians and used torture on prisoners. Why did the Algerians have to fight so long and hard for their freedom?

> By 1954 France had ruled Algeria for 124 years.

> By 1954 there were 1 million **pieds noirs** living in Algeria. They were totally against making deals with the native Algerians.

> Eight MPs represented 1 million Algerian French in the French Parliament. Another eight MPs represented 8 million native Algerians.

> In 1954 the French Army lost a war to keep hold of the French colony Indo-China. They were angry, embarrassed and determined not to lose another colony.

> One-third of the people who lived in Algiers were French.

Read and think

Historians help us to make sense of the past. One way they do this is to group pieces of information (like those in the boxes on Algeria) into themes or categories.

1 Read all the information boxes.

   a) On a copy, draw lines between the boxes that contain similar pieces of information.

   b) Label the lines with a category title that you think explains the link between the boxes. One example has been done for you.

Notes

- You might want to use the ideas you came up with when you looked at **source a** to connect some boxes.

- Some boxes might connect with others in more than one way.

- You might want to discuss the information in boxes with a partner before drawing lines.

- You could compare your lines with a neighbour after you have finished.

a

■ *This photo shows French troops resisting Algerian protesters. It was taken in Algiers, the capital city of Algeria, in 1955.*

Only eight out of 864 top government jobs were held by native Algerians.

The native Algerian population doubled between 1900 and 1950. Many lived in **shanty towns** called 'bidonvilles'.

The Front de Libération Nationale (FLN) was a group of Algerian terrorists who launched their first attack on 1 November 1954. They shot French military leaders.

The FLN began to kill French **civilians** with guns and bombs in August 1955.

The pieds noirs said that the French government was not doing enough to help them. They formed their own armed gangs to fight native Algerians.

In 1956 the French increased the number of soldiers in Algeria from 100,000 to 500,000.

In 1956 the French discovered oil in the south of Algeria.

In 1961 some members of the French Army and the pieds noirs formed the 'Secret Army' to attack native Algerian civilians.

In 1959 the French government tried to make a deal with the FLN to allow a public vote on freedom if the violence stopped. The FLN and the pieds noirs rejected this.

The French Army began to kill native civilians and arrest whole villages to try to stop the FLN in November 1954.

Ahmed Ben Bella was an Algerian who fought for the French in the Second World War. He thought the French did not reward Algeria enough after the war. He led the FLN.

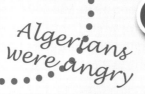
Algerians were angry

History detective

Apart from Ethiopia, every country in Africa has been under European control at some time in the past. Pick a country, then use the school library and the Internet to find out how and when they gained their independence.

Who or what was to blame?

We now have a good idea of the major reasons for the violence. However, historians like to argue about which reason was the most important to get to the root of the problem.

2 Look again at the information in all the boxes.

   a) With a partner, arrange the boxes in order of their importance to explain why there was violence in Algeria.

   b) Compare your order with another pair. Argue about any differences in the order and try to reach an agreement.

   c) Look at your final order.

   ● Do most of the important boxes belong to a particular category?

   ● What does this tell us about the causes of the war in Algeria?

Spot the difference

Today, many politicians and generals look back at the war in Algeria to learn how they might try to reduce violence in current struggles for **regime change**.

3 Imagine the Ministry of Defence has asked you to write a report about the causes of the war in Algeria. In your report you must decide which the most important causes were and use detailed evidence to support your argument.

Back to the start

Turn back to Lesson 3.5a. Use the same category headings you came up with in this enquiry to look again at Ghana's struggle for freedom. Why do you think there was peace in Ghana but war in Algeria?

How did African colonies gain independence?

Who is to blame for the problems in Zimbabwe?

The land that had once been known as Great Zimbabwe (see enquiry 3.5c in Book 1) was conquered by the British in the 1890s. It was renamed Rhodesia, after Cecil Rhodes, the man who led the British 'scramble for Africa'. Many whites liked the climate in Rhodesia and went there to set up farms. The land was taken from black families who were forced to live on poor land. In 1923 the British government allowed the white settlers to run the country, but kept Rhodesia as part of the Empire.

At the start of the 1960s, many blacks in Rhodesia, inspired by events in Ghana, began to press for change, and even black rule. Before 1961, you could only vote if you had a very high income. This meant that only 560 blacks could vote, compared to 52,000 whites! Between 1930 and 1950, 500,000 blacks had moved onto poor, overcrowded land to make way for white farms. The government feared the rise of black opposition and banned the first **moderate** black political parties. This led to anger and the creation of more **radical** political parties, such as the Zimbabwe African National Union, or Zanu.

The whites became more scared. In April 1964, Ian Smith, a man who had sworn to stop black rule in his lifetime, became the Prime Minister of Rhodesia. He banned Zanu and threw its leaders into prison. Smith opposed British plans to introduce black rule gradually. In November 1965 he announced a Unilateral Declaration of Independence (UDI). Just as a unicycle only has one wheel, the UDI was 'unilateral'

Key words

Guerrilla war
Type of warfare that relies on hit and run tactics rather than big battles.

Moderate
Person willing to compromise to achieve reasonable change.

Radical
Person who demands great change and is unwilling to compromise.

■ *A cartoon in a South African newspaper, 18 February 2001.*

IT'S ALL THE FAULT OF
MEDIA !...
UNPATRIOTIC WHITES !..
GAYS !...
AMERICA !..
BRITAIN ! ...
EXPATRIATES !..

because only one power, Rhodesia, agreed that Rhodesia was independent! Britain only recognised independence in April 1980 after the Rhodesian government finally agreed to hold elections that would allow black rule.

Robert Mugabe and Zanu-PF

Robert Mugabe was one of the Zanu leaders who spent ten years in prison. He was a radical who wanted to get rid of not just the white government but the whole white business system, especially the farms. He thought meetings to discuss black power were useless while Ian Smith was in power. Between 1974 and 1979 he led an increasingly violent **guerrilla war** to secure his aims. Under a lot of international pressure, Smith finally agreed to hold elections that would allow black power. In the January 1980 election, Mugabe's new party, Zanu-PF, won 57 out of 80 seats. Mugabe became the first black leader of a country now renamed Zimbabwe.

Mugabe in power

For the first two years in power, Mugabe treated the whites well. About 6,000 white farmers employed one-third of all wage earners in Zimbabwe and produced one-third of all exports. However, not all the blacks supported Mugabe. There are two main groups of people in Zimbabwe:

- the Shona, who are the majority
- the Ndebele, a minority who live in the south.

Mugabe speaks Shona, and the Ndebele worried that Mugabe would exclude them from power. Mugabe wanted total control. He began to attack members of rival black political parties, especially at election time, to scare people into voting for him. He used experts from North Korea to train his own guerrilla army, called 5 Brigade, to attack his enemies.

■ *A photo of a 100 billion Zimbabwe dollar note. In July 2008, one egg cost $35 billion. A loaf of bread cost $30 in 1998, $3,500 in 2004 and $200 billion in July 2008!*

On 30 December 1987, Mugabe made himself 'Executive President' with almost total control over the country. He now began to take the farms owned by whites without payment. Some of them were used to resettle the poor black families, but many were given to his friends and family. By 2000 almost all the white farmers had left Zimbabwe; they fled after Mugabe allowed so-called 'war veterans' (men who claimed to have fought in the 1974–79 guerrilla war) to take over their farms. Farming collapsed and the value of the economy fell by one-third between 1999 and 2004. Unemployment rose to 80 per cent of the population and paper money became almost worthless.

Mugabe blamed the remaining white farmers, Britain, the United Nations (UN) and even the churches for the problems. He has continued to hold power by beating up, starving and even killing his opponents, especially those in the Movement for Democratic Change (MDC), a party set up in September 1999 under Morgan Tsvangirai. In September 2008, a power-sharing deal was signed, whereby Mugabe remained President while Tsvangirai became Prime Minister. However, the situation is tense and is likely to change again and again in coming years.

Over to you ...

Mugabe blamed 'the West' for the problems in Zimbabwe. How convincing do you find this argument?

Next Lesson

In this lesson you will:

- discover why people moved from Africa to the USA in the 1960s

- discover that an event can by interpreted in different ways.

● Key words

GI Bill

Law passed in the USA in 1944 by which the government paid for the education of returning troops and lent them money to buy homes.

Senator

Person who sits in the Senate, which is part of Congress – the Parliament of the USA.

Why have they moved?

1 **Source a** gives a number of reasons why people within a family move. Explain in full sentences and in your own words why the members of this person's family have moved.

Why move from Africa to Hawaii?

On 27 July 2004, a **senator** from Illinois in the USA made a speech to the Democratic Party Convention.

? *Read source a. Can you guess who the person making the speech might be? Then look at source b, which shows the speaker as a child with his father. Does this help you to answer the question?*

a *My father was a foreign student, born and raised in a small village in Kenya. He grew up herding goats, went to school in a tin-roof shack. His father, my grandfather, was a cook, a domestic servant. But my grandfather had larger dreams for his son. Through hard work and perseverance my father got a scholarship to study in a magical place: America, which stood as a beacon of freedom and opportunity to so many who had come before. While studying here, my father met my mother. She was born in a town on the other side of the world from Kenya, in Kansas in the USA. Her father moved around to find work on oil rigs and farms through most of the Depression. The day after Pearl Harbor my grandfather signed up for duty, joined [General] Patton's army and marched across Europe. Back home, my grandmother raised their baby and went to work on a bomber assembly line. After the war, they studied on the **GI Bill**, bought a house through it and then moved west in search of opportunity.*

The father of the speaker at the Democratic Party Convention had moved from Kenya in Africa to the USA. From the sixteenth to the nineteenth centuries, people were transported from Africa to the USA as slaves. The reasons people moved from Africa to the United States in the 1960s were very different.

c

He was an African, a Kenyan of the Luo Tribe, born on the shores of Lake Victoria in a place called Alego. The village was poor, but his father – Hussein Onyango Obama – had been a prominent farmer, an elder of the tribe, a medicine man with healing powers. My father grew up herding his father's goats and attending the local school set up by the British administration, where he had shown great promise. He eventually won a scholarship to study in Nairobi; and then on the eve of Kenyan independence, he found out that he had been selected by Kenyan leaders and American sponsors to attend a university in the United States, joining the first large wave of Africans to be sent to master Western technology and bring it back to forge a new, modern Africa.

In 1959, at the age of 23, he arrived at the University of Hawaii as its first black student. In a language course he met an awkward, shy American girl, only 18, and they fell in love. They married and she bore them a son to whom he gave his name. My father won another scholarship to Harvard University but he did not bring his family with him. He then returned to Africa to fulfil his promise to the continent. The mother and child stayed behind.

■ *Adapted from the author's book,* Dreams From My Father, *published in 2004. This extract is about the author's father.*

d

My son was working as an office boy. He was deeply sad, almost desperate. Many of his age-mates had gone to university in Makarere [in Uganda]. Some had even gone to London. They could expect big jobs when they returned.

Then good fortune struck, in the form of two American women. They were teaching in Nairobi, connected to some religious organisation, I think, and one day they came into the office where my son was working. Your father struck up a conversation with them, and soon these women became his friends. They lent him books to read and when they saw how clever he was they said that he should go to university. He explained that he had no money and no school qualifications. These women said that they could arrange for him to take a correspondence course and, if he was successful, they would help him to get into a university in America.

For the first time in his life my son worked hard. Every night and during lunch he would study. A few months later he sat for the exam at the American university. One day, the letter came and he was shouting with happiness.

He still had no money though. My husband could not raise the money for university fees and transport abroad. My son wrote and wrote to universities in America. Finally a university in Hawaii wrote back and told him that they would give him a scholarship. After less than two years we received a letter saying that my son had met an American girl and that he would like to marry her. They married, had a son, but when my son eventually returned to Kenya we discovered that he had left his wife and child in America.

■ *Adapted from the author's book,* Dreams From My Father, *published in 2004. Here the grandmother tells her story.*

Why did he move?

2 Read **sources c** and **d,** which are extracts from the speaker's book *Dreams From My Father*.

a) What are the similarities between the two extracts?

b) What are the differences?

c) How do the extracts compare with the speech in **source a**?

Reporting the story

3 You might well have guessed by now the identity of the speaker and the author of *Dreams From My Father*. Imagine you are a reporter on an American newspaper. Write an article explaining how the father of the American President came from Africa to the USA.

History detective

Members of your family or your carer/guardian's family might have moved in the past 40 years. Try to find out who moved, where they moved and why.

In this lesson you will:

- find out about Barack Obama's life

- explain diversity and change.

A long road to the White House

On 4 November 2008, Barack Obama was elected as the first black president of the United States of America.

? *Read source a, in which Obama describes the changes in the lifetime of a 106-year-old lady called Ann Nixon Cooper. Which of these changes do you recognise from other enquiries in this book?*

a

She was born just a generation past slavery; a time when there were no cars on the road or planes in the sky; when someone like her couldn't vote for two reasons – because she was a woman and because of the colour of her skin.

At a time when women's voices were silenced and their hopes dismissed, she lived to see them stand up and speak out and reach for the vote. Yes, we can.

When the bombs fell on our harbour and tyranny threatened the world, she was there to witness a generation rise to greatness and a democracy was saved. Yes, we can.

She was there for the buses in Montgomery, the hoses in Birmingham, a bridge in Selma, and a preacher from Atlanta who told a people that 'we shall overcome'. Yes, we can.

A man touched down on the Moon, a wall came down in Berlin, a world was connected by our own science and imagination. And this year, in this election, she touched her finger to a screen, and cast her vote, because after 106 years in America, through the best of times and the darkest of hours, she knows how America can change. Yes, we can.

■ *Part of Barack Obama's election victory speech, 4 November 2008. Here he talks about the life of a black woman called Ann Nixon Cooper, to show the changes people like her have lived through.*

Why did Barack Obama move?

1 Barack Obama's life has changed many times as he has moved to different places. Read through boxes A–J and put them in chronological order.

2 Write a summary of Barack Obama's life in your own words, in under 200 words.

A Obama's parents separated when he was two years old and his father returned to Kenya. His mother remarried and, in 1967, Obama moved with his new stepfather and mother to Jakarta, Indonesia, where he lived from the age of six to ten.

B Obama graduated from high school in 1979 and moved to Los Angeles to attend Occidental College, where he studied for two years.

C Obama was elected as a member of the American Senate representing Illinois in 2004. In 2008 he won the American presidential election and on 20 January 2009 he and his family moved into the White House in Washington, DC.

D Obama travelled to Kenya for five weeks in mid-1988 to meet his African family.

E In 1981 Obama moved to New York City to study Political Science at Columbia University. He graduated in 1983 and stayed to work in New York for two more years.

F Obama returned to Honolulu in Hawaii when he was ten so he could attend the Punahou School. During this time he lived with his grandparents.

G Barack Obama's parents met at the University of Honolulu. He was born in Hawaii on 4 August 1961.

Barack Obama's inauguration as the 44th US president, 20 January 2009.

3 There are many reasons why people move.

a) Put each move in boxes under the appropriate sub-heading. Some points might go under more than one sub-head.

- Family reasons
- Education
- Work
- Improving lives of others

b) Which of these factors turned out to be the most significant in Barack Obama's life?

H In 1991 Obama returned to Chicago to become a lawyer and politician.

I In 1985 Obama moved back to Chicago to become a community organiser with a church-based group which worked to improve living conditions in poor neighbourhoods.

J From 1988 to 1991 Barack studied at the Harvard Law School in Cambridge, Massachusetts. There he was elected the first African-American president of the publication the *Harvard Law Review* in its 104-year history.

What does it tell us?

4 As you have read, Barack Obama has moved a number of times in his life.

a) Discuss the following question with a work partner.

What does Obama's story show about how moving can have a positive impact on people's lives?

b) Now answer the question in writing, using examples from Obama's life.

Back to the start

Barack Obama's story is amazing. What aspect of Obama's life do you find the most interesting and why? Discuss this question with a work partner.

Next Lesson

Why did people move around in the twentieth century?

The twentieth century saw people moving about the world in larger numbers than ever before. As the century progressed, millions took holidays around the world, in Ibiza and Tenerife, in New York and Sydney. The more adventurous explored the steppes of Russia and the game reserves of South Africa. These were people travelling for leisure and pleasure – for the fun that awaited for them at the end of their journey. But there were others who travelled for very different reasons. These people left everything behind: their homes and friends and sometimes their families. These were people embarking on life-changing journeys of enormous significance; many of them were looking for a fresh start and a new life.

Push and pull

Every movement of people involves two main factors: the push factor and the pull factor.

- The push factor refers to those aspects of life that make a person decide to leave. What is pushing them out? It might, for example, be fear of persecution.

- The pull factor refers to the attractiveness of the place to which they are going. What is pulling them to that particular place? It might, for example, be the desire to serve your country by fighting overseas.

Making links

1 Study **sources a–d**. They all come from enquiries in Unit 3.

a) What does each source tell you about the reasons the people involved made the journeys they did.

b) Talk about it to the person sitting next to you and draw up a joint list of reasons. Try to think of more than one reason for each source.

Push or pull?

2 Reflect on the enquiries you have covered in Unit 3. Working with a partner, list the push factors and the pull factors involved in the movement of the people in each of the enquiries.

For each factor you have identified, agree a score of 1–5 (where 5 = very important and 1 = not important at all).

3 Compare your scores with those of others in your class. Talk through any differences you have, and come up with scores for each enquiry which you all agree with. Which did you decide as a class were the more important – push factors or pull factors?

a

THE EMPIRE NEEDS MEN!

AUSTRALIA
CANADA
INDIA
NEW ZEALAND

All answer the call.
Helped by the YOUNG LIONS
The OLD LION defies his Foes.
ENLIST NOW.

■ Poster entitled 'The Empire Needs Men', 1915.

b

In deep gratitude
to the people and Parliament
of the United Kingdom
for saving the lives of
10,000 Jewish and other children
who fled to this country
from Nazi persecution
on the Kindertransport
1938 – 1939

■ A plaque in the Palace of Westminster, unveiled in June 1999.

c

One night our Hindu neighbour banged on our door and warned us that angry Hindu mobs were coming towards this area, wanting to kill Muslims. A few hours later my dad decided that we should leave for Pakistan. The journey was by bus. It was one of the most terrifying and heart-aching moments of my entire life. We left everything behind in a blink of an eye: all our friends, our house, our belongings.

■ From an interview with a Muslim woman in 2007. She was aged seven when she left India in 1947.

d

■ British orphans arrive in Australia in the 1950s.

In conclusion ...

4 Choose four sources from the whole of Unit 3 that support the statement below and four that disagree with it.

People in the twentieth century moved because they were afraid.

5 You are now ready to hold a class debate, using this statement as the motion to be discussed.

Why did people travel in the twentieth century?

> *In the twentieth century, people only travelled because they were afraid.*

How far do you agree with this view? Use the sources and your own knowledge in your answer.

a

■ *Crew of HM messenger ship Trent from the magazine British Seafarer, published in April 1916.*

b

Oskar suggested that they play one more hand. If Amon won, Oskar would pay him 7,400 zloty [Polish currency]. 'But if I win,' said Oskar, 'then you give me Helen Hirsch for my list.' Oskar won. Out in the kitchen, Helen Hirsch did not know that she had been saved by a game of cards. Rumours of Oskar's plan were heard all over the camp. There was a Schindler list. It was worth everything to be on it.

■ *From Thomas Keneally's book* Schindler's Ark, *published in 1982. Here he describes a game of cards between Amon Göth and Oskar Schindler. Helen Hirsch was Göth's Jewish maid, whom he abused.*

c

On the evening of 11 August 1947, Lahore railway station was packed with passengers when news came that the Sind Express, on its way to Lahore, had been attacked by Muslims. Panic spread. They found that men, women and children had been brutally murdered and were lying in pools of blood. The dead bodies were carried across several platforms while all that was visible in the city of Lahore was a huge tower of smoke.

■ *From a report by Justice Gopal Das Khosla in 1947, an Indian judge working in the Punjab High Court. Lahore was just on the Pakistan side of the newly drawn border between India and Pakistan.*

d

There are two principal aims in child migration, which I wish to bring before the House this evening. The first, which is common to all migration projects, is to increase the British population in the empty spaces of the Commonwealth, where there are unrivalled resources of fine farmland and mineral and industrial wealth, which remain relatively undeveloped.

The second aim, certainly not less important, is to rescue the children of broken homes and a bad environment in the United Kingdom and to open for them the door of opportunity to a happy and hopeful future in our great overseas Commonwealth. Instead of a cheerless, back-street existence, often unloved and unwanted, these children, if they go to Australia, are given the fresh air, sunshine and beauty of the countryside, a new start in a new country and the prospect of a full and useful life.

■ *From a report in* Hansard, *which records debates in Parliament, 9 February 1959.*

How will you set about a task like this?

Think!

The question needs you to do three things:

- **evaluate** the given source material
- **select** appropriate information from your own knowledge
- **judge** whether or not people in the twentieth century travelled only because they were afraid, by reflecting on and weighing up the evidence you have found.

Evaluate!

Take each source in turn and apply the **5xW** rule (see Skills bank, page 186). Now think particularly about the context (background history) of each source and work out how that helps you understand the source. Using your findings, link this to 'fear'. How far does each source support the view that people were travelling because they were afraid? Give each one a ranking on a scale of 1–5 to help you decide.

Select!

You have already thought about the context of **sources a–d** and considered how far they support the view that people moved because they were afraid. Now think about the overall impression you have gained from working through this unit. Did people travel because they were afraid? Skim through the lessons and pick out any information that would support this idea and any that would challenge it.

Judge!

- When you evaluated the sources in their contexts, you ranked them as to how far they supported the view that people travelled because they were afraid. Now do the same with the information you have extracted from the unit as a whole.

- You have now ranked both the information and the source material. Link them up so that you know which sources and which knowledge can be used fully to support the view in the question, which can't support it at all and which come somewhere in between.

You will need all this material to answer the question.

Plan!

Turn to the Skills bank, page 186. You will see there that a good plan is the secret of success. What sort of plan suits you best? You may, for example, like working with a spider diagram. It doesn't matter – what does matter is that you plan your answer. Sort your material into a plan that addresses the question. Remember to structure your answer so that it begins with an introduction, works through the points you want to make, one by one, uses evidence to back up the points you are making, and ends with a conclusion.

How will your work be marked? Have you:

Level 5

Described the reasons why people travelled?

Suggested how these reasons could be linked to fear?

Begun to evaluate sources to establish evidence for links with fear?

Selected information and **used** it to structure your work?

Level 6

Explained how the reasons people travelled could be linked to fear?

Considered how some reasons for travelling had nothing to do with fear?

Evaluated sources to establish evidence relevant to the enquiry?

Selected, organised and used relevant information to reach a judgement?

Level 7

Analysed the reasons why people travelled in the twentieth century and linked this analysis to fear?

Investigated the issue by asking and refining your own questions?

Evaluated evidence by considering the origin, nature and purpose of the given sources?

Selected, organised and used relevant information in well-structured work to reach a supported judgement?

What was the most important movement of people in the twentieth century?

The children in your local primary school have been working on a combined history and geography project 'People and Journeys'. This has focused on people moving and travelling within Britain in the twentieth century. The headteacher wants to widen this out and to get the children thinking about other people in other places who travelled, too. She has asked you and a friend to help by telling the children about what you consider to have been the most important movement of people in the twentieth century.

What a task! You've probably got lots of ideas already, but you need to look back over Unit 3 and the journeys people made. Here are some images to remind you of what you might choose.

■ *Some of the first West Indian immigrants arriving in Britain, 22 June 1948.*

■ *A photograph sent to Adam Rybczynski. On the back is written 'My dear brother-in-law, we send you our photograph for you to remember us by.' It is dated 1955.*

■ *Barack Obama and his father when Obama's father visited Hawaii in the early 1970s.*

How will you set about a task like this?

There are clearly going to be two main parts to this task:

- the **process**, by which you and a partner decide on the most important movement of people in the twentieth century
- the **product**, which is your final presentation to the primary school children.

The process

- How will you measure importance? You will need to draw up a list of qualities you will be looking for. You will need to think of such things as the impact on the people concerned; the impact on the societies they left behind and those they were joining; and the importance nationally and internationally of the journey made. What other qualities can you think of that will help you judge importance?

- Having drawn up your list of qualities (each one is also known as a criterion) you will need to apply these to the journeys described in Unit 3. Not every criterion will apply to every journey, and those that do apply may apply more strongly to some journeys than to others.

- How will you rank the journeys? You could apply a scale of 1–5 for each criterion when you apply it to a journey. The winner is the journey with the highest score! These could be set out on a table like the one below.

Journey	Criterion 1	Criterion 2	Criterion 3	Criterion 4	TOTAL
Soldiers to the Front					
Kindertransport					

The product

- How will you present your findings to primary school children? You could produce, for example, a booklet, a poster, a wall display, a PowerPoint presentation: the choice is yours!

- Remember that you must tell the children about the most important journey made in the twentieth century – and the reasons why you think it is the most important.

- Remember, too, to think about your audience. Your presentation should be aimed at children in primary school and so the explanation and language should be at a level they can understand.

Good luck!

How will your work be marked? Have you:

Level 5

Described the journeys made by some people?

Suggested reasons for the journeys?

Begun to ask your own questions about the importance of the journeys?

Selected and used appropriate information in your presentation?

Level 6

Explained the reasons for the different journeys made?

Asked questions to help you decide why some journeys were more important than others?

Selected information appropriate for primary school children, **organised and used** it in your presentation?

Level 7

Decided on the criteria to be used to judge the importance of the journeys?

Explained how the criteria have been applied to enable you to select the most important journey?

Selected information appropriate for primary school children, **organised** it, and **used** the appropriate level of language in your presentation?

Use this section to remind yourself of some important historical skills. These hints will be useful as you complete the tasks and activities in this book.

Being a historian

These are some of the things that a historian does.

- Tells the story of the past.
- Explains why things happened and the consequences.
- Shows that some things change while others stay the same.
- Works as a detective using evidence.
- Identifies why certain events and people are important.
- Understands how to extract evidence from a source.
- Explains why interpretations differ.
- Communicates about the past.

Throughout this course you will have the chance to practise and improve all of these skills. Read through the descriptions below to find out what kind of historian you are.

Level 5

You can:

- tell the story of the past
- begin to explain why things happen
- explain how some things change while others stay the same
- begin to explain why some events and people are really important
- begin to ask questions of source material
- use the right information to explain the past.

Level 6

You can:

- tell and explain the story of the past
- begin to explain how causes link together
- explain in detail why some things change and others stay the same
- ask questions about why some people or events are more important than others
- decide which evidence is useful
- use the right information and organise ideas clearly.

Level 7

You can:

- tell and fully explain the story of the past
- explain how causes link together and why some are more important than others
- show you understand that change and continuity (things staying the same) differ between people and across time
- explain how and why interpretations of the past have come about
- investigate historical problems by asking and refining your own questions and reflect on the process you have gone through
- question sources to establish evidence
- select, organise and use the right information and the correct historical words.

Evaluating a source

Evaluating a source means looking at it (or reading it) carefully and asking questions about it so that you can decide how valuable it is to a historian. Whatever the source, whether it's a diary or a letter, a photograph or a painting, you need to remember the **5xW** rule.

When you have the answers to these questions, you can then ask the final one: 'What is this source evidence of?'

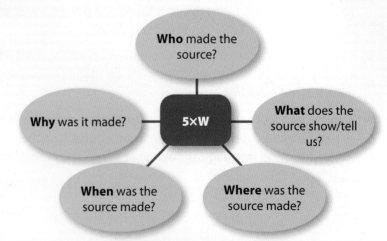

Now try this

You last saw this source in Lesson 2.3c.

What is this source evidence of? Is it evidence of:

- what people actually ate during the Second World War?
- what the government suggested people could eat?
- the food that was available in the country all through the war?
- the food that would keep people healthy during the war?
- the food women liked to cook for their families?

Think carefully!

Saturday, 24 February 1917

2.20pm: Afternoon's post brought me a circular from the Food Controller urging all ministers of religion to encourage a voluntary cutback in food consumption to avoid rationing. Suggested limits were four pounds of bread, two and a half pounds of meat and three-quarters of a pound of sugar per person per week.

■ *From the diary of the Reverend Andrew Clark, vicar of Great Leighs, Essex.*

Questioning photographs

It's very tempting to think that photographs, unlike paintings, must show the truth because they show something that was really there or really did happen. The photographer, again unlike most artists, really was there, pointed his or her camera, pressed a button and there was the image. Result! But was it?

Sometimes photographs can be set up. A photographer might ask people to pose in a certain way, do something (or make it look as though they are doing something) and then photograph them. In every case, the photographer will have made a deliberate decision to take that photograph, of those people, at that moment in time.

Look at **source b**. You last saw this photograph in Lesson 2.2c. The photographer didn't just happen to be strolling by this jolly group of women with German prisoners of war, carrying a camera. The photographer knew that German prisoners of war were working in the factory with English women. He or she asked some of them to come outside, stand in a row that was (more or less) alternate men and women, smile and look happy. They were genuinely doing this. But there are at

MONDAY
Breakfast (each day): Porridge or breakfast cereal. Fruit. Toast. Marmalade. Eggs occasionally. Milk or milky tea.
Dinner: Vegetable soup or Jacket sausages. Raisin dumplings with golden syrup.
Tea-Supper: Blackberry bake. Wholemeal bread and butter. Cocoa.
TUESDAY
Dinner: Mutton pie. Jacket potatoes. Baked apple.
Tea-Supper: Macaroni cheese. Bread and butter. Fruit. Milk or tea.
WEDNESDAY
Dinner: Braised beef (keeping bones for soup). Vegetables. Chocolate blancmange.
Tea-Supper: Scrambled eggs on toast. Stewed dried apricots. Milk drink.

THURSDAY
Dinner: Baked marrow with leftover beef. College pudding.
Tea-Supper: Vegetable casserole. Bread and jam. Tea or fruit-juice drink.
FRIDAY
Dinner: Bombay rice. Cabbage. Golden apples.
Tea-Supper: Vegetable salad on lettuce. Wholemeal bread and butter. Rice pudding.
SATURDAY
Dinner: Liver casserole. Mashed potatoes. Greens. Milk jelly.
Tea-Supper: Bread and butter pudding. Fruit.
SUNDAY
Dinner: Beef, carrots and dumplings. Greens. Sponge pudding.
Tea-Supper: Cheese and tomato sandwiches. Cake. Milk drink.

■ *A week's menus from a government information sheet.*

Your turn...

1 Read **source a**. What is this evidence of? Think carefully, make a list, but use the **5xW** rule first. Share your list with others in your class and draw up a list with which you all agree.

■ *German prisoners of war with women who worked at the tailoring factory. This factory made German uniforms for German PoWs and British uniforms to send to Germany for British PoWs.*

least six questions you need to ask before you accept this photograph as evidence.

- How did the photographer know who was working in the factory?

- Did the men and women volunteer to come out and be photographed or were they forced out?
- What about the people who didn't come out to be photographed?
- Are the jolly feelings shown in the photograph genuine or were the people told to smile and look happy?
- Why did the photographer take the photograph there and at that particular time?
- Was the photographer trying to make a particular point?

Using photographs as sources

2 Find another photograph in this book. What questions would you ask of it before you could accept it as evidence?

Thinking about paintings

Pictures can provide really useful evidence for historians. Sometimes they tell us far more than the artist intended them to. Sometimes they lead us to ask more and more questions so that the picture turns into a puzzle. First you need to think about the artist. This is called looking at the **provenance** of the painting. Remember the **5xW** rule! You need to ask these questions.

- Who painted the picture?
- When did they paint it?
- Were they there at the time? (Were they in a good position to know what was going on, or did they make it up afterwards?)
- Why did they paint the picture?
- Did someone pay them to do it?
- Were they trying to make a particular point?

You won't find answers to all these questions for every picture you look at, but you need to bear them in mind and answer the ones you can. This will help you sort out whether a picture is giving you accurate evidence of what happened at the time, or not.

Remember, too, that there are other things in paintings that the artist did **not** set out to show but which tell us a lot about the time in which the picture was painted. This might be information about, for example, clothes and fashion, buildings and bridges, cars and carriages. This is called **unwitting testimony**. It also, of course, applies to photographs.

Photographs again

3 Look again at **source b**. What unwitting testimony does this photograph give you?

4 Go back to another photograph in this book and work out what unwitting testimony this could give you.

Unpacking a written source

Remember the **5xW** rule! This applies as much to written sources as it does to pictures and paintings.

Read through **source c**. You read it first in Lesson 1.5e on Hiroshima.

C

The Americans were already aware of Japan's desire to end the war. But President Truman and his main advisers were keen on using the atomic bomb to speed up Japan's collapse. Why else was the bomb used? America and Britain's ally, the Soviet Union, was due to declare war on Japan on 8 August [1945]. The Soviet leader [Josef] Stalin had demanded to share in the occupation of Japan. The US government was keen to prevent this. The atomic bomb was used to help solve the problem; it was dropped two days before the Soviets were due to enter the war against Japan. The second reason for the bomb's use at Hiroshima was that it had cost a lot of money and simply had to be a success.

■ Adapted from Basil Liddell Hart's book History of the Second World War, *published in 1970.*

Using a written source

5 Apply the **5xW** rule to **source c** to help you answer this question: *How useful is this source to a historian trying to find out why an atomic bomb was dropped on Hiroshima?*

What else do I need to think about?

In order to answer a question like this fully, you will need to think about each of the following.

Bias

A source might be biased. This means that it gives you an argument or an opinion from one person's point of view and is not balanced. But take care. Just because a person may be biased about a particular event or individual, that doesn't mean to say that everything he or she writes or draws is automatically biased too.

Reliability

Once you have checked out the **5xW** rule you will be able to decide whether or not a source tells you accurately about the person, event or time it is describing.

Usefulness

Thinking about the **5xW**s, **reliability** and **bias** will lead you to consider usefulness (sometimes called utility). When you are thinking about whether a source is useful, you'll need to ask: 'Useful for what?' In this case, it is useful as part of an enquiry about the reasons why the atomic bomb was dropped on Hiroshima.

Remember, every source is useful at some time and for something. Biased sources are useful because they tell you a lot about the person who wrote, drew or painted them. Reliable sources are useful because you can count on them to be telling you accurately about the time, person or event.

Interpretations

Check out whether or not the source is an interpretation (sometimes called an impression). Sometimes the source will give different impressions. This is something that needs checking out before you decide how to use the source.

Communicating about the past

All historians need to be able to be able to communicate their ideas. This can be done in at least three ways:

- using writing   - using IT   - verbally.

Whichever way you communicate your ideas, you should do the following.

- **Plan:** map out your work before you start.

- **Structure:** every piece of work should be clearly structured, including the use of an introduction and a conclusion.

- **Use evidence:** all ideas should be backed up with accurate information.

The plan

A good plan is the secret to success. It will help you to work out what you want to say before you start. Your plan should have two parts to it:

- the main points that you are going to make

- what you will put in each paragraph/section.

You can set out your plan in a number of ways. For example, you might want to use a spider diagram like this one.

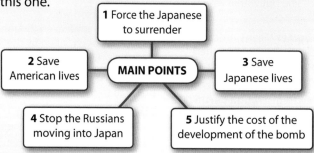

Structure

Think about your paragraph/section running order. You should prioritise, which means putting the most important reason first and the least important reason last:

Introduction: writing out the main points from the plan

1 The most important reason

2 The next most important reason

3 The next most important reason

4 The next most important reason

5 The least important reason

Conclusion: sum up your main points.

Using evidence

When you make a point, make sure you back it up with evidence. Each paragraph or section should include the following.

- **Point:** make your point.

- **Evidence:** back up your point with evidence from sources or your own knowledge.

- **Explanation:** explain why you have chosen that piece of evidence.

Putting it all into practice

7 Now you are ready to write an answer to the question: *Why was the atom bomb dropped on Hiroshima?*

Glossary

9/11 How the attacks on the World Trade Center are commonly known. In the USA, the dates are written with the month first, then the day; September 11 is the day the attacks took place.

Advanced dressing station First aid post behind the main front line but within easy reach of it.

Afrikaner Means 'African' in Dutch; the Dutch settled in southern Africa in the seventeenth century.

Alien Registration Certificate Certificate issued to all non-British people with permission to live in Britain after the Second World War. They had to show it to the police every time they moved house or changed jobs.

Allotment land Usually owned by local councils and rented out in plots to people to grow fruit and vegetables.

Al-Qaeda Islamic extremist group that has used terror to try to achieve its aims.

Amnesty An official pardon.

ANC African National Congress; a black political organisation.

Anti-Semitism Hatred of Jews.

Apartheid Means 'apartness' in Afrikaans, the language of the Afrikaners.

Appeasement Give in to demands to keep someone happy.

Army Group South A number of German army groups in the Second World War, further subdivided into smaller groups.

Balkans Area of south-east Europe that includes many present-day countries such as Albania, Serbia, Croatia and Bulgaria.

Barrage balloon Very large gas-filled balloon anchored to the ground in wartime to deter enemy aircraft.

Bay of Pigs Failed attempt by Cuban exiles supported by the USA to overthrow the government of Fidel Castro.

Bayonet Sharp knife that fixes onto the end of a rifle.

Billets Buildings given over to soldiers for them to live in when not at the front line.

Blackleg Person who continues to work even though a strike has been called by the trade union.

Black Marias Vans used by police to transport prisoners.

Black market Illegal buying and selling of officially rationed goods.

Blitz Concentrated and focused bombing.

Boycott To protest by refusing to do something (e.g. go to work or school).

British Mandate Power given to Britain by the League of Nations to run Palestine.

Capital punishment The legally permitted killing of a person as punishment for a crime.

Caucasus Mountain range that runs between the Caspian Sea and the Black Sea. It used to be part of the Soviet Union.

Censor Person who decides what can be published and what cannot.

Civil rights Rights that are considered to be unquestionable; deserved by all people under all circumstances, especially without regard to race, creed, colour or gender.

Civilian Anyone who is not in the army, navy, air force or police force.

Colony Country or area of land that is ruled by another country.

Common Market Large trading area made up of many smaller ones (such as countries). Members agreed to get rid of taxes on trade between themselves, and to have the same taxes on imports from outside the European Community.

Commonwealth Organisation of former members of the British Empire.

Commune Group of people who live together and share goods and chores.

Communist Person who believes in government by a single party that controls the country in order to bring about equality for the people.

Conscription Making someone join the armed forces.

Coupons Printed in ration books, clipped out and then stamped by shopkeepers to show that rationed foods had been bought.

Crematoria Furnaces or ovens used to burn corpses into ash. Modern cremations are nothing like the ones used by the Nazis.

Culture (cultural) Way of life of a group or of society.

Culture Material used to grow germs or bacteria in a controlled way.

DEFCON DEFense readiness CONdition is a measure of how ready the USA is for war.

Demobbed Someone who has left the armed services and has returned to civilian life.

Democratic System of government that elects its leaders by allowing the people to vote for candidates.

Deportation Forced removal from your home or country.

Depression Time when there are not enough jobs and people have less money to spend.

Devolution Transfer of some powers from central government to regional governments.

Dispensary Place where drugs and medical treatments are handed out.

DNA Deoxyribonucleic acid; the material that contains the genetic code needed to build new living cells.

Dockers People who worked at the docks to load and unload ships.

Economy Organisation of a country's resources.

European Community Organisation that binds the governments, laws, economies and people of Europe together. It is now known as the European Union (EU).

Evacuation Sending children away from the cities to the countryside or abroad to keep them safe from enemy bombs.

Extermination To destroy completely; to kill.

Fascist A racist who supports the rule of a dictator.

Flying picket Group of striking workers who move from place to place to block other workers from going to work.

Fusion Blending together the food, dress and ideas of different cultures.

Gangrenous When body tissue becomes infected and starts to rot.

General strike Refusal to work by those in many different industries.

Genocide Deliberate attempt to murder an entire national or ethnic group of people.

Gestapo The Nazi secret police.

Ghetto Part of a town walled off from the rest where Jews were forced to live.

GP General practitioner; doctor who provides a range of medical services at a local level.

Guerrilla war Type of warfare that relies on hit and run tactics rather than big battles.

Hijab Head covering worn in public by some Muslim women.

Holocaust Mass murder of Jews (and other groups) during the Second World War.

Hoovervilles Slum housing on the outskirts of US cities, named after President Hoover, who many blamed for the Depression.

Hypothesis Statement to be further investigated and proved or disproved.

Identity card Everyone living in Britain had to carry an identity card to prove who they were.

Immigrants People who move into another country to live there.

Infer Draw a conclusion from information without it telling you the answer directly.

Interahamwe Extreme Hutus in Rwanda who formed into groups armed with guns and machetes.

Intern To take away from the home and workplace and put into a camp until the war was over.

IRA Irish Republican Army; Catholic terrorist group that wanted a united Ireland.

Irgun Jewish terrorist group from the 1940s.

Isolationist Remaining separate from the political affairs of other countries.

Joining up Phrase used to mean joining the army or other armed forces.

Loyalist Supporter of the idea that Northern Ireland should remain part of the UK.

Luftwaffe The German air force.

Machete Long heavy knife, usually used to hack through jungle or to clear plants.

Mandate Orders that set out what a person or group has the power to do.

Martyr Someone who dies for a cause.

Moderate Person willing to compromise to achieve reasonable change.

MP or MPs An abbreviation of Member or Members of Parliament.

Munitions Military weapons, ammunition and equipment.

NAACP National Association for the Advancement of Colored People – an organisation in the USA that strives for civil rights for all.

Nationalist Supporter of the idea that there should be greater independence for Ireland from the UK.

Nazis Extreme right-wing Fascist party in power in Germany 1933–45.

Nobel Prize International award given to people who have made important advances in areas such as science and medicine.

Pacifist Person who does not believe in fighting wars of any kind.

Partition Division – in this case of India and Pakistan.

Pieds noirs Name given to French colonial settlers in Algeria.

Prejudice Judging people or events unfairly without considering the facts.

Prisoner of war Member of the enemy's armed forces who was captured and sent to Britain for the duration of the war.

Propaganda Information that deliberately misleads people about the true facts.

Proposition Statement that affirms or denies something and is either true or false.

Purge Flush something out. In Russia in the 1930s, millions of people were purged from society and sent to prison camps for little or no reason.

Racism Treating people badly because they are of a different race from your own.

Radical Person who demands great change and is unwilling to compromise.

Refugee Person driven from their home.

Regime change Replacement of one set of rulers with another set.

Republican Supporter of the idea that there should be a united Ireland.

Revolution Large and sometimes sudden change in the way things are done.

RUC Royal Ulster Constabulary; name of the police force in Northern Ireland until 2001.

Sanctions Measures taken to improve conduct or behaviour.

Segregation Separation of groups of people based on race.

Senator Person who sits in the Senate, which is part of Congress – the Parliament of the USA.

Shanty town Area on the edge of a city where people live in very poor conditions.

Shrapnel Fragments of a bomb that scatter on explosion.

Slav Ethnic group from eastern and central Europe with several related languages.

Slum housing Housing that is badly built, in bad condition and is often overcrowded.

Soviet Formal unit of local and regional government in the USSR (the Union of Soviet Socialist Republics).

Stasi Secret police of communist East Germany.

Suffrage The right to vote.

Suffragettes Women who used militant, and sometimes illegal, ways of persuading people that women in the UK should have the vote.

Suffragists Those who used peaceful, legal ways of persuading people that women in the UK should have the vote.

Superpower World power: a state powerful enough to influence events throughout the world.

The Derby Important horse race held once a year at Epsom, near London.

Total war War involving the civilian population as well as the military.

Trade unions Organisations set up to represent the interests of workers.

Treason Betraying your own country.

Treaty of Versailles, 1919 Treaty that set out the terms for the end of the war between the Allies and Germany. It also identified the main features of the League of Nations.

Turning point Event after which things are never the same again.

U-boat German submarine.

UVF Ulster Volunteer Force; a Loyalist terrorist group.

Untouchables People who did the dirty jobs in India. Many Hindus believed you could be 'polluted' by their dirt if you touched them.

US Congress Parliament of the United States of America. It consists of two Houses: the House of Representatives; and the Senate.

Veto Negative vote that blocks a decision for action.

White House Place in Washington, DC, USA, in which the president and his team work and make decisions.

Women's Institute National women's organisation (UK) that co-ordinated the evacuation of children.

Zeppelin German airship, sometimes called a dirigible.

Index